AF632643

Lifequake

Lifequake

A Story of Hope and Humanity

A Memoir by

Tarini Mohan

juggernaut

JUGGERNAUT BOOKS
C-I-128, First Floor, Sangam Vihar, Near Holi Chowk,
New Delhi 110080, India

First published by Juggernaut Books 2025

Copyright © Tarini Mohan 2025

10 9 8 7 6 5 4 3 2 1

P-ISBN: 9789353453930
E-ISBN: 9789353451950

The views and opinions expressed in this book are the author's own. The facts contained herein were reported to be true as on the date of publication by the authors to the publishers of the book, and the publishers are not in any way liable for their accuracy or veracity.

All rights reserved. No part of this publication may be reproduced, transmitted, or stored in a retrieval system in any form or by any means without the written permission of the publisher.

For sale in the Indian Subcontinent only

Typeset in Adobe Caslon Pro by R. Ajith Kumar, Noida

Printed at Thomson Press India Ltd

To my family, whose unconditional love makes living a pleasure (and a possibility) once more.

"I know it sounds absurd, please tell me who I am."

– "The Logical Song" by SUPERTRAMP

"A bend in the road is not the end of the road ... Unless you fail to make the turn."

– HELEN KELLER

"We walk the same path, but got on different shoes,
Live in the same building, but we got different views."

– "Right Above It" by DRAKE and LIL WAYNE

"The doors of the deformed man are always locked, and the key is on the outside ... He may have treasures of charm inside, but they will never be revealed unless the person outside cooperates with him in unlocking the door."

– RANDOLPH BOURNE

Contents

Prologue

The wind whipped through my hair as I dug my feet firmly into the footrests on the sides of the motorcycle taxi, ensuring that I was tethered in place. Now, I could spread my arms wide to really revel in the thrill of my newfound freedom. I tilted my head back, enjoying the breeze. It was October 8, 2010, and at twenty-three, I had never felt freer. Six weeks earlier, I'd traded the sleek glass towers of New York City for the vibrant chaos of Kampala, the capital of Uganda. It was a leap of faith, a wild adventure, and in that moment, I was soaring.

Sandwiched between my new friend, Sujal, and the driver of the motorcycle taxi, I felt the wind in my hair as we cruised down Yusuf Lule Road.

Then, in a heartbeat, everything changed.

Screeching tires. Blaring horns. Shattering glass. The sickening thud of three bodies hitting the ground. I drifted into a chasm of oblivion. Time froze. And just like that, three months of my life dissolved into nothingness.

I woke up in India, my consciousness piecing together fragments of my surroundings in snatches. Mumbling some gibberish here, uttering half-formed curses there, I was lost in a sea of confusion and consumed by profound discomfort. My short-term memories slipped away like wisps of smoke. Once sharp and agile, my mind now moved at a sluggish pace. Emerging from another realm, I confronted the jagged contours of my new reality. With my body and brain altered, I found myself dwelling in an unfamiliar home.

Thus began the afterlife of a severe traumatic brain injury.

It was reading *I Am the Central Park Jogger*, Trisha Meili's uplifting story of healing and recovery after devastating injuries, including brain injury, that sparked the thought, a few years ago, that I, too, could and should write about my own experience. Trisha had spent several days in a coma after being brutally assaulted in New York's Central Park, and had to learn to read, write, walk, and talk again. Trisha's story also resonated with me because of the multiple connections we shared. She had attended Wellesley College many years before I did, but we shared an economics professor, David Lindauer, who was beloved by both of us. He had put us in touch when I began my recovery from my injuries, which were remarkably similar to hers. Also, we both worked on Wall Street and got our MBAs from the Yale School of Management. The following sentences from her book have stayed with me:

"Healing is the process of moving toward wholeness. Healing isn't becoming exactly the same as we once were. We move toward wholeness, certainly, through our physical health, but also through our emotional and spiritual health."

Reading Trisha's story stirred something deep within me, helping me to begin the slow journey to truly accepting and owning my limitations. If a woman like Trisha, who shares much of my background, could transform the tragedy that she endured into something beautiful, something everlasting, then what was stopping me? Despite the different contexts of our injuries, I heard echoes of myself reverberate from the pages of Trisha's book. But it would be another nine years before I began writing. The catalyst was Suleika

Jaouad's memoir, *Between Two Kingdoms*, another story of illness and recovery. Suleika's words flowed like vivid watercolors, painting the landscape of a life interrupted, inspiring me to create the time and space to tell my own story.

Straddling two worlds, that of India and the United States for many years, I've learned that while much of the experience of disability echoes across borders – even the most robust systems in the United States can crumble without warning – it is much, much harder experiencing a disability in India than in the West.

Though countless wonderful people here, as in the United States, carried me through my darkest days, and Western visitors marveled at the thoughtful care I received in Delhi, if one steps beyond the borders of my "village" – that magic circle of family, friends, and caregivers – empathy often dissolves into patronizing pity. This book seeks to piece together two parallel lives – the before and the after. And to communicate to readers that life for someone like me can still be beautiful. *Is* beautiful.

To write this book, particularly about the time I was in a coma in Uganda and India, I bombarded many of the people who appear in these pages with questions, and pieced my story together bit by bit. The details presented here of those moments are based on their accounts and are as accurate as reported. However, with their consent, I have taken some artistic license for crafting dialogue and scene-setting. Even while doing so, I have aimed to recreate events as faithfully as possible.

From Chapter 4 onward, the narrative primarily draws on my own recollections, thoughts, and feelings. However, when I was uncertain of the accuracy of certain details, I drew upon the memories of others to refresh my own.

The characters in my memoir have given me permission to name them, write about them, and quote emails, blogs, and so on, a few of which have been lightly edited for brevity. To protect the privacy of certain individuals, I have altered their names, but other details are intact, allowing this story to endure while respecting norms of confidentiality.

I would like to emphasize that what follows is *my* story. It should not be generalized to represent the experience of any other person with a traumatic brain injury (TBI) or disability. Every brain is unique, and the effects of every brain injury are distinct for each individual. Likewise, each person's journey with disability is their own, each being true in its own right.

1

An Ever-Burning Candle

It was a Friday. The mood in the office was light and breezy. Yet, nerves and excitement made knots in my stomach. I had recently started my new job in Uganda at the Bangladesh Rural Advancement Committee, or BRAC, a nonprofit organization with global reach, and had been consumed by work all week.

Outside, the sun, still a couple of hours away from vanishing below the horizon, beamed its unsparing rays upon the kitchen staff scurrying down the red dirt paths of the office compound, wrapped in their colorful traditional lesu.

Having moved out of my comfort zone to the breathtaking beauty of Uganda's capital city, Kampala, nestled amidst undulating hills and lush greenery, I sat in my chair, exulting at the prospect of the adventures that awaited me in this unknown land, thousands of miles away from home.

I often wonder if I would have done anything differently that day if I'd had some premonition that it would be the last day I would experience such lightness and ease for a long time. Might I have taken a break from staring at my laptop to soak up some sun with my colleagues? Booked a flight to return to my comfortable life in New York with my partner?

Or maybe – hopefully – hopped onto a matatu[1] to purchase a helmet.

The day had begun with a meeting with the visiting CEO of the US branch of BRAC, Susan Davis – a confident, middle-aged woman with short, brushed-back blonde hair. She had seemed surprised yet pleased when I'd sought her out in New York a few months earlier and told her I wanted to resign from my Wall Street job and work for BRAC in Uganda.

I'd approached her when the time finally felt right to begin moving out of the world I then inhabited, before it came to define me. It's difficult to overstate just how surreal that existence had become – to have the means not merely to live comfortably, but to party or frolic most weekends without a second thought about the thickness of my wallet.

Living in a shoebox-sized apartment in downtown Manhattan in your early twenties makes you feel you have it all. And yet, paradoxically, I often came home feeling incomplete, unfulfilled by days spent making rich people richer. I had always seen myself as creating a larger social impact than the smiles on millionaires' faces – I believed I was destined for the social sector. However, I remember feeling bewildered when I witnessed a bunch of women – my classmates – strutting around campus, their heads held high, decked out in business suits to interview for sought-after jobs. What was I missing? These women were smart, were they onto something that had escaped me?

A short while later, after some well-crafted emulation, I felt elated when I managed to get a job on Wall Street amid a global financial crisis; reveled in the thought of being able to afford to live in New York City, where my partner would also relocate. Though my days at Morgan Stanley gleamed with corporate polish, I kept my true compass hidden, but unwavering: I was there to study the intricate machinery of private sector success, collecting tools that would one day serve a greater purpose. I gathered each lesson knowing I would reshape these silver spoons into something that could feed more than just profits.

In two years, I felt I had learned enough. If pivoting away from my current client base meant a big pay cut, so be it. I set my sights on working to help smallholder farmers in Africa – this became my pole star. It wasn't long after that I discovered BRAC, a global non-profit, uniquely headquartered in the Global South, in Bangladesh – working on poverty alleviation in some of the world's most conflict-torn countries.

I won't pretend I didn't have any wisps of doubt about the trade-off I'd made, particularly in those final days after I'd put in my papers, when it was already too late. Was I really trading Morgan Stanley for BRAC? What doors might now stay closed?

And then there was Uganda – so far removed from anything I knew. Each passing day there brought new questions.

But after just thirty minutes of talking to Susan on the morning of October 8, 2010, everything clicked into place. Having her assure me of the endless opportunities that awaited me in Kampala and of the boundless potential she saw in me to create real impact did the trick. I had a challenge to scale.

As I walked out of the meeting, I spotted my colleague, Meri, a serene yet vivacious twenty-six-year-old Armenian, seated at her desk, her curly auburn hair flowing past her shoulders. Meri worked as a research associate at BRAC Uganda. She had worked with Susan at BRAC USA and the Center for Child and Family Welfare at Duke University in the US before coming to Kampala. The following day, October 9, was a holiday marking Uganda's Independence Day, and we had an extended weekend to look forward to, to cap off a hectic week.

I walked up to her and suggested that we kick off the long weekend festivities together at my place before we set out for the night. The tiny apartment I shared with our colleague, Saif, and his wife, Jouty, was a five-minute walk from the office in Nyanama, a sparse suburb about a thirty-minute drive from downtown Kampala. The couple were both Bangladeshi. Saif was my colleague at BRAC while Jouty worked at Nyumbani Decor, a furniture store in Kampala.

I had arrived in Kampala six weeks ago and had soon connected with an idealistic crew of young expatriates, mostly working on some form of poverty alleviation with various development organizations. The group I was part of had decided to meet to make the most of the long weekend. We had planned to begin with a barbeque at the home of a young man called Matt, and later, we intended to explore one of the many hotspots in a city I was still discovering.

There was one thing I needed to do before I left Nyanama for the evening – call Nikhil, my partner of the past five years. When I had taken a flight east to Uganda from New York, Nikhil had flown west to enroll at Stanford Law School, returning to the San Francisco Bay Area where he had spent most of his life. He only moved away in 2004, when he gained admission to Harvard University as an undergraduate. At the same time, I left India to study at Wellesley College, also in the Boston area. We met in 2005 and were inseparable.

Dhaval, my best friend at the time, like me, was also starting college at Harvard in 2004, and I would often spend time with him on the weekends. To be honest, it wasn't just Dhaval I wanted to visit but his charming male friends. With a (deserved) reputation for being easily smitten by the opposite sex – I had my first crush as early as the third grade – I was, in that sense, an unlikely candidate for Wellesley, the reputed women's-only liberal arts college that had offered me the best deal for undergraduate study. I had no regrets about my decision since Wellesley proved to be an empowering place. But I longed for male companionship.

One weekend, Dhaval had invited me to a concert at which his band was playing. Students thronged the auditorium, and there was an energetic buzz in the air. Soon, the band started playing, the tempo of the music picked up, and the audience began moving to the beat. "My gosh!" I yelled, leaning closer to Alex, a close friend from Wellesley, to make sure she could hear me over the din. "The lead guitarist's solo is *fiiine*. He's so damn attractive, too!" I had been a fan of rock music since the age of fifteen when Dhaval introduced me to Led Zeppelin. Suffice it to say that I knew a good guitarist when I saw one. This one's finesse had me mesmerized.

Later that night, we went to a party in a cluttered dorm room, with music blaring from speakers of sub-optimal quality. Dhaval introduced me to his friend and bandmate: Nikhil. Soon, we were dancing and every time our bodies touched, my skin tingled, the sensation growing stronger as the night progressed until our lips finally met. He wasn't the best dancer in the room, but that was the last thing on my mind.

The more I came to know Nikhil, the more I felt pulled to him. I was fascinated by how lightly he wore his razor-sharp intellect, combining it with a surfer-casual demeanor vaguely reminiscent of the Dude from *The Big Lebowski*. He was majoring in Social Studies, a prosaic name for an exciting interdisciplinary major at Harvard, in which subjects like politics, economics, sociology, anthropology, and philosophy were applied to a narrow topic in your final dissertation. Nikhil, whose interests were wide-ranging even though he was a true child of the Bay Area, traveled to Egypt to conduct thesis research on the Muslim Brotherhood. He studied advanced Arabic, and researched and wrote on the transformation of modern Islam. As we grew closer, my friends became his, and his mine. Our time together was filled with love, laughter, shared dreams, and endless shenanigans.

Now, in 2010, we had mutually agreed to pursue our individual paths while holding onto our relationship, with the shared belief that giving ourselves space to grow would strengthen our future together. The idea of putting our relationship to this test felt both terrifying and exciting. Could it really survive the miles between us? "If we're still together after a year of a long-distance relationship, we will get married after I graduate from law school," Nikhil had declared before I left. I remember wrapping my arms around him, imagining our wedding at the destination of my dreams – the Neemrana Fort Palace, a historic fort-turned-hotel in Rajasthan.

Nikhil and I would chat regularly. I felt a sense of incompleteness if even a day passed without his involvement in my life in some small way. Advice, commentary, feedback, conversation – I wanted any or all of it. Five years of togetherness that began when we were just eighteen had bound us tight to each other. This co-dependence felt almost innate. Sometimes we talked about the most mundane things. You could do that with Nikhil. He was both brilliant and utterly unpretentious. Perhaps his Punjabi–American roots shaped this blend. Most of his larger clan was spread across California, with some sprinkled far away in Florida. They combined American traditions and Indian ones with gusto. The centerpiece of their Thanksgiving feast was always a masterfully spiced tandoori chicken. Earlier that week, Nikhil had advised me to cook and freeze bulk quantities of keema (minced goat meat) after I told him that I'd bought some for lunch. On another day, I might have asked him to look up a couple of Kampala restaurants or bars for a fun weekend night with my friends.

"Bye, babes, have fun tonight," Nikhil said.

"Yeah, I really gotta go. I wish you were here," I replied. "Love you, Nicky," I added before reluctantly ending the call.

Meri, with an inexplicable sixth sense, had chosen to head to her own place to get dressed and run errands before our night out, giving me some alone time.

Now, I saw her approaching from the open landing outside my apartment. She warmly complimented me on my outfit – a navy blue dress with silhouettes of beige and white flowers, worn over black trousers, if I remember correctly.

As Meri and I chatted about who we might see that night, a sudden thought struck me: we hadn't invited Kizito Davis, a Ugandan man, whom one of our colleagues, Amar, had met a short while ago. They had met at the aptly named Good African Coffee – a sanctuary for English Premier League (EPL) fanatics – where both men had independently sought refuge, each hoping the coffee house would meet their expectations. But it didn't. The cafe wasn't airing the game they'd come to watch.

Two defeated fans. One shared obsession. In desperation, Davis led Amar to a nearby ramshackle structure, its roof made of corrugated iron. He insisted it was a church. Davis knew that the rickety building contained an unexpected treasure: a TV. Amar couldn't believe his luck. He'd found a local friend when he needed one most. To their surprise, entry was ticketed. But the fee was modest.

Within minutes, Amar and Davis were squabbling over which team would win, Manchester United or Tottenham Hotspur. Before Amar left Kampala, he made sure to introduce us to Davis.

I reached for my phone.

"Davis! What are you doing tonight?" I paused, then plowed ahead. "Oh, forget it, you don't have a choice. You're coming out with us!"

"Ah, trust me, I really want to," Davis sighed, "but I have to work..."

"Noooooo!" I wailed. "The night will be no fun without you."

I loved dancing and Davis was my dance partner in Kampala. I nagged him relentlessly until he agreed to join us. "Okay, now that's sorted, let's grab a boda to Matt's house," I said to Meri.

Boda bodas, or motorcycle taxis, are ubiquitous on Ugandan streets for the undeniable convenience they provide to passengers. It's not as if folks taking bodas are unaware of the numerous collisions they are involved in, sometimes resulting in grave injuries and even death. But such tragedies only happened to others.

Just that morning, I had sworn to my parents that I'd buy a helmet the following day and had really meant it this time. I had, myself, witnessed a boda accident just the previous Sunday, with a man rolling on the ground, shrieking in agony.

Despite my desire to purchase a helmet, I simply hadn't made the time during the hectic workweek, and I was in desperate need of a night out – read, buying a helmet was not top priority. That week, I went on a field trip to the rural hinterland of Iganga, located two hours away from Kampala, to visit a group of maize farmers BRAC was training through its agriculture program. As the program manager for agriculture interviewed them, I listened attentively, notebook in hand. BRAC's mission here was clear – to enhance farmers' livelihoods by forming informal groups, promoting fertilizer use, providing storage solutions, educating them on crop life cycles, and offering training. My role was to document these realities by crafting compelling fundraising proposals and concept notes for donors to secure the necessary funds for these critical projects.

I had been moved by the struggles of the women farmers I'd met. Even when I returned to the office, their words echoed in my mind. Despite their productivity, their frustration at being unable to transport their bountiful harvest to the market was palpable. I found myself fidgeting with the plastic folders on my desk, overwhelmed with a feeling of helplessness. But then, I reminded myself that I had moved to Kampala for a reason – I must act, I told myself. After two days of brainstorming, I conceptualized a project for a bus service that would enable these women to transport their crops to market, alleviating their struggles and reducing market inefficiencies.

I was in the early stages of designing this new program, and it had consumed my mind. The thrill of providing a potential lifeline to the women I'd observed toiling under the sun filled me with a strong sense of purpose. I knew I had done the right thing by coming to Uganda. I was planning to spend a full year in the country at BRAC, after which I had ambitions of enrolling at a business school in the US which emphasized nonprofit management and social entrepreneurship. But it was my project I was focusing on, right now; the business school applications had taken a backseat.

As the sun set behind the hills, tinging the sky with a golden glow and illuminating Nyanama's bare landscape, Meri and I scurried to hail a boda.

After haggling with the third boda driver, we settled on a price that would get us to Kitante, an upmarket suburb of Kampala, without carving too deep a hole in our non-profit pockets. Even though the fare into Kampala in 2010 was only three thousand Ugandan shillings – less than one US dollar – the frequency with which we took bodas made haggling a necessity. Besides, price negotiations were expected when taking bodas.

The sun had dipped below the horizon, but the night was young. Meri and I had learned a hack that added a little extra fun to our boda rides while also saving money. Rather than each of us getting our own bodas, we had discovered that two people could share one. I hopped on behind Meri, feeling like a feather being swept up by the wind as the scooter picked up speed. Meri whooped in glee and spread her arms wide like she was flying. We zipped into Kitante, and before long we were stepping into Matt's garden, where laughter and the smoky scent of barbeque greeted us.

Meeting such a diverse group of accomplished and passionate individuals in just the first six weeks filled me with a sense of hope and endless possibilities. Uganda was already shaping up to be more than just a place for meaningful work – it was becoming a place where I would surely make lifelong friendships.

With a quick hello to Matt – who seemed preoccupied with his hosting duties – we strolled over to a group assembled around a table, ready to dig into the food. Nearby, another cluttered table displayed an array of cheap liquor bottles. We tended not to splurge on alcohol. Because of the work we did, we were acutely aware of the pervasive inequality and poverty in Uganda, and it felt brash to buy expensive alcohol when the World Bank's estimate of Uganda's per capita income was a mere $825 per year back then, in 2010.

I had been planning to organize a TEDx Kampala conference with Sujal, another of my new friends, an Indian American who was in Kampala to conduct scholarly research on psychosocial and cognitive rehabilitation for children with HIV/AIDS. Slim, with chiseled features and large eyes, he was personable, extremely intelligent, and fun-loving. I was now waiting for him to arrive so that we could discuss the theme and potential venues for the event. Soon, I spotted him chatting with others in the distance. Upon seeing me, he attempted to tear himself away from the group he was surrounded by. But just then, a couple of other muzungus[2] accosted him. I shrugged and moved on. He'd be back.

As I looked around, I saw several familiar faces. I waved enthusiastically to Eleanor, a young woman who worked at the Clinton Global Health Access Initiative (CHAI) in Uganda. She was working on a pediatric diagnosis of HIV/AIDS at CHAI and was also managing teams from the US Agency for International Development (USAID) and the Centers for Disease Control and Prevention (CDC). I enjoyed her company because of her wealth of experience in global health and always cheerful demeanor. Eleanor pulled me into a hug. Sujal, who had finally managed to extricate himself from his fans, soon joined us.

As we chatted, Jack's booming voice erupted from behind me.

"Let's head to Just Kicking tonight." This was a sports bar with good music, and very popular with our lot.

Sujal turned around, cupping his palms around his mouth, forming a megaphone.

"An executive decision has been made. We are heading to Just Kicking! If anyone objects, speak now or forever hold your peace."

I fished out my phone from my bag and called Davis to find out where he was.

"I'll meet you at Just Kicking soon. I still have to finish working and close the shop," he said.

Like me, Davis was twenty-three years old at the time, his energy as infectious as his easy smile. He walked with a spring in his step. Slight of build, his boyish and good-natured appearance only added to his charm. He had grown up in a family of modest means, and had turned his studio apartment into a barbershop, which he began running when he was just sixteen.

Davis had become a breadwinner at a young age. After his father had passed away, his mother, a stay-at-home mom, struggled to make ends meet. Since money was short, Davis was forced to drop out of school in the sixth grade. Despite the weight on his shoulders, he never let it dim his spirit. He threw himself into our carefree adventures and frivolous activities. He seemed always to be brimming with the knowledge of how to navigate life's curveballs.

Meri and I had grown attached to him in the short time we had known him, and we were already thinking of encouraging him to pursue higher education.

After speaking to Davis, I made a call to Walter, the reliable boda driver who'd handed me his business card on a previous ride, promising us that safety was his utmost priority. Having availed Walter's services on several occasions, I asked him for his help ferrying me and my friends to Just Kicking. Soon enough, Walter arrived with his friend, Denis, another boda driver, and we got ready to navigate the lively streets of Kampala.

2

That Frenzied Second

Of the three of us riding on Denis's boda, only one of us was wearing a helmet: Denis, the driver. As a result, he had minor injuries, like broken bones. Sujal had bought his helmet about ten days before, and since then, had never been seen traveling on a boda without it. He even wrote about it on his blog[3]: "Bought a helmet for my boda-boda rides. Very, very happy about this, partly because I'll be safer and partly because I won't show up to work with a thick layer of red dust on my face anymore." But on this night, of all nights, it was not on his head.

The three of us were violently thrown off the bike when an unknown vehicle collided into us from behind. The impact was brutal. The moment gravity pulled us to the ground, our consciousness slipped away. Meanwhile, the offending vehicle vanished into the night.

Or so I'm told.

All I can recall – will ever recall – are the moments preceding the crash. My sensations during the accident and my memory of it remain elusive, relegated to the realm of imagination.

Despite its many flaws, the human body is a miraculous work of art. In accidents as severe as mine, our bodies instinctively shut down at the moment of impact to protect us from a world of pain. That's what happened to Sujal and me when our heads hit the unforgiving tarmac. The world went dark, our bodies shattered, and our systems shut down in that split second when our brains registered the devastating impact. I felt nothing. It would be another three months before memories would begin trickling back in. Not of the crash, but the day, full of promise, that had preceded it. The crash I would never remember.

Meanwhile, Davis, already at Just Kicking, hopped off his boda, mumbled a quick "*asante*" to the boda driver, and made his way inside. It was 11 p.m. Outside, the night pressed dark and silent against the windows, but inside Just Kicking, the room was buzzing – a mix of familiar faces and unfamiliar names. Davis surveyed the room, looking for Meri and me, then reached for his phone when he came up empty.

He stepped out just as Meri disembarked from her boda, with Jack in tow.

"I don't want to get into what took you so long," Davis teased. "I'll wait for Tarini to explain."

Minutes crawled by. Clutching his phone, Davis tried calling me again. Even now, fourteen years later, his voice still cracks when he recalls that night. Four rings. Five. Six. He cut the line and tried again, resisting the impatience, if not rising panic, bubbling within. Still nothing. He would later tell me that he could hear his heart beating inside his chest, beating harder with each passing minute.

A feeling of cold concern was growing inside Meri.

"Have you tried calling Sujal?" she asked, suddenly realizing that she hadn't paid her boda driver, Walter, his fare. Glancing around, she noticed that everyone from the barbeque had arrived – everyone except Sujal and me.

Meri walked up to Walter and spoke with urgency in her voice.

"Walter, please wait till we hear from our friends. We will pay you extra for your time."

Walter waited, shifting his weight from one foot to another. More time passed. At the fifteenth minute, he tapped Meri's shoulder lightly. Meri hurriedly gestured to Davis to tell her if she could let the boda driver leave.

Davis, his phone still to his ear, said, "No reply from Sujal either. I want to try Tarini again." As he waited for me to answer the phone, Davis pictured my boda speeding through the blackened streets of Kampala, the gritty exhaust fumes filling my lungs. No answer. He tried Sujal again. He had a feeling Sujal would answer his phone this time.

The call was indeed answered, but not by Sujal. He heard a gruff, unfamiliar male voice instead.

His heart sank.

"Who's speaking?"

"I'm a police officer," the man said, speaking with urgency. "We found this phone lying on the road near a motorcycle accident."

Davis almost choked.

"What? What do you mean? Where are the two people who were riding the boda? Are they okay?"

Hearing his questions, Meri rushed over to Davis and gripped him by the shoulder as he stumbled backward. Her eyes searched his face for clues.

"There were three people on the boda who have been hurt: a young man, a young woman, and the boda driver," the police officer said. "At this time, we can't say if the two young people are alright. They are both unconscious."

Davis felt like he'd been punched in the gut.

"Oh my god. Where are you? I'm coming."

"The accident was at Yusuf Lule Road," the officer said, his voice steady. "As soon as we found them, we called for an ambulance. It took your friends straight to the ER in Mulago Hospital. That's where you'll find them."

Before he finished speaking, Davis had jumped on Walter's boda with Meri following closely behind.

Meri and Davis were ushered into a chaotic emergency room, where Sujal and I had been rushed and kept at opposite ends in a room stripped bare of privacy – not a curtain in sight. Patients lay helpless on stretchers on the floor, signaling a shortage of beds. My friends' eyes swept desperately across the room, searching for any trace of me. According to Davis and Meri, the few medical staff present hurried past, leaving questions hanging in the air.

Finally, they spotted me lying motionless on a bare leather stretcher, strapped to a ventilator, with blue and white tubes protruding from various parts of my body. I lay in an unnatural posture, stiff, with arms bent, fists clenched against my chest, legs stretched rigid. The wrist and fingers of my right arm were flexed and held to my chest. My left arm flailed in the air, making jerky, involuntary, inward movements, and my eyelids flickered without seeing. Blood stained my skull, belly, and mouth.

Knowing Meri and Davis, once they'd located me, their first instinct would have been to search for Sujal, but the shock of what they saw hit them so hard, it froze them in place. It was only later that they would go to Sujal, whose roommate had been called in the meantime.

Davis was trembling. He took a step closer to me, afraid of shattering the fragile stillness around my being. He searched my face for any hints of recognition – even a familiar flicker of the eye would do. Nothing. Tears sprang to his eyes. Meri ran out of the room, unable to breathe, unable to hold back tears.

Composing himself, Davis noticed my clothes were badly torn, exposing me to the world. He quickly pointed this out to Meri, who took off her jacket to drape across my torso.

Wiping her puffy eyes, she said, "One of us should go search for a shop nearby that sells clothes and buy some basics to put on Tarini."

Pointing out that no shops would be open at this hour, Davis said he would go to the homes of two women he knew who lived in the area, instead.

Before Davis could leave for his friends' houses, a nurse informed him and Meri that Sujal and I would soon be taken for X-rays and CT scans. These scans would help in diagnosing any unseen injuries in our bodies and determine what treatment we needed.

Digesting this information the best he could, Davis left and soon returned with a bag full of clothes. How was he to know that, amid all the chaos, they wouldn't even have a moment or the mind space to think about changing my clothes? Meanwhile, Meri had been calling our colleagues and friends, telling them about the accident, asking for people to come to the hospital to help.

Another nurse appeared. She stripped off my pants to insert a catheter, not stopping to drape a cloth over me. It feels like a shocking detail, but it is what poor, sick people go through in busy public hospitals in the developing world all the time. Meri was distressed to see injured and sick patients left on the floor, surrounded by broken machines in the hospital. But she did find solace in the remarkable dedication of the hospital staff, who worked through the night, making the best use of the limited resources at their disposal.

Saif and Jouty, my flatmates, arrived shortly after they received the soul-crushing news, bringing a fresh burst of support for my two weary and anxious friends.

Jouty's hands flew to her mouth when she saw the state that I was in. She and Saif quickly went back home to our apartment to pick up sheets, blankets, and some of my clothes.

After tending to me and taking care of my immediate needs, Davis and Meri went to Sujal.

Crossing the room, they found Sujal's roommate standing at the foot of his bed with a furrowed brow and trembling lower lip. While my injuries came from the impact with the ground, Sujal had borne the full force of the vehicle that struck us from behind. Being seated at the rear, he took the first and hardest hit. Unlike me, he was visibly unconscious, his eyelids were gently shut and his body was utterly still.

Though shaken, his roommate – who, like Sujal, was also in Uganda for medical work – set aside his own emotions to focus on Sujal's condition. He gathered his thoughts and made a few calls to his contacts who he believed might have access to competent Ugandan doctors.

At around midnight, in a hospital ward that had imperceptibly transitioned from frenetic activity to the eerie stillness of a cemetery, Sujal's roommate placed a call to his supervisor, a seasoned medical professional of Asian American descent working in Uganda. She rushed to Mulago Hospital at once to perform a quick, sighted assessment of Sujal and me, then immediately reached out to one of just four neurosurgeons in all of Uganda (that number, I would read later, had only grown to thirteen by early 2020). In a stroke of luck, one of the four neurosurgeons, Dr. John Baptist Mukasa, happened to work at this very hospital.

Dr. Mukasa wasted no time in expediting the CT scans that had been ordered for us.

As a nurse pushed my stretcher toward the X-Ray and CT scan rooms, Meri rushed to my side. Another nurse had already asked Sujal's roommate and Davis to move Sujal onto a stretcher and take him for his scan.

Meri and Davis remained at my side, forming a protective shield around my stretcher as we moved down the hallway to stand outside the room where Sujal was undergoing his CT scan. I was next. Although I was unconscious, my left arm continued its rapid, jerky movements, like a ship lost at sea, tossed by tumultuous waves with no port in sight. It was almost as if I was rebelling against my state of suspended animation.

"I am going to stay with her," Meri said to the nurse.

"Okay," the nurse responded, gently handling the silver necklace around my neck, a gift from Nikhil that I never removed. "Let's make sure we remove all the metal from her body."

Meri scanned me from head to toe. She unfastened my necklace, unclasped my watch, and slipped the bracelet off my wrist.

"All done," she announced to the nurse.

Double-checking Meri's handiwork, the nurse ran her eyes up and down my body and then shook her head, pointing to my blue nose pin. "Sorry, but that will have to go as well."

Meri examined the delicate blue gemstone studded in my nose and came to the realization that taking it off was easier said than done, because of an intricately woven coil of wire that kept the nose pin in place. No matter how hard she tried to dislodge it, the blue stone remained stubbornly immovable.

"Are you not able to figure it out?" the nurse asked.

"No, but I know who can." Meri whipped out her phone to call Jouty, who was already waiting downstairs in the hospital lobby.

"Jouty, Tarini needs your help." Jouty ran up, and Meri's tense shoulders relaxed when she saw that Jouty was indeed able to remove the intricately wound nose pin often worn by South Asian women.

Stripped of its final trace of metal, my lifeless body was ushered into the CT scan machine. My fate hung in the balance, to be decided by machines and their readings.

While Sujal's roommate had managed to speak to Sujal's parents, mine had no idea I was lying comatose in a hospital bed. In the mere six weeks I had been in Kampala, I had not yet had a chance to talk to Meri and Davis about my family. To make matters worse, my phone was missing, having likely fallen out of my bag during the collision.

Before my friends could decide how to reach my parents, Davis caught sight of two fraught-looking nurses walking out of the CT scan room toward them.

Meri bolted upright. What now?

"There seems to be a problem with the CT scan machines," one of the two nurses said, her voice calm but concerned. She paused, before adding with a reassuring smile, "But don't worry, Dr. Mukasa is getting your friends transferred to a private hospital with working machines and spare ICU beds."

Six years later, in a private chat on Facebook, Dr. Mukasa confessed to me, "I keep wondering how I took the decision to transfer such sick people to another hospital." Perhaps the answer lies in doctors' instincts. When confronted with decisions fraught with risk, they lean toward whatever is best for their patient's health and safety.

Dr. Mukasa moved fast. While Davis and Meri were preparing to tell Sujal's roommate about the latest complication, a team of medical professionals marched down the hallway toward them, two grim-looking doctors escorted by four nurses.

"We have arranged for an ambulance to take both your friends to International Hospital, Kampala – IHK," one of the doctors said. He turned to Meri and added, "There is space for only one of you in the ambulance. Which one of you will ride with your friends?"

Davis jumped at the chance to exercise his local know-how to help his friends.

The ambulance set off with a jolt, bouncing and swaying over the rough roads of Kampala, dodging potholes and weaving through traffic. Crouching between our supine bodies, Davis used his arms to help stabilize both of our stretchers. He held on tight to protect Sujal and me from being jolted too severely by the bumps and turns in the road. Meanwhile, Meri and Sujal's roommate followed close behind in a second vehicle.

Upon arriving at IHK, the scene from Mulago essentially played on repeat, albeit this time in a hospital with actual sheets. The medical team at IHK asked a slew of personal questions about me to fill out the admission forms, answers to which Davis and Meri obviously didn't possess. However, due to the critical nature of the situation, they expedited our CT scans without insisting on the forms being completed. Thankfully, my body was already metal-free.

The results of our scans would take a few hours, which provided my friends with the headspace to consider how to contact my parents, whom they knew nothing about. Meri had spent enough time with me in my tiny room to know that my laptop, in all its password-unprotected glory, was just sitting there.

"I can hop on a matatu to fetch the laptop from Tarini's apartment," Davis said. It isn't hard to understand why he suggested the more sedate shared taxi over the expeditious boda boda, which would normally have been his preferred mode of transport.

"No, Davis, I would rather you stay here with me. We can ask Saif or Jouty to bring her laptop to us."

Davis softened, understanding Meri's fears.

"Okay. Don't worry, I'm not going anywhere."

When Saif and Jouty returned with my laptop, Meri checked my Facebook profile for clues. She wouldn't have had any idea just how averse my parents are to social media.

Coincidentally, October 8, the date of the accident, also happens to be my aunt Peggy Mohan's birthday, and she'd recently joined Facebook. Since it was 2010, it was still common to post "Happy Birthday" on people's walls, as they were called then (later they became timelines). I'd done exactly that earlier in the day. As Meri went through my Facebook feed, she chanced upon the birthday message I had posted for my aunt and deduced from her last name that we might be related. She sent her a cold message.

But Meri could not just wait for my aunt's reply. Her mind raced with the difficult tasks that lay ahead of her. The responsibility of informing my loved ones seemed too heavy for her to carry alone. Obviously, Nikhil needed to know at once, and he could help her contact my family as well. But who would tell him? The thought of informing my partner crushed her like a ton of bricks.

Suddenly, an idea struck her.

"Let's reach out to Santhosh," she suggested.

Curious, Davis asked, "Santhosh? Why?"

"He's one of us. He knows the situation; he's dependable and wise," Meri explained. "Plus, he has a way with words. He can break the news to Nikhil, who can call her parents."

The idea was sound – Santhosh was our colleague and friend. Originally from India, he was now based in New York City, working as a senior project manager at BRAC USA. At the moment, he was involved in scaling BRAC International's microfinance company in

Uganda. Everyone at BRAC trusted Santhosh. You always had the sense that he would go out of his way to help you, if you ever needed it. Meri and Davis felt a weight lift off their shoulders as they set their plan in motion, knowing that they could now rely on one more person to help them navigate this impossible situation.

Dr. Hussein Ssenyonjo, the second of the country's four neurosurgeons, also miraculously on duty at IHK at the moment, cleared his throat.

"We have run the necessary tests and, unfortunately, the results are not what we had hoped for."

Meri's world tilted. She felt Davis's hand grip hers.

"Your friends have severe traumatic brain injuries. They are both in deep comas. The young lady scored an 8 on the Glasgow Coma Scale, or GCS," he informed them solemnly.

My friends didn't have to know what the Glasgow Coma Scale was to understand that the doctor had just delivered dire news. Meri and Davis stood in silent shock, grappling with the gravity of the situation as the doctor's words washed over them. The GCS is a tool used to assess and calculate a patient's level of consciousness, using a triple criteria scoring system to do so – best eye-opening (maximum of 4), best verbal response (maximum of 5), and best motor response (maximum of 6). These scores are added up to result in a total score between 3 and 15.

Traumatic brain injuries or TBIs are tricky terrain – caused by a forceful blow, bump, or jolt to the head or body, or from an object that pierces the skull and enters the brain. My case was clearly the first of these. The injury to my brain is diffused, affecting not just a single region, but several niche areas. It was as if a tornado had ripped through my brain, leaving behind a trail of destruction in its wake. Dr. Ssenyonjo believed the consequences could be fatal if he did not act swiftly.

He also discovered a fracture in my skull. The ruptured blood vessels had allowed a crimson river to flow freely between the skull and the outer lining of the brain. Without hesitation, he diagnosed it as an epidural hematoma, a clinical term referring to blood accumulating between the skull and the dura mater, the outermost layer of the membranes protecting the brain.

The right side of my body took the brunt of the impact of hitting the ground, yet it was my left brain that bore the real damage – its neurons shattered by the violent jolt.

"Tarini is currently being prepared for emergency surgery. I hope you have been able to contact her parents." It was more a statement than a question. Without waiting for an answer, Dr. Ssenyonjo signed a form a nurse placed in front of him, and strode briskly into the OR.

Despite the crippling news Dr. Ssenyonjo had dropped on my friends, they couldn't help but notice the strange sense of peace they had felt in his presence, with his calm demeanor and quiet confidence.

And just like that, within a span of a few hours, I managed to be operated on by half of Uganda's entire crew of neurosurgeons.

3

Heart-Stopping News

Out in San Francisco, Nikhil had been looking forward to a much-needed respite from his law school routine in the company of his childhood friends. As I write this, I imagine him in his signature blue T-shirt with "STOP WARS" in yellow lettering splashed across the front, a playful nod to his love for Star Wars. He clutches a pint of beer in one hand while queueing up classic rock tunes with the other. Suddenly, his Motorola flip phone buzzes in his back pocket; his eyes light up upon seeing the Uganda area code, and he quickly answers.

It was Santhosh.

As his words registered, Nikhil went still. Later, he described feeling as if he were floating in space, untethered from the ground beneath him. His friends drew near, forming a constellation of quiet support.

A heavy silence ensued as the word "coma" reverberated in the air.

Another friend broke the silence: "Don't worry, she's a fighter." Two of Nikhil's friends sensed the depth of his despair and hugged him tight, offering whatever comfort they could muster at that moment.

"I … I gotta go home," Nikhil stammered, his voice trembling with uncertainty. "I have to think of the million things I need to do to help." He took a quick gulp of his beer in an attempt to steady his nerves.

"I'll take you to your parents' place. You really shouldn't be alone, Nikhil," one of his friends said. Nikhil felt lucky to be with the four friends who best understood what he needed; they knew his parents were his biggest source of comfort. Also, his father was a gastroenterologist – he might know other doctors who could help.

Nikhil climbed into the passenger seat beside his friend and took a deep breath, bracing himself for the call he'd have to make to my parents.

My parents were winding down for the night in New Haven, Connecticut, when they heard Papa's cell phone ringing. It was unusual for Nikhil to call, especially at such a late hour. Papa took the call, with curiosity rather than dread, only to be confronted with the kind of news that is every parent's worst nightmare.

In those first terrifying moments, my parents considered racing to the airport – but paused, knowing they needed more information about my condition. Papa wasted no time in dialing Santhosh's number, which Nikhil had shared.

"This is Rakesh Mohan, Tarini's father," he said, introducing himself in a measured tone, despite the turmoil within.

"Yes, hello, Rakesh. I am glad you called," replied Santhosh. "Tarini is in a critical condition and is comatose in the ICU at International Hospital, Kampala. The neurosurgeon says her reports are not looking good," he said bluntly. Later, he said he felt it was important at that moment to be as direct as possible.

My father was rendered almost speechless with shock. He replied, with difficulty, in a choked voice, telling Santhosh that he and my mother would fly out at once.

Back in Delhi, my aunt, Peggy, had read Meri's message and rushed to inform her husband, my father's older brother, Dinesh Mohan, about my accident. It's truly ironic – and shameful for me to admit – that my uncle was, at the time, one of India's pre-eminent road safety experts. (Later, COVID-19 was to tragically claim his life.) His expertise spanned transportation safety and injury prevention. One of the many things he had focused on, in his efforts to protect road users at higher risk, was designing motorcycle helmets.

My family isn't overly sentimental, or even openly affectionate. It's almost like we are all allergic to saying "I love you" to each other – as if the words might send us into some kind of emotional anaphylactic shock. But in moments of real need, they're there.

Dinesh Tau (uncle) immediately contacted his dear friend, a pre-eminent Indian orthopedic surgeon based in Delhi, Dr. Matthew Verghese, and another friend at the World Health Organization (WHO) in Kampala. He informed Matthew of the situation and that they'd be calling him for advice and with questions. Dinesh Tau also requested the friend at the WHO to visit the hospital to check up on me. Shortly afterwards, he called my father, telling him what he had done. Before ending the call, my uncle calmly added that he would see my father in Kampala. He had already bought his flight ticket.

In New Haven, my parents set aside their emotions for the time being and got to work. There was no time for anxious thoughts. Just three months ago, my father had been appointed professor in the practice of economics at Yale University. It was his first foray into academia after a career as one of India's foremost economists in public service. Nikhil's phone call had come at the end of a long day of high-profile meetings with Larry Summers, the director of the National Economic Council of the United States, for which my father had flown to Washington, DC. The meeting had occurred against the backdrop of then-President Barack Obama's upcoming trip to India, but none of that was important now. My parents' priority was taking care of everything they needed to do before flying to Kampala.

The top priority was reaching my younger brother, Rasesh, or Rasoo, as I lovingly call him. Rasoo was in his final year of college, also at Yale, majoring in political science. That night, he was in New York City with friends. Rasoo and I have always been like two peas in a pod, despite the three-year age gap. Unbelievably, we never squabbled as kids and would instead happily play with one another or read side by side; we even created an imaginary world and populated it with residents who spoke a language that only the two of us understood. When he was little, he would position himself on the floor of the passageway between the room we shared and my father's study, where my mother had taped a giant world map on the wall. Crouching on the cool stone floor tiles, holding a marker in his left hand, he wouldn't tire of noting down the capital cities of each country.

My parents did not have the time or mental space to worry about how Rasoo would take the news of my accident. They tried, in vain, to contact him that night. He wasn't answering. They continued trying even while attending to the countless other tasks still needing their attention. Papa glanced up from his laptop, the blue glare concealing the pallor on his face. He'd realized they also had to call Nikhil back to tell him they were leaving the next evening for Kampala, for he planned to travel with them to Uganda. From Nikhil, they learned that Rasesh was in a bar with Darshini, my friend Pallavi's sister.

Pallavi is one of my closest friends. We shared an apartment in downtown Manhattan after we graduated from college. Our younger siblings, Rasesh and Darshini, followed in our footsteps to study at the Mahindra United World College of India (MUWCI), an international boarding school in Pune. Darshini and Rasoo were in fact in NYC for an unofficial reunion with school friends.

In a relatively quiet corner of the bar, away from the blare of the speakers, Darshini cut the call she had been on.

"My sister just called to tell me that your parents have been trying to reach you, but you aren't answering your phone," Darshini blurted out. She was at a loss for words. She took a moment to compose herself before continuing. Rasoo looked at her quizzically.

"Tarini has been in a serious accident," her voice cracked as she spoke. "She is in a coma, in a hospital in Uganda," she rushed to explain, before attempting to soften the blow. "We are all in this together. You know that Tarini is like a sister to me."

She placed her hand on Rasoo's shoulder to steady him. My brother immediately made a series of phone calls, to our parents, and to Nikhil, focusing on whatever facts he could extract from them.

After hanging up, he muttered, "A traumatic brain injury," testing out the phrase for himself, unsure of what to make of this diagnosis he had just heard.

"I'm fine, guys," he insisted when his friends tried to hug him.

It didn't take long for Rasoo's logical brain, resistant to catastrophic thinking, to take charge.

"Darshini, tell me everything you know about traumatic brain injuries," he pleaded. Darshini, who was pursuing a PhD in neuroscience at Columbia University, suggested they continue the conversation in her apartment, where she knew Rasoo would have more privacy and freedom to react. The reunion had taken a form no one could have predicted. The group congregated in Darshini's small Upper West Side apartment. Once they settled into her cramped living room, she mustered the courage to broach the topic of my injury again. Despite my brother's calm manner, his friends could sense how deeply affected he was. They stayed by his side through the night.

The last time my parents had spoken to me was two days earlier when I had chattered non-stop about my new lunch routine of walking with my colleagues to the shed in which nearly all fifty BRAC Uganda office staff ate together. At the time, more than half the employees were Bangladeshi and the rest local. The lunch menu was reliably rice and watery yellow dal – not exactly gourmet, but Amar, Meri, and I would devour it like a delicacy.

With a giggle, I recounted how earlier that day, Jackson, the warm and ever-cheerful kitchen boy, had entered the compact lunch shed, holding up a platter of … fish heads. Grinning from ear to ear, he'd placed it at the center of our table with a flourish. Catching Amar's eye, he pointed toward the fish heads and then pressed his index finger to his lips, as if sharing some grand culinary secret. Once Jackson returned to the kitchen, Meri leaned in and whispered conspiratorially that Jackson probably wanted to fill us up with fish heads so that there'd be enough of the "actual" fish for others. We sat upright, adamant we would wait for the fish's body to arrive, along with the customary dal and rice. No fish heads for us.

While our colleagues chomped on the fish heads – the only source of protein on the table – we waited, confident our superior tactics would give us the last laugh. But after twenty minutes, it finally dawned on us: there was no "rest of the fish". Clearly, Jackson had bought only the heads, and the vendor was still waiting for wealthier customers to purchase the bodies. I'd narrated how we'd returned to our desks, stomachs growling, while Meri, ever the optimist, tried turning the experience into a life lesson: never make assumptions based on just a part of the picture.

My parents had chuckled, amused by the odd experiences I was having. When I'd announced quitting Morgan Stanley months earlier, they'd taken it in their stride, as true, old-fashioned liberals who valued meaning over money. Though strict in my childhood, especially Mama, they'd loosened their grip after seeing me thrive at boarding school, college, and in New York. I'd earned a reputation for being meticulously organized, a trait confirmed when they later found my Kampala room in perfect order, every file in its place.

Now, their world lay shattered. Yet in their responses – each distinct, each fitting – I see our family's essence: how they found strength in ways uniquely their own. In their different but complementary responses, you can read the story of my family.

My father activated his most essential self – the methodical problem-solver. He worked his way through the tasks on his mental to-do list. One of his first actions was reaching out to an acquaintance, the Ugandan ambassador to India, to confirm that visas could indeed be obtained on arrival. To his relief, the ambassador promised to connect him with her friends in Uganda who would provide my parents with any help they needed.

Mama is a natural pragmatist, a trait that has served her well through decades of adapting to new countries and changed circumstances. She immediately rushed to pack their suitcases, trying to anticipate what they would need in Kampala. She had no sense of how long their stay would be. Would it be cold in October? What kind of shoes should she pack? Should she take something for me? There were no proper answers but each folded shirt, each travel document arranged in sequence, was a small act of control in a situation that could have spiraled into chaos. "Sitting there howling," as she put it later, with her characteristic directness, "wasn't going to help".

Papa knew he needed to inform the university, but it didn't feel like it was the right time. It had only been two months since he'd started teaching at Yale. Finally, after a couple of agonizing hours, he made the calls. Professor Levinsohn, the head of the School of Global Affairs, immediately reassured him that a substitute teacher would take care of his classes, and offered him the university's full support.

Several miles away, in New York, Rasoo trudged to the train station at dawn, his eyes puffy from lack of sleep. As he boarded the train, the ride felt interminable, each passing mile stretching out like a lifetime. He emerged from the station determined not to consider the possibility that I might never wake up. He instead willed himself to believe that I would return to my boisterous self in no time, perhaps even before my parents arrived in Kampala.

This signaled an extraordinary capacity to hold on to hope. The pivotal fact was, I was alive, and as long as there is life, there is hope. My parents' extraordinary composure, too, was driven not by blind optimism but by holding on to this most fundamental of life's truths: as long as breath flows, possibilities exist. Their hope was also fueled by experience. They had witnessed other families recover from similar traumatic injuries. A friend and another family's daughter-in-law had both managed to pick up the threads of their lives after traumatic brain injuries. They held fast onto these experiences as they prepared for Kampala.

Less than a day after the catastrophe that was to change their lives, my parents were on an airplane, huddling close together. Amid the haze that his thoughts had become, after all the organizing had been done, Papa heard his cell phone ring in Amsterdam, where they had a layover. It was the Indian family, Bina and Shaishav Nanavati, to whom the Ugandan ambassador to India had connected my parents.

Coincidentally, just a few weeks ago, Meri, Davis, and I had met with the Nanavatis' son, Akshay, for dinner at a Chinese restaurant. He'd introduced us to his parents at their home that same evening. Upon hearing my name, the Nanavatis immediately rushed to IHK. They found me comatose but stable, having just emerged from emergency brain surgery. The Nanavatis' phone call to my parents helped quell the storm raging in their heads.

Looking back, what strikes me isn't just how vulnerable we were as a family then, but also the many comforts we had that helped us cope. I was lying comatose in a country in which over half the people live in deep poverty, sometimes described as multidimensional poverty. It's a type of hardship that includes struggles with education, healthcare, and all the things from food to drinking water to electricity, needed to lead a decent life. Nevertheless, I was fortunate enough to have access to not only half of Uganda's neurosurgeons, receiving care in the relative comfort of a private hospital, but was also benefiting from my parents' skillful leveraging of their social network to ensure I received the best possible attention under the circumstances.

Nikhil traveled to Uganda with a return ticket in hand. Struggling with a tidal wave of emotions, he clung to hope with Pavlovian tenacity. He willed himself to believe I'd regain consciousness within a week. After all, he told himself, this was reality, not a movie. And he wanted us to have at least one week together after I "woke up", so he booked a flight for two weeks later.

Once in Kampala, he politely declined my parents' offer to have him share a room with my uncle in their hotel. Instead, Nikhil and Meri obtained permission to stay at the hospital, in a spare room on the floor above the ICU, where I was.

Nikhil's reason for choosing to stay in the hospital was simple – he wanted to be as close to me as possible. Living in proximity to me on the hospital premises would make life easier. In reality, the entire experience was, I heard from him later, like staring into a chasm of bleakness. He had hoped that his unstinting presence by my bedside would bring relief to my unconscious mind and that I would wake up. But he was hoping for too much, too soon. He clasped my hand and talked to me, love radiating from his body despite my limp form and changed appearance. Lying before him was not the Tarini he knew – an attractive woman with long, wavy black hair – but a patient with a shaved head, in an overflowing hospital gown, and white and blue tubes snaking from her arms and nose – tubes to help her breathe, and restore blood volume, and blood pressure in the face of trauma and hemorrhagic shock.

His routine in Kampala was relentlessly grim. Gradually, he grew accustomed to shuttling between his bare hospital room, the ICU where I lay comatose, my parents' hotel nearby for his daily shower, and the shed outside the hospital where everyone gathered for dinner. Dining with my family and friends was the only break from his routine. The dinners were provided by numerous acquaintances in Kampala, none of whom my father had previously known. The Indian ambassador to Uganda, who heard of Papa's predicament through a common friend, went out of his way to provide home-cooked Indian food, and thus, a semblance of familiarity and comfort. Day after day, my visitors awaited the food sent by the Indian ambassador.

For every imaginable reason – and the myriad reasons that cannot possibly be imagined – Nikhil grew more forlorn with each passing day, sitting by my side with slumped shoulders and an averted gaze. Those two weeks felt like an eternity to him.

During one of those relentless days, Nikhil stood before the bathroom mirror, his eyes fixed on his reflection. He noticed the puffiness around his eyes and the worry lines etched across his forehead that betrayed his growing anxiety. His scruffy appearance startled him, signaling that a change of plan was in order. Right then, he made the tough decision to take a year off from law school. He knew he could always return to complete his degree later. He wouldn't graduate with his current classmates – a small price to pay for the relative peace of mind he was confident would follow. Nikhil felt the clouds in his mind lifting. He could fly to New Haven or India – wherever I'd be next – to visit me once every few months. He felt infinitely lighter now.

Soon, his two weeks were up, and it was time for him to board his flight back to San Francisco. But I still hadn't regained consciousness. He now had to admit it to himself – my condition was more serious than he'd thought. I hadn't stirred for two entire weeks, and although he thought he'd glimpsed glimmers of improvement, there was no saying if it was real.

4

Fractured Stillness

As for me, although my body insisted on ticking on, I had vanished into an abyss. Minutes, hours, and days had all merged into an indistinct blur. In a comatose state, I was not beholden to time or to anyone, and even if I was, I was beyond the reach of accountability. It was as if I had surrendered to the ebb and flow of existence. Might as well swim with the tide.

For three long and harrowing months, my parents' world twisted into a labyrinth of uncertainty. In Kampala, they kept vigil, navigating the unfamiliar hum of a foreign hospital, drawing comfort from the silent warmth of my unconscious form, and waiting for a sign of consciousness. In my first comatose month there, the doctors had deemed my condition critical and judged me unfit to travel. While IHK became my parents' sanctuary, they were all too aware that they had to think ahead. Mama tended to me and Papa orchestrated a series of phone calls, seeking the counsel of various medical experts. Rick Levin, the president of Yale University, generously connected my father to an expert neurosurgeon in the university system for his guidance.

Armed with information, my parents deliberated on the next step: should they fly me to the US or to India? President Levin offered to arrange a private medical evacuation flight to fly me back to Yale. This plan would let my parents oversee my care while allowing Papa to continue his teaching responsibilities. But after a lot of back-and-forth, they made the tough choice to return to India. The thought of being surrounded by family and friends whom they could lean on was a source of immeasurable comfort to them.

I flew on a stretcher aboard a regular commercial Emirates flight while still comatose. A doctor and nurse accompanied us, standing guard by my stretcher through the duration of the flight. It was all so well orchestrated that it was almost like a covert operation. Dinesh Tau, my parents' anchor, arrived at the airport to receive them. First, I was put into an airport ambulance, then another ambulance, which took me straight to Max Hospital. When I ask my parents now what it felt like to arrive in India with me in that state, they look at each other and shrug. Hours, if not days, seem to have slipped from their memories. Vinod, our trusty driver, remembers them coming out of the airport in a shell-shocked trance.

Now back home, they held their breath, suspended between hope and fear. For two more months, they danced on the precipice of despair. As in Uganda, in India too, doctors could offer no solace, no glimpses into the future, for the brain's secrets remain as vast as the night sky and as personal as fingerprints. Their hearts ached as they stood witness to this mysterious battle.

It was after three months of dormancy that I first felt a flicker of sensation in my body. Though the exact moment I emerged from endless sleep is lost on me, the raw intensity of my awakening is seared into my memory: the harsh hospital lights, the weight of my own body feeling foreign and wrong, my mind struggling to grasp where and when I was. Every sensation was overwhelming – my nerve endings had forgotten how to process the world.

I tried to move my arm, but it remained stiff and immovable, resisting my efforts to budge it. *Why is my arm locked in a cage?* My right leg lay equally mutinous, bound in an even crueler contraption – a medieval-looking brace that climbed from ankle to knee like ivy choking a tree. Yet, it was my arm that screamed the loudest; that feeling was more acute, closer to the core of me.

A gentle lady dressed in pristine white uniform, pressed crisp despite the late hour, moved with the practiced grace of someone who had tended to thousands of broken bodies. Her hands found my arm, each adjustment whispering compassion and care. The way she held herself, the quiet authority in her movements, told me she was a nurse.

Have I gone crazy? How can that be? This is just a nightmare. Before I know it, it will be morning, and I'll open my eyes and find myself under my red comforter in my bed in Manhattan.

Awareness came and went. I drifted into hazy wakefulness. And then I drifted back to sleep. And so on. For me, nothing felt real yet either, and it wouldn't for a long time to come. Time ticked on.

Still, the absence of an epiphanic moment of re-emergence didn't diminish my parents' joy when they noticed my fingers twitching with purpose. Each small victory – a finger bend, a hand squeeze, a slight turn of the hand – wrote itself across their features in a language of cautious hope. These small gestures, at the very least, signaled my presence.

On the fourth day, my heavy eyelids finally won the battle with gravity. I blinked into a world that made no sense. Women clad in white. Sterile surroundings. Imposing machines. Everything gleamed with that harsh hospital shine. There were long moments when nothing existed. Space felt confined, constricting. The edges of my dreams blurred into a strange, unsettling haze, until I couldn't tell which was which.

None of this matters because this is just a dream. It shall pass.

During my absence from this world, I surely must have floated to my happy place – the place where it seemed like I had all the pieces of my life seamlessly assembled, where the building blocks of my dream life appeared to have fallen into place. That place was New York City …

I glanced at the hands of the clock above my cubicle and groaned out loud. The constant tick-tock was an unwelcome reminder of how slowly time passed in the office, particularly on Friday evenings. I had another half an hour to endure before I could leave the dreariness behind and return to my comfortable East Village haven. Though my Morgan Stanley office was usually quite cheerful, it took on a sickly feel at the end of the work week, with the overhead tube lights emitting their fluorescent glow, sucking out any remaining vestiges of life.

Tomorrow was the weekend, and Nikhil, Zak, Jon, and I were getting ready to host our group at the boys' spacious apartment. I felt a spark of joy when I thought about how our little group – including Pallavi – resembled the group in the sitcom *Friends*. *Friends* was more than just a sitcom for me – it was the blueprint of urban young-adult life, a seductive ideal of what friendship could look like in your twenties. The characters worked in wonderfully improbable jobs – a waitress turned fashion buyer, a masseuse, a chef, a paleontologist – that seemed to give them all the time for coffee-shop conversations and endless shenanigans. Unlike them, the people in my real group of friends sustained our New York lifestyle by doing occasionally soul-sucking corporate jobs. Still, our time together had the same vibe, all of us constantly gathering in each other's apartments or venturing out together, enjoying each other's company, savoring a carefree existence.

Back at the office, I rummaged through my bag and retrieved a crumpled paper ball containing a shopping list of party essentials. The paper was creased and worn, with the ink smudged from being handled countless times. I had volunteered to pick up the snacks for our get-together from Trader Joe's on my way back from work.

The hands of the clock above my desk refused to budge. I sighed and shifted my gaze back to the monitor to study the chart I had constructed on FactSet. We were considering adding a Brazilian telecom company to our portfolio. I stared at the price movement of the stock, depicted by a downward-sloping red line and an upward-sloping blue line, signifying its price-to-book ratio. Examining the graph, I realized that my initial hypothesis was incorrect and that presenting a value-for-money case to the portfolio managers for adding the stock to our Latin America portfolio would be a faulty proposition.

It felt unreal that financial experts on Wall Street trusted fresh college graduates with limited experience, like me, with work that seemed to require a modicum of expertise. I reminded myself that while I may not have a deep passion for the *purpose* of my work – designing stock portfolios to increase the wealth of institutional investors and high net-worth individuals – I *did* find the work involved in constructing stock portfolios in emerging market countries intellectually challenging. It was a step toward adulthood.

It was finally 6.02 p.m. My heart leaped. Freedom to live my life the way I wanted, if only for the next two days. My mind switched gears to the night ahead as I shifted in my chair, feeling my small toes pinch in my black heels. I promptly took off my shoes and tossed them into the bottom drawer. The relief was palpable as I slipped into my soft brown Rainbow slippers, feeling their cushioned soles mold to my feet. I exited the office and practically skipped to Grand Central Station to take the 4 or 5 train down to Union Station.

Once there, I spotted Nikhil waiting for me at the entrance of Trader Joe's. Like me, he had it good; working decent hours in New York City as a paralegal at a major corporate law firm. Both of us were in the corporate sector for now – it was just for the "experience", we promised ourselves and each other. He planned to attend law school after this job. Like me, he had no appetite for a long-term corporate career. I ran to Nikhil, wrapped my arms around him, and planted a kiss on his full lips. A chuckle escaped me as I felt his beard tickle my face. We entered the store, grabbed two green plastic baskets, and joined the sea of weekend shoppers. Despite the crowded aisles, the cheerful chatter of shoppers and the bright colors of the fresh produce around us made it worth it.

With grocery shopping out of the way, we walked home. When we reached Nikhil's apartment building, he motioned for me to hand him the shopping bags I was carrying, and we arranged to meet back there at 8 p.m.

In my apartment, a block away from his, in the same housing complex, the thumping bass of music filled the air. Pallavi was sitting on our brown couch, swaying to the rhythm, her laptop open on the coffee table. What was I going to wear tonight, she asked me as I entered.

In my room a moment later, with Pallavi at my heels, I eyed my wardrobe, tilting my head as I considered my black, yellow, and white dress, recalling the compliments I had received when I wore it last.

"No!" Pallavi protested as if she could hear my thoughts. "Have you forgotten that you wore that outfit just two weekends ago?" Rummaging through my closet, she stopped at a classic choice, a cute short white tube dress. "I love this dress. Believe me, you will turn heads. And just picture Nikhil's face when he sees you – especially after I touch you up."

Laughing, I submitted to Pallavi's impeccable fashion sense. She was more than a friend; she was like a sister I turned to for everything, from fashion to work to love, to family matters, or even things as obscure as Uruguayan politics (the country was the homeland of her partner at the time). We even shared a deep desire to create a lasting social impact in the world, constantly bouncing ideas and plans off each other – ones shaped by our half-baked dreams.

"Tarini, are you awake? Are you trying to say something? I am your Mama," a voice said to me. It had to be my mother, Rasika, who would determinedly bring me back from the depths of my unconsciousness. She had kept a constant vigil by my bedside, enduring countless sleepless nights in the hospitals in both Kampala and New Delhi, where I lay in deep catatonic slumber.

The second time I stirred awake, my parents happened to be at home. The excited nurse, who had been giving me an early morning sponge bath, rushed to call them and reported that when asked my name, I had answered, "Mohan, Tarini Mohan", channeling 007 himself.

Soon after, they had rushed over, overwhelmed with joy and relief. There, they found their once-ebullient daughter lying motionless, her right hand and leg strapped up in a brace. Her speech was unintelligible, her eyes clouded with confusion and pain. Yet the fact that she was awake and speaking was nothing short of a miracle. Asked by my mother what I wanted, I am said to have croaked, "Mmmm ... JELLY."

However, staying awake proved too taxing for me, and I retreated into hibernation for several days, so much so that my parents began doubting whether I had actually regained consciousness. They were just beginning to discover that emerging from a coma isn't marked by a sudden "Aha!" moment like movies have us believe, but is instead a painstakingly slow and frustrating process, one that generally unfolds in three distinct stages: post-coma unresponsiveness, a minimally conscious state, and post-traumatic amnesia.

This was when my mother remembered what the neurologist had told her: that she should speak to me about an experience only she and I shared. My mother being my mother, immediately reached into the world of Bharatanatyam.

A trained Bharatanatyam dancer, she had insisted on teaching me the dance form from the age of five and I had thereafter spent a decade under her tutelage. She had grown up in an unconventional home, a beautiful mirror of India's diversity. Her father, a Punjabi Hindu who gave up a secure bank job to paint full-time, eventually becoming an artist of great renown, and her mother, a Bengali Christian schoolteacher, were modern in their outlook, and supported their children in chasing their own dreams. Intellectual curiosity and artistic expression were as important as breath in this household. So, my mother followed her calling and moved to Madras – the birthplace of Bharatanatyam – after she completed her BA, and steeped herself in the dance. But, for me, growing up with a strong-willed mother – who was also my dance teacher – wasn't always easy, especially during my rebellious teenage years. Looking back, I realize it must have been a struggle for her, too. She must have hoped her daughter would share her passion but had the joy of contending with an obstinate teen instead.

But unquestionably, Bharatanatyam was a source of shared connection. So she began singing the notes of the "Kalyani Jathiswaram", a dance piece she'd taught me when I was eleven. Now, in the hospital room, she started tapping a complex rhythm with a teaspoon on the bedframe, each note a gentle summons: *Sa Ni Dha Pa Dha Ma Ga Re Ni Re Sa*. The notes either served as invitations back into a world I once knew or – as I now say with a mischievous glint in my eye – I was rudely jolted out of my tranquil reverie and dragged, unwilling and restless, into the dreaded dance class of my teenage years. Or it could have been the irrefutable force of a mother's love that the sound carried. The reason remains a mystery, but the music found its way through the fog. Seeing my eyes flicker as she persisted with her singing, tears streamed down her cheeks.

"*Nyari*," she whispered, using her special name for me, which means beautiful, unique, rare, "I love you". As if this moment was too intense for me, I slipped into slumber yet again.

The next morning, I woke up, my face twisted into a nasty scowl, looking like a wild animal.

But my mother couldn't care less about the faces I was making. Instead, she felt like her heart had leaped out of her body. She rushed to me and held my head close to her heart.

"What's wrong, Tarini?" Mama asked, her voice catching in her throat, overwhelmed with emotions. "Don't worry, *nyari*. Everything will be okay. I am with you."

I mumbled, groaned, winced, and finally spoke.

"Teripkkkjoyar ueneey ofahelemmmaruurryjh zfvvvnklklklkl vroooosh. . ."

My mother didn't care that it was gibberish. I was alive and speaking with purpose once more. A purpose that would yet need deciphering. Drawing my bare head to her heart, she said, "Find your way back to your Mama. There is no life without you." My mother, now more familiar with the thick, ever-shifting fog of uncertainty around me, thought I had seemed more lucid the first time I awoke and hoped my current state wasn't a sign of regression. Yet, she chose to anchor herself in the now, letting love illuminate each passing moment.

But I was incredibly weak. My eyelids drooped, heavy with exhaustion after having spoken a long sentence composed of complicated words, gibberish though they might have been. I was lulled back into limbo.

After another day of wakefulness, I slipped back into a deep slumber, only to be followed by more days in slumberland, in a minimally conscious state. The doctors had refrained from offering my parents any prognosis on my recovery since there was no way for them to predict how long I would remain unconscious, whether I'd regain full function to return to my pre-accident state or remain a vegetable for life. My parents refused to rely on Google for fear of being led down a spiral of despair. Instead, they simply clung to hope.

For me, the hospital room was a blur of white, and time seemed to have lost all meaning. Occasionally, a familiar, soothing voice would break through my fog of slumber. It was my mother, caressing my left arm, when I awoke again.

"You are in a hospital in your home city of Delhi, but don't worry, both your Papa and I are with you. Papa is at home, but will be here in the evening."

"That makes no sense," I protested, struggling to articulate coherent words. It felt like I'd been gone for a truly long time. *But where could I have gone? Where am I?* "I'm going to get in huge trouble for missing work for so long. Morgan Stanley is going to fire me."

Tears of joy welled up in Mama's eyes. She didn't pay heed to my slurred speech or my nonsensical talk and would wonder only later why it was that I thought I still worked at Morgan Stanley, a job I had left before I moved to Uganda. But not just yet. At that very moment, Mama couldn't care less about where *I* thought I was, she was just thrilled that I was back with her.

The TV blared in the background, and the urgent voices of news anchors filled the room, talking about a crackdown in Syria.

Syria sounds familiar; haven't I been there?

I had indeed. Nikhil and I had backpacked there just a few months earlier in July. Syria evoked myriad images and sounds ... *old bazaars, souks, the old city, dotted with beautiful houses, a silk market, and a fabric market, customers haggling in Arabic ...*

Despite my confusion about the time and place, I was certain of one thing.

"I miss Nikhil. Can you call him for me and hold the phone to my ear?" When I saw Mama's eyes squinting in uncertainty, I thought I better be more direct.

"Dial Nikhil," I implored. I couldn't wait to wake up from this nightmare, in my bed in New York City.

"Did you say Nikhil?" Mama asked gently. "I'm sorry, *nyari*, I don't have his number with me ... " her voice trailed off. If I'd had my wits about me, I would have known that Mama didn't have Nikhil's number – I'd never felt the need to share it with her. I could feel frustration building up in me.

"I can give it to you, no problem." And just like that, I rattled off the number.

The relief on Mama's face at seeing that I could remember Nikhil's phone number was palpable, a thing come alive. A small smile broke out on her face at the thought that at least my memory was not impaired – that is, if the number I'd provided wasn't a figment of my imagination. It wasn't.

Our exchange was interrupted by two nurses who came in to change my diaper. It hurt when I moved any part of my body. My eyes brimmed with tears as they rolled me from side to side to stabilize my body. After they were done, one nurse adjusted the locks of the prison my hand was fastened in, while the other did the same for my leg. They finally left me feeling fresh, but my body felt as if it had been dragged through a battleground.

It doesn't matter. I'm in a dream. I know where I actually am – asleep at home in NYC, with Nikhil by my side.

5

The Loyalists

Hospitals unnerve my father – the sight of suffering overwhelms him. He still marvels at my mother's strength in that numb void of suffering. Yet, he found his own way to show love: orchestrating my care from behind the scenes. He tracked down specialists for second opinions, maintained meticulous records of my treatment, coordinated with insurance, arranged for medical equipment, and managed the stream of concerned calls from family and friends. Yet, every evening, without fail, he'd appear at my bedside.

Shortly after I came to, my father brought pictures of our extended family and a photo collage featuring several of my college friends to the hospital with him, hoping to understand the impact of the TBI on my memory and the true gravity of the situation. Brain injuries, like storms, don't follow a single path – their impact varies wildly, depending on the severity and location of the injury. In my case, the unpredictability was amplified by the diffuse nature of my injury, touching multiple areas of my brain. Nothing could be predicted – not the effects on my motor skills, the depth of cognitive impairments, the emotional or behavioral shifts, nor the long-term repercussions.

As I looked at the faces of my friends, my mind struggled to remember their names. But then, like a dam bursting, the memories flooded back, each name and face bringing me closer to the world I had left behind.

"Yes! You are right, that is Sahar, and wow, you got Courcoulas right too!" Papa exclaimed, unable to contain his elation that not only could I remember my college friends but also recall and pronounce my Greek friend's relatively complex last name. He would have done a little jig, if not for his two left feet, when I named everyone in the next photo of my father's side of the family. I wagged my left index finger towards the photo, recognizing the familiar faces of Papa's sister, his brother, and their spouses. "That's Mun Bua [father's sister] and Joy next to her. And there's Dinesh Tau and Peggy Tai [Tau's wife]." Even though I wasn't yet aware that anything had happened to me, as always, my father's approval lent me enormous comfort and confidence.

For Papa, my recognition of family and friends was half the battle won. My long-term memory proved to be intact. "Papa's Pom is a champion!" he said, eyes twinkling. Pom is Papa's nickname for me, one he coined over three decades ago now, back when I'd been more interested in playing with the Pomeranians in the hospital yard than welcoming my baby brother into the world. The nickname has stuck as a reminder of Papa's love and sense of humor, while my aloofness toward my brother is ancient history.

Papa turned to Mama, who was sitting in the easy chair at the far side of the hospital room, and said confidently, "No need to worry about any regression."

While my parents rejoiced, *my* mind was in turmoil. It would be much later I would understand that what I was experiencing was post-traumatic amnesia, leaving me only half present. I had yet to formulate to myself all the questions I had that needed answering. Instead, I remained befuddled. I looked around, squinting at the unfamiliar surroundings. I didn't remember having curtains of such a dull shade of beige in any room I had lived in. *I haven't been here before. Why can I not remember coming to this place? It must be somewhere in New York.*

I noticed my mother hovering around me and turned to her, ready with my burning questions. Fear knotted inside my chest as I worried, again, about losing my Morgan Stanley job, without which I wouldn't be able to afford to live in New York with Nikhil. I felt dead certain about one thing – my life couldn't be devoid of Nikhil.

Papa pulled out another photograph he had brought with him. It was a picture I had taken in Uganda, of a little boy with big round eyes clutching a yellow watering can on a dirt red path. My parents and I had loved that photo, exuding hope and potential. But now I didn't remember it.

Papa held the photo up to me.

"Where is this picture from, Pom?'

The photo blurred before my eyes, my mind a blank canvas.

Undeterred, Papa moved closer and nudged me gently.

"Don't worry. When I tell you, you'll remember. You took this photo in Uganda."

I stirred. My mouth gaped open. My facial muscles were weakened by my injury, and it was the only expression of disbelief I could manage on my otherwise expressionless face. I remember being flummoxed. *This photo looks very familiar.* It surprises me now why it didn't strike me as odd that I needed assistance with remembering so much.

"No," I protested, "that's India made to look like Uganda! Why would I have been in Uganda when I work and live in New York City?"

My parents exchanged worried glances.

"Pom, don't you remember? You moved to Uganda to work there?" Papa asked, trying to jog my memory.

"I've never been to Uganda," I replied firmly.

Then, in a moment of inspiration, my father decided to use my laptop to show me more of my own photos of Uganda, ones with me in them, too. Despite the glaring evidence before me, I remained skeptical of what I thought was his trickery. If I didn't remember having lived a life, how could I have possibly lived it?

Papa carried on, insisting I had been working in Uganda.

"Fine. Show me proof," I conceded, but not without a challenge.

My befuddled father decided to sleep on how to produce more "proof" beyond the visual proof he had already presented me with.

The next day, Papa came to me with my offer letter from BRAC.

"Here is the proof you asked for. *Now* do you believe you were in Uganda?" He seemed to believe that he could reach me through logic. Logical thinking forms the crux of my father's personality and at least half of mine. He'd decided to appeal to that half.

I stared at the document as if it was an alien thing. It couldn't be denied that I had indeed been offered a job at BRAC, in Uganda's agriculture program. But why could I not remember my time there? It made no sense.

My head swam as I glanced at Papa, then back at the offer letter lying before me.

"Yes, now I believe you," I said in a voice barely above a whisper.

I was dragged willy-nilly into the world of physiotherapy, or at least that is what they called it. Two male attendants came to my bedside, one morning. With careful coordination, they lifted me up from my bed in the bedsheet I was lying on. They placed me on the wheelchair seat, bedsheet and all, to take me downstairs for physical therapy. Upon reaching the physiotherapy room, a place I had been to once before, the therapists got to work, stretching my stiff muscles. My eyes moved to the metal standing frame with trepidation, knowing what was in store for me. Minutes later, I was buckled into a harness and strapped into the frame. As the therapists helped me stand upright, I vividly recall thinking I would prove them wrong in their belief that I required the support of parallel bars to walk. Aided by my strong long-term memory, I visualized myself running. *When I show them I can run, this nightmare will finally end.* But when I attempted to take a step, my body would not cooperate. I lost my balance and had to be caught.

Once I was transported back to the confines of my hospital room, waves of agony coursed through my body, causing me to squirm in discomfort. *This couldn't actually be happening, could it?*

After spending a disturbed night paralyzed with fear and uncertainty, I awoke the following morning with a newfound determination to seize control of my life and do whatever little I could to put an end to this madness.

The next morning, I found I was being sent right back to the physical therapy room. My eyes widened in horror as Mama's words registered. She actually expected me to go back to that place? I couldn't believe it. *Mama can't be so old-fashioned as to call a gym a physiotherapy room.* In an effort to align my current reality with the reality I had known, I reasoned that the physical therapy room was really just a gym, like the New York Sports and Racquet Club where I was used to going at least twice a week. Maybe I just didn't remember the discomfort that gyms could cause. That so-called physical therapy room was nothing short of a hellhole, a torture chamber designed to inflict as much pain as possible. The "gym instructors" there were clearly incompetent – the only plausible explanation for the intense agony that had wracked my body during each of the two sessions I'd been dragged down for. My mind flashed back to my gym in New York City, where everything was state-of-the-art, designed to maximize results and give its patrons the best experience. Compared to that, what I was being subjected to here was nothing short of medieval. There was no way I was going back.

"Nurse, please dial the gym for me," I pleaded to the nurse in the room.

Hats off to that nurse for not only understanding what I meant when I spoke of the "gym", but also for making sense of my slurred speech. And most of all, for giving me a sense of agency.

She dialed the number of the physical therapy room and handed the receiver to me. A man answered the phone.

I cleared my throat and spoke as firmly as I could manage.

"Yes, hello. This is Tarini Mohan. I'm resigning from the gym. I won't be coming back." I took a deep breath and added, "Goodbye." Relief washed over me. Finally, I'd taken the first step toward taking charge of my life.

As I hung up the phone, I turned to face Mama and saw Papa had entered the room, too. Their amused expressions made me feel victorious. However, my elation was short-lived. I was bundled up and wheeled to the dreaded "gym" again, where I'd sworn to never return. That day, I was given the childishly simple task of sitting up without support, which turned out to be anything but simple for me. Unaware of the damage to my brain's neural pathways, I sat before the occupational therapists with my right hand tightly clenched in a fist. Despite my reluctance to believe I had any injury, they pledged to help stretch my tightly shut hand open.

Because in their resting state, my muscles contract instead of expanding, to this day, my right hand remains clenched. However, after a decade of rehabilitation, it now rests in a slightly looser fist but still curled up. This condition leads my extensor muscles, responsible for extending and straightening various body parts, to be underused, and consequently weakened, putting them at risk of atrophy.

I gritted my teeth as the therapist coaxed my fingers open. *Here we go again.*

Later, the story of me resigning from the "gym" was retold countless times. My parents' eyes sparkle as they share it with friends over dinners, their laughter drowning out my playful protestations. To me, the story is just one of many hazy memories. In this particular instance, my parents say I was quite the conniver. On occasion, snatches of this incident flash in my mind's eye. It's like trying to recall a dream after waking up – an ephemeral image, then nothing.

Slowly, my world began to be peopled. I hadn't lived in New Delhi since the age of fifteen and had naturally drifted apart from most of my childhood friends. I had done the latter part of my schooling at MUWCI, perched on a hilltop on the outskirts of Pune, a boarding school with a mix of Indian and international students. After that it had been Boston for college and later, working on Wall Street before joining BRAC in Uganda. Hearing about the profound, life-altering impact of Papa's college experience in the US, along with countless stories of his time there, it felt only natural for me to follow that path. Scholarships had paved the way for my father's education in London and the US, and my scholarship to MUWCI set me on a similar journey. I became part of a small but growing Indian elite choosing to attend college abroad.

As a result, the names on the roster Mama prepared of people who had graciously offered to be with me at night to give her a break were largely those of relatives rather than friends – Seeta Bua, Malati Masi (mother's sister), Valli Chachi (father's younger brother's wife), Paro Masi, Radhu Masi – and they unflinchingly stayed night after night. But friends from the past did re-enter my new life. Himali was one. She had been at my school in Pune and we had grown close there. As we had pursued our separate paths through college in the US, and then together in New York City, we found ourselves living starkly divergent lives. While Himali was a laid-back artist, I lived a fast-paced life on Wall Street. Yet, we would meet up on weekends to either stroll through flea markets in Brooklyn or for home-cooked brunches, and more. Aristotle would have called our friendship a virtuous one, built on mutual admiration for each other's good qualities – indeed he believed virtuous friendship to be the highest form of friendship, transcending both friendship of pleasure and friendship of utility.

Himali came in one day with a cloth bag that carried a set of spare clothes. Like me, she'd left NYC and was back in Delhi now.

"Hi, Uncle and Aunty! I've got this now. You both need to rest. Please go home and get some sleep. You can come back tomorrow."

My father smiled.

"Hello, Number Two!" he said affectionately. Papa's playful nickname for Himali had its genesis in the fact that she had been a light in the darkness of my comatose days, giving my entire family a much-needed dose of strength and positivity. According to him – at least half-seriously – I was his Number One and Himali his Number Two.

While I'd been lost to the world, Himali had been a constant, visiting me in the hospital, and she even practised Reiki on me with quiet spiritual reverence. She would delicately place her hands over my heart and forehead, and softly recite invocations as she felt for subtle shifts in the energy fields around my body. Had I been awake, I would have probably teased her for all the hokey-pokey she believes in. But she got the last laugh since there's no saying if her Reiki had some part to play in bringing me back from the netherworld.

She stayed by my side, talking to me even when I couldn't respond, sharing stories of our past adventures, and reciting poems in the hope that the cadence and beauty of the words would penetrate my unconscious mind. She was a patient source of comfort and strength through my darkest days, never losing faith that I would make it back.

It was Himali who composed an email that day to a group of our childhood friends – Sahil, Manak, and Gayatri – from whom we had technically drifted apart, but who had been showing up to the hospital to see me every week regardless.

I would love for you guys to go in and bear some of your love and some of my silly dances to deliver unto Tarini.

She reflected for another minute before adding: *You are The Loyalists.*

Responses began trickling in. As Himali read Sahil's response, she placed a hand on her heart and a small chuckle escaped her lips. Sahil's antics always seem to lighten the mood, whatever the situation. In a matter of minutes, Sahil had suggested a surprise visit to me in the hospital, since I was more alert and had been talking more lately. He also suggested throwing a "party" in the hospital room in my honor and even joked about sneaking in bottles of booze past the guards. Each of them held true to their word – although I'm not so sure if their bottles of booze made it past the hospital guards.

Amid my hazy memories of the hospital, I vividly remember Himali's presence beside me. Her familiar warm smile, the sound of her cheerful voice, and the reassuring touch of her hand in mine provided a much-needed sense of familiarity and comfort. Her voluntary presence day after day made me feel whole. She reminded me that the people I loved weren't going anywhere. I was not alone.

One day, Sahil asked me what he could bring me during his next visit, and I wasted not a minute before rattling off a list of all the things I was craving. I usually leaned toward savory and spicy foods, but my injured brain craved sugar, and I couldn't resist the temptation of Nirula's hot chocolate fudge ice cream, popularly known as HCF.

With my long-term memory remaining surprisingly sharp, clearly allowing me to recall the joy that HCFs had brought me as a child. The daughter of the Nirula family was my classmate, and it followed that we often enjoyed an abundance of complimentary HCFs through the years. Even now, the rich, creamy, velvety chocolate sauce coating scoops of vanilla ice cream holds a special place in my heart.

Sahil kept his HCF promise. As I savored each bite of the latest HCF he brought for me, my father entered the room, his forehead creased. I had, apparently, been taking advantage of the kindness of my visitors, using them to indulge my new sweet tooth. I wanted to tell my father I was doing nothing wrong; I was merely telling them the truth when they asked me to please let them know if they could do anything to help. Feeling the ice cream melt on my tongue, I gently shut my eyes. For just a moment, I felt like a child again, free from the weight of my injury and the worries of the world.

My father shook his head, but he approached me with his characteristic, rationality-fueled gentleness. "Tarini, please put down that hot chocolate fudge. You have had far too many today," he said.

"Why, Papa? This is the only pleasure I have in my life these days," I replied, my eyes pleading. It was as though my injury had also rolled back the years I'd lived on this planet. I must have seemed like a child, begging for her lolly, rather than the adult who had traveled the world with her partner and then lived alone in a remote and distant land. I was still fundamentally the same person – my essence intact. Parental love is remarkable in the way it allowed my father to see this truth. Despite all the evidence to the contrary, my core self was alive and apparent to my parents. But right now my father was having to reason with me as if I was a child.

"Oh, Pom, I know it's difficult, but trust your Papa. Put that down or I will have to forcibly take that cup away from you. You know I would never make such a request of you, but you have been going berserk with the sweet stuff lately." He inched closer to my bed.

Avoiding eye contact with him, I placed the cup on the table, frowning, but the creamy vanilla ice cream and the warm fudge topped with crispy walnuts still called out to me. I watched as the fudge dripped down the sides of the cup.

The taste of goodness was now replaced by the bitter aftertaste of guilt. I wanted to protest, to tell Papa that I was not overindulging, but it appeared my actions spoke louder than my words. I looked at the half-eaten cup of ice-cream on the table beside me, and couldn't bring myself to believe that I'd actually eaten so many desserts that day.

"Okay, here you go," I said, pointing at my cup. "But how could I have eaten too much dessert?" I frowned. "I don't even have a sweet tooth! You know I love spicy food," I added, averting my gaze. "I'm just craving an HCF *right now*, that's all."

The left side of my lips stretched out, while the right remained limp. I couldn't tell whether the lopsided smile was a consequence of my facial muscle weakness or if it was just my wry smile. Either way, I felt satisfied at having shifted the blame where I was certain it rightfully belonged.

"It's not for me, it's for you," Papa said, his eyes soft.

"Papa, make a list of every sweet thing I've eaten today. Show me proof," I said.

"That's a good idea. I will do that soon. But in the meantime, try being more disciplined."

Later that day, Papa sat in the armchair in my room, holding up a large piece of paper on which he'd written what looked like a number for me to see. I cocked my head, as I struggled to make out what was on the paper. I could somewhat discern the number "13" scrawled in Papa's barely legible handwriting.

"Can you guess why I'm showing you this?" Papa asked, his voice cracking.

I remained motionless and expressionless, as was my new normal.

Undeterred, Papa continued engaging with me.

"Do you remember you asked me to count the number of desserts you've been eating in a day? You might have been wondering why your Papa was sitting in your room for so long today. I was here, carefully making a list of all the desserts you ate."

Silence.

There was so much going on at the time that I didn't have the wherewithal to keep track of everything. I was grappling with being stuck in my nightmare, where I appeared to be living a new life that I had almost no control over, and the very concept of time itself was an alien thing. I couldn't even process my changed appearance or the relentless pain shooting down my right leg just yet, much less Papa's presence in my room or just about anything else.

"I took your request seriously, and this is the number. THIRTEEN. The doctors and nurses have emphasized that you need to regain the weight you lost when you were unconscious. But thirteen? You have had thirteen hot chocolate fudges in twelve hours, to be exact."

I grew concerned about the number, but my weak facial muscles prevented me from producing an appropriate expression.

"That's shocking," I said, in a voice lacking any intonation or emphasis. "You're right, that's way too many." I paused to consider how to remedy this. Right there, I decided to seize the reins of my life, gripping them in my working hand, feeling strangely empowered. "From today, I won't eat any more desserts, Papa. Not one, I promise," I said firmly, in my new lifeless voice.

My father leaned back, his shoulders easing.

"Everything in moderation, Pom. Your body obviously needs sugar."

"Can you guess who is coming to visit you tomorrow?" Papa asked, his eyes sparkling. It was now about a month after I awoke.

I wished the correct answer was Nikhil, but I knew it couldn't be him because we spoke on the phone fairly regularly when my mother offered to hold the phone to my ear and stand ready in case she needed to translate my slurred speech. Nikhil had gotten somewhat accustomed to my speech and could usually decipher what I was saying. But we still required my mother's translation services on occasion. If he was flying to India to visit me, we would have been talking about it for days.

"Himali?" I guessed.

"She will also probably be here tomorrow, of course," my father said. "But I am talking about Chhottay! It's his spring break, and he wants to visit his didi [big sister]," he announced. Chhotay is the Hindi moniker for "little one" that Papa uses to refer to my brother.

My heart soared upon hearing of my brother's visit.

"Really?" I asked. "We haven't seen each other in forever!" My joy would have likely been imperceptible to those outside my inner circle. Because of my weakened facial muscles, it became difficult for my face to reveal my true feelings.

"No," my mother quickly interjected on my brother's behalf to set the record straight. She spoke slowly, each word clear and deliberate. "*You* haven't seen *him* since before you left for Uganda, but he has come to see you here twice already – once while you were still in the ICU, and again when you woke up from your deep slumber. You won't remember."

In fact, my brother was using all his senior year vacations to come and see me. A political science major, now on the verge of stepping into the real world, he was looking for meaningful work, though – unlike his sister – the non-profit sector was not for him.

Despite the monotone of my voice and the weakness of my facial muscles that masked my feelings, my soul was yearning for my brother's visit. I couldn't wait to hug him and feel the comfort siblings bring.

My parents were eager to see a glimmer of joy in their daughter. Dr. J.D. Mukherji, the neurologist assigned to my case, had, apparently, witnessed the magic that my brother had brought into my life on his previous visits. "We neurosurgeons and neurologists are nothing compared to the super-doc that your son is," he'd said to my mother.

Our super-doc finally arrived with his jar of good-spirit fairy dust. I have no memory of his arrival and only the broadest outline of much of his visit, but others tell me that Rasoo's presence helped me to be more present. However, he disagrees, insisting, "Didi, you can't imagine how out of it you were."

Unconcerned by my altered state, my brother caught up with me rather quickly and kept me engaged in our usual brother–sister banter. Our secret code, reserved for when we're alone in each other's company, kept us connected as we engaged in playful conversation. The sound of our nonsensical language spoken in slurred speech must have been alienating for Rasoo, but he did not leave my side.

Rasoo later informed me he was in cahoots with my parents about wanting to see me smile, so he decided to watch *Friends* with me, hoping it would do the trick.

How wrong he was!

I sat before the TV screen, transfixed, my gaze locked without so much as a blink. Rasoo craned his neck, hoping he'd get to share a laugh with me, but nothing.

In moments like these, my mind was consumed by the gaping hole in my life. Where was Nikhil? Watching the characters on the TV screen lead full, enjoyable lives had only served to remind me of the emptiness of my own. Yes, I talked to Nikhil nearly every other day, when Mama would succumb to my demands and call him for me. Every time Mama held the phone to my ear and then translated my slurred speech for Nikhil to understand, I felt a pang of frustration at needing my mother's assistance to communicate with my partner. While I appreciated the connection her help provided, I didn't much care for the lack of privacy it afforded. I'm sure this wasn't fun for my mother, either.

Now that Rasoo was here, I could converse more freely with Nikhil. Even if the assistance provided was identical, I felt more like a helpless child when my mother helped me than when my brother did.

While I was unconscious, the well-qualified doctors on my case, both in Uganda and India, had refused to offer any predictions about whether I would ever regain consciousness. Predictions were off the table even after I re-emerged. Uncertainty hung heavy in the air, casting a shadow over my loved ones' hopes and dreams. There was no word about how long it would take me to recover from my immobile state. When would my short-term memory be restored, if ever? Would I remember my stay in Uganda? What other cognitive limitations could my parents expect to see in me?

Despite the overwhelming weight of these unanswered questions, my parents remained resolute. They clung to hope and took action to transform their wishes into reality. The doctors in both countries, while avoiding pessimism, also refrained from raising expectations. Maintaining silence on my prospects for recovery appeared the safest course of action. Science, with all its incredible advances, still cannot provide a credible prediction of how an individual human brain might respond – such is the enigma that is the essence of what makes us human.

Amid all this uncertainty, my parents found a shot of magic in the realm of neuroplasticity. The idea that neural networks can regenerate themselves to form new connections, potentially restoring lost functions, was one my parents clung to, believing that this could support the reorganization of my brain. Therapies would be organized accordingly.

Now, two-and-a-half months after regaining consciousness at the hospital in India, the medical professionals completed the necessary CT scans and declared that I no longer required continuous monitoring by a doctor at the hospital. However, I would still require 24/7 care for basic tasks and safety in my daily life. Still, since I was no longer a high-revenue patient for the hospital, the doctors urged my parents to take me home.

On hearing this news, my parents exchanged glances, their bewildered expressions mirroring one another's. Their eyes filled with a mixture of apprehension and quiet desperation. How would they possibly care for me, their adult bedridden daughter? I still couldn't sit up unsupported and required help just to transfer from my bed to my wheelchair. I would also need daily physical and occupational therapies. Who would lift me into my wheelchair and into the car at home?

For people of means, hiring support staff in India is usually a straightforward affair. However, it was proving challenging for my parents. After returning from Uganda, they had, in fact, hired a new domestic worker to help in the house – but that person chose to return to his village, leaving his work responsibilities behind. My parents were left with nobody to assist them at home. Mama spent most of her time at the hospital with me, while Papa resumed his teaching duties remotely from India. These all-consuming tasks hadn't left them with enough time to relaunch a search for a new domestic worker.

With their minds elsewhere, my parents had soldiered through the necessities of life without complaint for as long as they could, but now, they yearned for reliable support at home. Caregiving is a deeply challenging task in its own way, one demanding enduring patience, utter selflessness, and deep reserves of resilience. Caregivers often find themselves navigating a complex web of emotions, from love and compassion to frustration and exhaustion. For my parents, managing their own needs and responsibilities, alongside the demands of caregiving, would be grueling, with no hands beyond their own to assist them. If I was to be transferred home, they felt that hiring two female nurses – a day nurse and a night nurse – was a must. I required round-the-clock care with everything from feeding and sponge baths to transfers and disposing of diapers.

In the middle of all this brainstorming, it also struck them that they had overlooked the basics. Installing a ramp at the front door was essential. Mama glanced at the wheelchair, noting it was unlikely to fit through our narrow bathroom doorway. What then? After much investigation, my parents discovered a potential solution – a customized wheelchair that could be used for bathing and could fit through the narrow bathroom door at home. The waterproof wheelchair even doubled as a commode!

Their heads spun with ideas, while their bodies sagged with exhaustion. The tasks ahead were daunting, but my parents discovered ways to not be intimidated. For now, all they wanted was to spark joy in their daughter's life in whatever way possible.

If only my parents had the presence of mind to arrange for a waterproof wheelchair that came in different colors, preferably with built-in speakers; one with flow controls and a jet spray for the commode facility. A waterproof wheelchair cum five-star commode cum remote concert venue hybrid would have been the best household luxury – give or take a champagne dispenser.

One evening, before my parents took me home, Mama decided to give me an "outing" down the hallway of my fourth-floor hospital room with the help of an attendant. Butterflies of excitement fluttered in my stomach at the mere suggestion of an outing. I longed to break free from the monotony of my hospital room, to get a taste of life outside my drab daily routine at the hospital.

Sitting in my wheelchair, I peered cautiously through the large glass windows at the end of the hallway. Underneath the yellow round-headed flowers of the kikar trees at eye-level, I saw boys playing cricket, running back and forth between stumps, while in the distance, a bevy of young women made their way home from work. It made me remember what it felt like to be out there, in control of one's own life. *I'll get there soon, as soon as I'm allowed to leave the confines of the hospital.*

Far in the distance stood the majestic Qutb Minar, which I had visited on numerous occasions during school trips. I spent a few moments marveling at the monument, reflecting on all that life had to offer beyond the confines of the here and now. I imagined myself as one of those girls I was seeing on the streets, leading busy lives, shaping their own destinies. It had been five long months since my incapacitation here, but I had not had the headspace to worry about my future.

After all, what is there to worry about? Even if it takes three months, say – that is just the length of summer vacations in college. And I have everyone important right here: I have Mama and Papa with me; Rasoo will graduate from college in a couple of months and be with me; and I have full faith that Nikhil will come visit me soon.

Nikhil and I talked daily, and though my speech remained fairly garbled, we persisted until we didn't need Mama's help to communicate.

"Soon, babes. It's just a matter of time. We will look back at how we overcame this bump in the road," Nikhil said on more than one occasion.

I believed it. Until my accident disrupted the path I had carefully laid out, my life had been unfolding as I had envisioned. I wasn't about to let anything steer it off course.

While they made tedious preparations to move me home, my parents began taking me out of my hospital room more frequently. In addition to Mama taking me on "walks", Papa took me downstairs to the hospital coffee shop with him. During these outings, Mama would stop and point out the funny faces of the yellow-and-blue pansies blooming in the shallow clay pots that were arranged with precision throughout the hospital grounds. Her earnest efforts to bring beauty into my life were not lost on me. Despite my disinterest in flowers, the vivid colors of the pansies were spellbinding, a welcome escape from the energy-sapping hospital room with its eerie white light. It didn't strike me what a child I had become.

When Papa first suggested we go on a trip to the hospital coffee shop, I was beyond excited. Improbable though it sounds, I was transported back to the dynamic SoHo streets in downtown New

York, where Nikhil and I used to saunter while sipping on cups of coffee. Now, watching the barista craft my cappuccino with care, I could barely contain my happiness. My elation, yes, elation, only grew when Papa brought me the steaming mug, with frothing foam spilling over onto the plate like a cascade of fluffy clouds.

Not daring to interfere with the beauty of the cappuccino, I stared at the little design the barista had made on the foam.

"This is heaven. Thank you for bringing me here, Papa. Life already seems more glorious than it did ten minutes ago"

There is no medicine like hope, no incentive so great, no tonic so powerful as the expectation of a better tomorrow. In the eye of memory, it's laughable but endearing now, that a simple cup of coffee could bring me as much delight as it did.

Only years later did Papa reveal to me that he had felt overwhelmed with emotion at my excitement over such a mundane daily occurrence. He confessed that he "may" have gone home and shed a few tears. Oh, Papa.

6

Coming Home

Mama reached into a bag and pulled out a pair of grayish-blue pants with an elastic waistband. She held them up for me to see.

"Seeta Bua sent these for you. The elastic waistband will make it easier for you to put them on with your working hand."

A wave of emotions hit me at the sight of the pants in Mama's hands. This was the first time in six months I would wear regular clothes. My life had been defined by the hospital gown I wore day in and day out. It was an ever-present reminder that I was a patient, that my life was on hold until I got better. But now, those pants Mama was holding were a flash of hope. Maybe, just maybe, I could start feeling my life was "normal" again.

Finally, in March 2011, six months since I'd first been hospitalized in Uganda, I was going home. Instead of feeling joy, my mind had raced with unexpected fear and uncertainty.

"Aren't you excited?" my parents had asked, exchanging quizzical looks.

How could I be excited about leaving the hospital? Things are so secure and predictable here. The hospital was a place where I was surrounded by expert medical staff who knew my every need. As the prospect of leaving drew nearer, I couldn't shake the feeling of vulnerability that gnawed at my insides. How could I go on without the constant support under the watchful eyes of those who had become my lifeline? The return to "normalcy" that had once been a driving force for me now seemed like a distant memory, replaced by a terrifying sense of exposure and unease.

But I had a new pair of pants.

A shift had begun, though I couldn't see it. This was the beginning of a new chapter in my life, practically a different realm.

The mundane details of everyday life that had once been straightforward now seemed downright formidable. I perched on the edge of my bed as the nurse helped me slip my legs into my new pants, the muscles of my torso still lacking the flexibility to bend and straighten up. Her hands moved with practiced care. Despite performing the same tasks for patient after patient, not a trace of frustration marred the nurse's face. All I saw was gentle focus. I would miss her. I would miss the other doe-eyed, gentle-faced nurse from Kerala, who had a knack for instantly putting me at ease every time she slipped through the door to my room. She was my favorite – nothing ever seemed to go wrong when she was around.

Sitting in my wheelchair on the porch, I felt stranded. The attendant steering my wheelchair positioned me at an odd angle near the car's back door. I looked at my parents, hoping to catch their eye, as I wondered if this particular attendant knew what he was doing.

A group of people seemed to materialize out of thin air and now surrounded us. My curiosity was piqued, and I watched my father exchange pleasantries with a man who appeared to be leading the unexpected entourage. I did not recognize him, but my father seemed acquainted with him. It wasn't until later, when the day's chaos settled, that my parents explained the situation to me. A friend of my father knew the founding chairperson of the hospital, Analjit

Singh. A friend had requested special attention for me during my hospital stay, and this man had helped organize it.

My parents say that while they don't know how Max Hospital treated its other patients back then, I certainly received exceptional care during my stay there. I wonder if Max Hospital specializes in a superior level of care for all, or if my father's social capital influence the quality of care I received? I have a sneaking suspicion I know the answer. I am grateful to have been born to parents whose rich professional lives and extroverted, friendly personalities have resulted in them having a wide network they can reach out to when life demands it. Yet, staring at the sea of faces around me, it was dizzying to think about the vast number of people who were tasked with helping to make my stay comfortable. My privilege was not, and still isn't, lost on me.

Despite the cushion, the invisible tension between living with multiple disabilities and maintaining adult autonomy weighed heavily on me. Privilege eases trauma, but it cannot eviscerate it.

As the hospital management arranged for my transfer to the car, I glimpsed a youth, peeking out at me. I saw my parents gently nudging him forward, encouraging him to approach me directly. Stepping out from the shadows, the boy held out a single rose in his trembling hand.

"*Aapke liye* [For you]," he said, in a voice barely above a whisper. His words, "*Didi, aap jaldi hi theek ho jaogi. Khyal rakhna* [You will get better soon, take care]," held a certain grace that reporting the incident here doesn't capture.

Before I knew it, the boy ran off, vanishing from sight. The two aides and my physical therapist had gathered around me, their sturdy frames helping me stay upright.

The attendants positioned themselves around me, ready to hoist me up from the hospital wheelchair. As they lifted me, the therapist cautioned them not to assist me "too much," encouraging me to contribute to the effort myself. I gritted my teeth and strained with all my might. One of the attendants reached around me, his hands gripping my waist tightly as he pulled me upright. The other one positioned himself on my left side, ready to support, letting me grip his arm with my working hand. With a deep breath, I pushed myself off the chair and rose, unsteady on my feet. As I stood, my right arm curled inward, toward my chest, my fist clenched, the extensor muscles too weak to fight gravity.

Despite my physical injuries – including a fractured collarbone, broken right rib, bruises, and a sutured wound on my face – having healed, the mobility of my right limbs remained limited. The diffuse brain injury had damaged both hemispheres, but scans showed that the damage to the nerve pathways in my left hemisphere was greater than that in my right. This was because despite the impact occurring on the right side of my head when it had hit the ground, the reverberations were felt in my brain's left hemisphere. As a result, my left limbs still functioned as they did before the crash, while my right limbs became hemiparetic.[4]

The intricacies of voluntary movement include a lot more than meets the eye. The coordination between the muscles and the nerves that enable us to move our limbs at will is a delicate dance between the body and the brain. In my case, this dance has been disrupted by the trauma to my brain, meaning that I have limited control over the movement, tone, and strength of the muscles on my right side. The tightness of the muscles in my right arm is because they are now in a constant state of contraction, making it impossible to release my fingers from the clenched fist they were trapped in. When I lay in the hospital bed, my arm was stretched out at my side, confined by a heavy and outdated hand splint. The archaic device, holding my hand open, lent me relief. It eased the strain from the constant struggle against the force exerted by the tight muscles trying to ball my hand into a fist. Hand splints support my weak extensor muscles, preventing my hand from curling up. The dedicated therapists and neurologists continued to assure me that though it may be slow, with hard work and perseverance, I would experience improvements.

Due to the disruption in the nerve pathways of my left brain, my right biceps, to illustrate with a single muscle, continuously receive the wrong command, leaving them in a perpetual state of contraction. Picture a seesaw stuck at one end: while my biceps remain locked in their endless embrace, their counterparts, the triceps, lie dormant in an eternal exhale, waiting for a command that never comes. The result is weakened muscles, including several in my right hand, arm, and leg. The disparity in muscle strength affects my body balance – my right side is weaker than my left. In those early fog-filled days of recovery, I couldn't begin to grasp this complex choreography of cause and effect. Back then, I was barely able to recognize myself in the mirror, let alone understand how this invisible tug-of-war between muscles had rewritten my relationship with balance and movement.

Getting into the car that day, the sensation of standing upright was an unexpected relief, but the effort it required was monstrous. I had practiced getting up countless times during physical therapy sessions, enduring the torturous time spent in the standing frame and the parallel bars. And yet, standing outside the door to the back seat of our car, with two attendants on either side of me, I felt overwhelmed by the complexity of the task at hand. The helpers' voices floated around me with gentle guidance, their hands hovering nearby as I fought to stay upright. My mind raced through calculations – how many steps to turn, which way to pivot, how to maintain my precarious balance while maneuvering into the car seat. What had once been an unconscious process now demanded the utmost focus.

After ten minutes of awkward maneuvering, I successfully turned to place my buttocks on the seat, my legs dangling out of the door. Climbing into the car facing outward rather than inward was a new experience, and it left me feeling disoriented and made me question myself.

This wasn't who I'd been, wasn't who I was inside, or who I wanted to be – I didn't want to live curled up on my parents', or anybody else's, lap. Gazing at the hospital building looming above me, a part of me longed for the security I had felt within its walls. It was a place where skilled caregivers were always on hand to help with even the most basic needs.

As I watched my parents hop into the car with ease, I couldn't help but feel envious. My memory of climbing into a car, which ought to have otherwise been a non-event, was still fresh. It had taken me twenty minutes of mental and physical exertion to accomplish what they did in mere seconds.

On the bumpy, potholed journey home, I was transfixed by sights I had not seen for years. On the pavements were squatting vegetable sellers dressed in vibrant saris. As they bargained with customers, their hands flailed in the air. Amid the commotion, a frail-looking construction worker wearing a sweat-soaked white vest called out to his fellow workers to pass him a bag of bricks. In front of the half-built house, a long line of men and women jostled as they waited their turn to board the crowded bus that pulled up. I drank in these sights whooshing past my window.

It was as if I had been given a second chance. Before, I'd always chased the next horizon, convinced that was where fulfillment lay.

This, right here, was life. At that moment, the ordinary had its own magic.

The car crept forward, trapped in Delhi's morning traffic. Beside me, my mother's hand found mine, her grip gentle and loving.

"Do you know who that sweet little boy is, who gave you the flower? You have seen him every day for the past three months."

Three months had passed since I returned to the realm of the living and my short-term memory was much improved.

I furrowed my brow, thinking hard.

"I don't think so," I replied. "Who was he?"

"He was the sweeper who cleaned your room every day," Mama said quietly.

I still feel moved when I think of that sweet informally employed boy – probably juggling a hundred problems of his own every day – who felt compelled to give me a rose on my last day. His simple act of kindness has stayed with me since. His identity remains a mystery – I can only hope he is rewarded for his big heart, which saw past my disabilities.

Mama peered out of her window.

"Look, Tarini! That's your old school, where you studied until class one. Do you recognize it?"

"What a silly question, Mama. *Of course,* I recognize Mother's International School."

"Very good, Pom!" Papa said from the front seat.

Mama continued pointing out different landmarks, some familiar, and others unfamiliar to me.

I sighed in frustration when Mama pointed to a familiar-looking market area and asked if I remembered its name. I drew a blank.

"I don't really recognize the sights of Delhi any more. I haven't lived here in seven years, Mama."

"Don't get annoyed, *nyari*, we are just reminding you," Mama gently chided.

"Thank you, Mama and Papa, but can you please stop talking to me like I am a child, asking me if I recognize places that I obviously do."

Confusion flickered on my mother's face and probably on my father's too, but rather than argue, Mama simply pointed silently to another familiar sight visible from my window.

"Montessori School!" I exclaimed, recognizing my pre-primary school, to Mama's delight. She motioned for the driver to stop the car for a few minutes to allow us time to drift into memory-land.

"I remember those days when we would come for your school function to watch you sing and dance," my mother said wistfully, refraining from adding a "do you?" at the end.

With my long-term memories intact, I gazed at the steps leading up to the school and pictured the days when I would run up and down them without a care in the world. They seemed like they were from another life. I closed my eyes, and saw myself in a yellow Winnie the Pooh dress, climbing the jungle gym with my other toddler friends before scurrying off to the nearby sandbox. I remembered being that little girl so distinctly. No, not another life. My life. I longed for the freedom of mobility but didn't dwell on that thought. I was at the very beginning of my recovery, and things would all work out in time.

The car rolled on. A few minutes later, we pulled up to my house, and my heart swelled with joy at the sight of my childhood home. Three homes on one plot – two side by side on the ground floor, and one on the second floor – this was an arrangement my late paternal grandfather had thoughtfully set up for his children and their families. A civil engineer, working as the chief engineer in Uttar Pradesh's Public Works Department (PWD), building roads and bridges, he retired as chairman of UP's State Bridge Corporation.

His wife, my paternal grandmother, was the first woman to receive a college education in the city of Hissar in Haryana. His children helped pay for the land he acquired for them. My father and Dinesh Tau had contributed to the construction of the house as students. I took in the sights before me – my aunt's garden, overgrown, yet lush, the plain white cement walls, a lone basketball hoop jutting out of the wall, the net long gone.

"I'm finally home!" I screeched, my face breaking out into a lopsided grin.

As the car door opened, I caught sight of the members of my extended family: Dinesh Tau, standing slightly apart. Mun Bua, her eyes, flickering with relief and uncertainty. Her husband, my uncle Joy, stood by her side, his quiet presence exuding warmth. Peggy Tai was moving toward the car with the determination of a general on a mission. My heart bloomed with happiness as I caught sight of my cousin Meghna, clutching a bouquet.

Without hesitation, they all rushed to the car. I was enveloped in hugs and kisses. When not overwhelming, familial affection can be a balm to the soul. This welcome was just what I needed after the sterile monotony of hospital life.

My parents enlisted both my aunts' cooks to help with my transfer to the wheelchair. Mama mentioned that we'd hire a new cook soon, but in the meantime, my two aunts would send us food from their homes next door. Mama would lend a hand with the cooking, too.

I was wheeled up a newly installed ramp at the front door of my house. Biting my lip, I wondered how I would climb the stairs to my room. But before I could ask, Mama pointed to the right. "Look, Tarini, the guest room will now be your room. We've set up everything for you."

I felt the tension I didn't know I was carrying lift from my shoulders when I saw a hospital bed placed in the center of the small room. The bed came complete with adjustable settings to help me sit up and lie down, which I couldn't manage on my own. On the wall hung a new TV, and I imagined my brother joining me to watch movies after dinner when he returned after graduating from college. A small smile crept across my face, but as usual, my weak facial muscles prevented it from being fully expressed. *My life is returning to me.*

My weak facial muscles struggled with even simple tasks like chewing on the right side. But in those early days of my recovery, I was blissfully unaware of all my limitations – apart from what was most obvious – and focused solely on getting my life back on track. Understanding would come slowly, one small revelation at a time.

Meanwhile, my mother gestured toward a young lady standing beside her, smiling at me.

"Meet your day-nurse, Sandhya," Mama said. "You will have a different night-nurse."

I introduced myself to her in Hindi, hoping she would understand my slurred speech.

Whether Sandhya understood me, or not, she responded with a warm smile. Although I can't remember what we could've possibly talked about, it wasn't long before we were chatting away. Sandhya assisted me throughout the day, feeding me meals at the dining table and helping me take a bath on a plastic bench in the shower area. She even retrieved items that were out of my reach. I'm not sure I was grateful enough. In those days, I was too consumed by the struggle of being unable to do even the simplest tasks on my own. I had no mental space for self-reflection. I was merely living each day as it unfolded.

A warm feeling of comfort washed over me at the sight of the bright patterned sheets on the hospital bed instead of plain white ones. The grim vibe of my hospital room was still fresh in my mind, making my small room seem cozy in comparison. I motioned for Mama to guide my wheelchair to the bed.

"I just want to lie down and take a snooze in the comfort of my own room."

Well into the afternoon, I cracked open an eye to find Papa standing at the door. With a flick of a switch, I adjusted the hospital bed to lift me to an upright position so that I could speak to him eye-to-eye. Once I was up, I beckoned him closer; I needed to clear up something that suddenly plagued me.

"Papa, you say that I had a motorbike accident in Uganda. Was I alone, or did someone else also get injured?"

"Don't worry about that now, Pom," he said calmly. "You've just come home after a long time. You need to rest and recover."

"Papa," I pleaded in a strained voice, "please tell me. I need to know if my friends are safe." I spoke words I hoped would tug at his heartstrings, but they did not express the full truth of what I was feeling then. In that moment, I craved a companion with similar injuries, one with whom I could share my thoughts and who could truly understand me. It may sound morbid, but when we are vulnerable, we often seek mirrors of our deepest, darkest experiences.

He hesitated for a moment.

"If you're feeling up to it, you can check your email. Nikhil says that many of your friends have been emailing you and would love to hear from you," he told me, clearly trying to change the subject. "I can help you type, if you find it tough."

A surge of excitement coursed through me at the thought of hearing from my friends. Human connections are my life force, and the visits of half-a-dozen school friends in the hospital had helped me look forward to the next day. It was love, friendship, and hot chocolate fudge that had kept me going. Without them, I might have withdrawn from the external world.

Therapy after therapy. Physical therapy, occupational therapy, speech therapy. If not for the pressing and all-consuming acute nature of my physical needs, I might have also considered mental health therapy. But the truth is that in those early days, I couldn't spare any space in my mind for dark thoughts. My focus had shifted entirely to making my body obey me, as best I could.

In the elevator at the hospital one morning, heading to my therapies, I was greeted by a balding middle-aged man dressed in a worn-looking mustard kurta–pyjama, tufts of hair sprouting above each ear. He looked down at me, his gaze lingering. The man turned to face Mama.

"What happened to your daughter? I saw her just last week, and she was running down the hallway, and now . . ."

My face grew hot, and my cheeks flushed. With gritted teeth, I spoke up, "You know, you can ask me your question directly."

Mama attempted to pacify me by placing a gentle hand on my shoulder before addressing the man.

"Ji, you must have seen somebody else. My daughter had a motor vehicle accident and has been immobile for over six months."

Ji? Why in God's name was Mama addressing this ignorant man so respectfully?

The man's eyes swept over me, and his persistent stare at my immobile arm, which lay curled in a fist on the wheelchair's armrest, was unnerving. He opened his mouth and spoke in Hindi in an almost cooing, high-pitched voice, "You poor little doll. Don't worry, the Lord above will shower His blessings on you, and you'll be running and jumping in no time."

My blood boiled. I wanted to scream. Instead, tears welled up in my eyes. The elevator doors swooshed open as we arrived at the rehab center's floor, and Mama steered me away.

This wasn't the first time a stranger had made me feel like I had no agency or spoken to me, largely through my parents, as if my injury had also chopped off my years on this planet. I stopped my mind from spiraling into negativity – maybe, just maybe, the man simply thought he was showing concern or compassion. I tried teasing the subtle, yet significant, difference between the seemingly intertwined notions of pity, concern, and compassion. It was only after thinking hard and deep about this that I understood why pity leaves us feeling small and inconsequential, while concern and compassion help lift us. Pity is laced with condescension, and reinforces helplessness and inferiority, while compassion and concern foster connection and understanding. The latter two emotions can be taken forward, but pity is an end in itself. Pity is a passive emotion, with the potential to create a power dynamic, whereas concern and compassion are active emotions that promote dignity and respect.

I struggled to keep a straight face, troubled by how little the world understands about disabilities. I would be the first to admit that being in a wheelchair does come with its own set of peculiar perks, like never having to find a chair at crowded venues and getting away with mischief – "*the cute girl in a wheelchair couldn't possibly have done it.*" But my disability is only one part, even if an all-too-visible one, of who I am, a footnote to the larger story of my life, albeit a footnote that makes my life more meaningful. Above all else, I am a woman, a daughter, a sister, a friend, a thinker, a dreamer. I am a person with my own hopes and fears, my own autonomy and agency, my own TBR,[5] and my own Netflix watchlist.

I refuse to forfeit my agency. Yet, despite the acceptance I have found in my own world of family, friends, and caregivers, beyond its borders, I am often seen as a person to be pitied. This creates a power dynamic between individuals with disabilities and those who are non-disabled that is akin to that between children and adults. The truth is the world does not fully understand what it means to live with a disability, to navigate a world not designed for us, while also having a fierce independence burning within. It's not just about accessibility – ramps and elevators – or Braille or sign language interpreters. It's about recognizing that people with disabilities, too, have dreams and desires, fears and frustrations, joys and sorrows, just like everyone else.

The label of disability doesn't provoke any contentious feelings within me. It holds the same significance as each of my other labels – such as being a woman or a person of color and an "international" when overseas at a university. Collectively, our labels, along with our experiences, and memories, shape our identities. But when just one label is thrust upon us, we feel reduced and limited, unable to evolve and adopt new identities as we desire. Taken together, I wear each of my multitude of labels with pride, knowing that they represent different facets of my life, and contribute to my unique story.

We entered the rehab room to see my therapists, Geeta and Deepak, busy with two other patients. Geeta, deeply committed to her work, often stayed well past closing time to help her patients regain lost functionality. Her dedication was matched only by her deep empathy, and in her presence, I felt truly seen. Deepak sir, as he insisted I call him, was in the same age group as us. Steeped in American casualness, initially, I couldn't help but scoff. Despite his quirks, I soon discovered that Deepak "sir" was an amiable therapist. But I still found his request comical, especially since he bore a surprising resemblance to one of Nikhil's closest friends, a friend I had bantered with over countless games of beer pong.

The patient whom both my therapists were attending to at the time was a young woman, about my age, who had a stroke during childbirth – her ailments were similar to my own, but milder. I watched her progress carefully as a barometer for what I could expect from my own rehabilitation.

The second patient was a boy with cerebral palsy. Despite his speech difficulties, this particular boy reacted to the world around him with his emotions plastered on his face. He held on fiercely to his outgoing personality and refused to be cowed down by stares that lasted longer than appropriate. I recall being envious of his indifference to judgment. His family had brought him from Bahrain for medical treatment, drawn by the affordable services offered in India. The boy lacked the fine coordination of the muscles around his mouth and tongue required for speech. However, with no speech therapy available at this branch of Max Hospital at the time, the boy was left without the support that he desperately needed.

Time trickled by, and the rehabilitation room grew emptier. Whether the other patients had found their way back to the world or simply lost hope, I couldn't say. But I stayed the course, a lone wanderer still trudging through the dunes of recovery.

Under the cautious scrutiny of my physical therapists, I continued the grueling routine of physical therapy. Simple mat exercises became the foundation of my strength-building regimen, demanding that I push my body to its limits. I would lie on my back, determined to raise my right leg against the force of gravity. Then, with my feet planted firmly on the bed, I would lift my buttocks and squeeze my glutes until my muscles screamed for mercy.

I had no other option. I had to persist.

Fortunately, my progress in those early days was visible and steady. The mat exercises soon gave way to walking between the parallel bars. After what seemed like years – but was only months on the calendar – I graduated to walking with a quad cane, flanked by two physical therapists to catch me if I faltered. And falter I did.

The rush of motivation that accompanied even the slightest visible improvement was palpable. I could feel the ember of hope burning within me, a spark in the darkness. I was emboldened by my progress, no matter how small. And as my quad and gastrocnemius muscles regained some strength, I could climb into the car unaided, relying on my own strength and the support of my quad cane. I still needed my walking shadowed in case I lost balance, but the independence I craved felt within reach.

I made a vow to myself then that I would give my all to therapy, no matter how grueling. The promise of a return to my former life was too sweet to ignore. I would push myself further, and not give up.

I have always relished scaling challenges, but this one was in a league of its own.

At this stage, occupational therapy primarily entailed exercises for my right hand and arm. Much like physical therapy, this stage of my recovery was centered on rebuilding strength, with a particular focus on my right upper limb. Fine motor movement was also a key component of the exercises, as I had lost all use of my right hand.

I would later learn that the distinctive feature of the human brain is its inhibitory function or the ability of the brain to regulate the firing of certain neurons that prevent the hyperexcitability of muscles. Our brain communicates with our muscles via motor neurons in our spinal cord, which, when fired, causes our muscles to contract. In severe TBIs, nerve pathways carrying inhibitory neurons, which tell muscles to relax or elongate, are often disrupted, leading to uncontrolled tightness, or hyperexcitability, in various affected muscles.

This uncontrolled tightness, or spasticity, is most pronounced in my right upper extremity. As a right-handed person, regaining the use of my dominant hand would be a boon for my achieving independence once again, especially since my poor balance continues to need supervision for safety concerns. During the initial period, the goal of occupational therapy was to restore functional movement to my right arm and hand. I knew I could be independent even in my wheelchair if I just had the use of both my upper limbs. Independence typically requires control over at least one set of limbs – either upper or lower – but I had neither. My right arm was immobile, and the weakness on my right side made it nearly impossible to use either leg on my own.

The damage to my nerve pathways is irreversible, but I still held onto hope for a full recovery; hope fueled by naïveté. I couldn't imagine being in a wheelchair forever. How would I lean against Nikhil on the grass at Summer Stage concerts in Central Park? How would I navigate my way through the crowds in a wheelchair? Still, thanks to my efforts, and to the remarkable adaptability of the brain, the therapy proved to be a game-changer. The unrelenting pressure of therapy after therapy pushed my brain to rewire, forcing me to attempt moving my right arm and hand tens of thousands of times. Every twitch, every extension, was a battle against the crushing tightness in my muscles. It was a Herculean task, but I had to persist if I hoped to regain even a modicum of functional movement.

As one of the fundamental laws of neuroplasticity elegantly states, "Neurons that fire together, wire together." I realized that recovering what I had lost wouldn't be a matter of sudden epiphany but of dogged persistence. To rewire my brain, I needed to repeat the desired actions over and over to give my brain the mental experience it needed to change itself.

With its intricate network of synapses and neural pathways, the human body's information processing system is a marvel. As an agnostic, I later found myself reckoning with the complexities of our existence and contemplating the possibility of an unknown force shaping our existence.

7

Reconnecting

My spirits lifted when I noticed Nikhil's name flashing on my basic Nokia feature phone. As he inquired about my therapy, his calm, measured tone reached me from oceans and continents away. The mere thought of his presence, his existence, his care, brought me immeasurable solace. Then, Nikhil slipped in the main reason he'd called: he was planning to visit me in March. I could hardly contain my joy. I practically screeched at the prospect of seeing him in person for the first time since the accident. I learned only much later that I'd apparently seen Nikhil soon after regaining consciousness, in December 2010, on his visit to India, but reality was no more than a blur back then. I would now be seeing him nearly a year-and-a-half after I last fully remembered being in the same room as him.

My excitement was soon tempered by a new fear – that he wouldn't find me attractive anymore. After my head was shaved for brain surgery, my long locks became a thing of the past. They were replaced with a pixie-cut-like regrowth, and my body carried an additional fifteen pounds. I couldn't shake off the worry that I wasn't the attractive woman Nikhil had fallen in love with.

Of all people, it was him I confided in.

"Babes, you should know that your physical appearance is not what matters. I will always love you," Nikhil reassured me. "*I* am chubby, but you still love me!"

His words melted away my insecurities. I passionately wanted to believe that our relationship was deeper than physical appearances, and when I looked back on our time together, this felt true. All those long hours spent at the Quad Library at Harvard, both of us working on our papers, liberally consulting each other. All that time discussing issues that felt so urgent and immediate to us, from post-9/11 politics to the Iraq war; and, a topic we often returned to, how economic liberalization was reshaping India, for good and for bad. Nikhil was also my guide to life in America, taking me to Fenway Park to see the famed Boston Red Sox in action, introducing me to American sports, something entirely foreign to a "fresh off the boat" Indian like me. Nikhil leaned further left than me – he was more attuned to anti-capitalist and anti-neoliberal economics, and usually more likely to be critical of the IMF and the World Bank than I was. But mostly we were intellectually on the same page. When we argued it was about silly things like why wasn't he spending more time at Wellesley, which was not as exciting a place as Harvard and its environs, but still, home for my friends and me (to be fair to Nikhil, we did end up spending *quite* a lot of time at Wellesley). We argued, as lovers do, about not calling the other often enough or not communicating enough when we were not together.

A recurring argument was whether we should live in India or the US. I vividly remember a particular day when this came up in New York. We had woken up to a perfect sun-drenched July day, and instead of lingering in bed, had set out immediately to explore the city, taking in our favorite brunch spot, and then walking endlessly along New York's streets before ending up on a blanket in Washington Square Park discussing our future. Nikhil was clear:

he eventually wanted to settle in the Bay Area, where his entire family was – an idea that only raised my irritation levels. How could he then say we would always be together? He knew I wanted to live close to my parents in India, in their old age. "Well then, it looks unlikely that we can be together," I blurted out, letting go of his hand. When he asked me not to be irrational, I got madder still. "Here we go again," I said, "with the rational Nikhil, irrational Tarini narrative. Sure, voice your thoughts, but if they make you look like a hypocrite, just know that I am going to call it out." Nikhil reached for my hand again and spoke a few soothing words – that we would sort it all out, and so on, and then we sauntered into the Whitney Museum for a Georgia O'Keefe exhibition. I felt myself relax. Despite our differences, I knew our love was real. We weren't "adulting" by a long shot, but had learned the give and take of cohabitation. Through every phase of my life in America, Nikhil had been there. He had supported my decision to go to Uganda. Even now, during the darkest days of my life, he was there. I had no reason to doubt his words.

After the call ended, I had three hours of free time after lunch, during which I settled into bed with my Kindle, eager to finally have time alone to read the book, *Poor Economics,* by the economists, Abhijit Banerjee and Esther Duflo, who would go on to win the Nobel Prize. Nikhil had recommended the recently published book as a step toward "normalcy" in my life, as he reckoned it would help me keep up with my area of interest – development economics – after my prolonged absence from the field.

As I reached for my Kindle, I was relieved at the ease it provided. Where turning paper pages calls for the use of both hands – one to hold the book while the other turns the page, now a single touch could unfurl entire worlds.

I was so lost in the book that when Mama interrupted me by coming in to tell me that my speech therapist would arrive in just five minutes, I was stunned – where had the three hours gone? I had barely made it through the short first chapter on my specific area of interest, food security. How was it that I couldn't even get through twenty-two pages in *three* hours? *Why do I have to reread passages multiple times to understand them?*

My thoughts were cut short by the raspy voice of my speech therapist, Amit, speaking to Mama outside my door. I let out an audible sigh, knowing that of the three therapies I had to endure, speech therapy was the hardest for me to bear.

The sound of the words that formed in my mind did not match what actually escaped my lips. Speech relies partly on the imagination and partly on the three layers of the ear responsible for hearing sound. It was as though my voice belonged to a stranger, one who spoke in a sluggish, slurred manner, and over whom I had no control when it came to inserting expression into her speech. This was not me. The discrepancy between my thoughts and my speech left me biting my lip in frustration, as though the words I spoke were not truly my own. I would smile and nod along with the surrounding conversation, but inside, I felt alone.

After one such session, I once again longed to share my experience with someone who could truly understand, someone with an injury similar to mine. I vowed to get Papa to tell me if, by any chance, one of my Uganda friends had been on the scooter with me that day in Kampala and was going through a similar experience. Maybe he or she remembered the accident. Doctors had informed me I never would. We could be sounding boards for one another, and connect on a deeper level.

As Amit entered the room, I was reminded of the other problem I had with speech therapy – it was all in Hindi. English is both the language of my thoughts, my dreams, and my speech, the default I had switched to when my family moved to the Netherlands for a year for Papa's job when I was six. Amit did not speak English, and he was the only therapist my parents could find. He reassured me that practicing sounds in Hindi would help my English speech as well, since Hindi has a wider range of sounds than English does. Although his explanation made sense, it didn't make our sessions any less irritating.

I would clench my teeth when Amit would throw in a word or two of English into his session. He would instruct me to say "vater" instead of "water". This was because Hindi lacks the W sound and instead utilizes only the V sound. With an exasperated sigh, I would devote the rest of the session to coaching *him* on the correct pronunciation. It wasn't until later that I discovered that a lot of the more qualified English-speaking speech therapists in India leave the country in search of higher pay, leaving the less qualified behind. It was no wonder my parents had such a hard time finding someone who was a good fit for me.

When Amit finally left, I let out a sigh of relief, the tension in my body dissipating like smoke. Mama went to the kitchen and returned with a tall glass of cold coffee for me, with beads of condensation clinging to the outside. The refreshing drink signaled the beginning of my break time, a respite before the next task in my therapist-advised, self-imposed regimen of practicing my walking in my long driveway.

By now, my days had settled into a pattern. To start with, I left for occupational and physical therapy at 10 a.m., and finished at 12.30 p.m. After returning home for lunch with Mama, I permitted myself to take a break, during which I usually tried to make progress on one of the many nonfiction books about the brain that I devoured, albeit slowly – these books helped me address my unquenchable thirst for knowledge about what was happening to me.

At 3 p.m., I had my twice-a-week speech therapy session, after which I had a window of two hours for visitors. Himali was far and above my most frequent visitor. Afterward, I would do therapy homework with my brother, who had graduated from college and got a job with Dalberg, a global development consulting firm.

In those in-between days, after his graduation and before Dalberg, Rasoo shared our home once more. Each morning, he'd become my compass, guiding my steps and the movement of my right hand with the same steady patience as always.

Like clockwork, Pallavi's voice would bridge the distance from New York every day, whether on her way to work or from her office desk. In those pre-Bluetooth earphones days, when wires were everywhere, our conversations still managed to find their way around life's daily rhythms, including therapy homework. Friendship has its own magic that way.

Evenings brought my father's steadying presence, calming the anxieties I openly shared with him. As night settled in, the remaining time was dedicated to conversing with Nikhil either on the phone or through the time-consuming process of typing out an email with just my non-dominant left hand.

Though others marveled at my unflagging discipline, the truth is that my tightly structured schedule was both a cure for boredom and a carefully crafted veneer of purpose.

I stuck to the daily grind with inflexibility, leaving no spare time in which to ponder my life, dwell in self-pity, or step into the bottomless pit of comparison. The moments when life took a turn from the daily schedule, however, were the ones that truly made me feel alive.

Among such moments were the ones when my darling college friends traveled from far-off places to see me in 2011 and 2012.

In Wellesley's stone corridors and wood-paneled common rooms, we international students had found each other. Over plates of steaming Nepali momos and Maggi noodles, in canoe rides around Lake Waban, and during visits to the communal basement kitchen at midnight, we had swapped stories and became close friends. And now they came to me, from Bhutan, London, and yes, even from Lahore. Sahar, my Pakistani friend, who lived in my dorm for three of my four college years, managed to leverage her father's prominence in Pakistan to obtain a tourist visa.

On each of their visits, my college friends pulled up chairs by my bedside to hear what I had to say and assure me of their love. As we reminisced about our shared experiences, their jokes lightened the atmosphere, brightening my day. Despite being geographically scattered, my college friendships continue to be an ever-present and empowering force in my life.

On those visits, my friends insisted on hearing stories about my time in Uganda working with smallholder farmers, and my lively social scene there. Just like that, by trying to remember my Uganda experiences, memories began trickling in slowly like fragments of a dream returning piece by piece. At first, it was just flashes – blurry faces, places, moments of laughter. Gradually, the memories grew clearer. The fields where we worked with smallholder farmers, the nights frolicking with friends, the sense of purpose that defined my time in Kampala. As these memories returned, so did the faces of Meri and Davis, two people whose presence in my life had been anything but fleeting.

And then one day, Skype's distinctive ringtone shattered the calm. Skype's blue icon had become my window to the outside world. With only my non-dominant hand available for typing, emails felt like a marathon but Skype made the possibility of connecting just a little bit easier, despite my difficulties with speech. When online, my name would light up to alert my contacts of my presence. Now, a name that stirred something deep in me was dancing across my screen. I watched Davis's name blur and sharpen, blur and sharpen, for another few seconds before I fumbled to press the correct button.

"Is this really you, Davis?" I asked in disbelief. "Kizito Davis, turn on your video and show yourself."

I heard a warm chuckle, a true Davis chuckle, and then he said, "It really is me, but I can't turn on the video to prove it. Don't you remember the kind of internet we deal with here?" Did I remember the fun times we had in Kampala, he asked me, in a voice tinged with nostalgia and tenderness. I felt comfortable enough to tell him there was a lot I did not remember about those days, and pleaded with him to remind me of our escapades.

Between bursts of laughter, he recounted scenes from a legendary goat race we'd attended. We had watched oddly decorated goats trotting past, with their owners marching behind, their eyes shining with pride. Then came the tale of our culinary misadventure with the Nanavatis' son, Akshay, at a Chinese restaurant chosen by him, where the prices on the menu had our eyes growing wider by the second, and the arrival of the bill elicited a collective gasp. The memory came rushing back, and I howled with laughter.

Davis instinctively seemed to know how to keep the conversation light. I learned later that my father had asked him not to talk about my accident at that time. He first wanted to be sure my mind was strong enough to take it. Luckily for Davis, I did not inquire. Otherwise, I doubt he could have resisted my insistent, if not incessant, and nagging pleas.

"Can you ask Meri to call me?" I said hopefully. He promised to try. So just two days later, the same story played itself on repeat. Meri's retelling of Davis's stories came with a female flourish, and I couldn't help but smile. She also added the detail that the absurdly expensive Chinese restaurant was called Fang Fang.

Less than a day after our joyous reunion on Skype, an email from Meri landed in my inbox, with the subject line Kampala Kronicles. I let out a gasp when I saw the length of the email. Meri had amassed detail upon detail to craft an account of three of our cherished Kampala memories. Each memory felt like a gift wrapped in thoughtfulness. I felt insanely lucky that our paths had crossed in Kampala.

As time went on, they kept in touch, refusing to step back from the difficult reality I inhabited. Even when I was in a coma, they had connected with my parents, getting updates on me. Now, no matter how garbled my speech, they called me regularly on Skype, and emailed me.

I have an email from Davis from 2012 in which he writes:

"Sometimes I just can't believe it's you writing to me, my friend I never hugged a good bye, never said a good bye she could hear, being stretched off to an ambulance!!!? That day, I locked myself in my room when I got home and cried with little hope! It's super amazing we are writing to each other now."

Those calls and emails were more than just a lifeline – they were a bridge to a past I thought might be lost forever. Ever so gradually, my Uganda puzzle began piecing itself together, and in that, I found a part of myself again.

One memory made us laugh non-stop. Meri reminded me about Babu, the middle-aged gent who was staying in the room next to mine at the BRAC guesthouse where I had lived before moving in with Saif and Jouty.

He had taken on the role of my unofficial guardian, always asking, "Tarini madam, where are you going? When are you coming back?" as though I needed his permission.

One night, he even locked the gate and wouldn't let me in until I nearly begged. He had somehow decided that I was a "good girl" who'd want to join him at the Hindu temple every Sunday, even after Amar chimed in with, "She eats beef." Meri recalled how we turned it into a joke, deciding that if someone at a party asked for my number, I'd say my name was Babu and give them his number instead.

Memory is a puzzle, or maybe it's better to think of it as the brain's personal library, where each book represents a particular memory. A new book is added each time we either experience or learn something new. In cases of injury or damage to the personal library, rubble and debris can accumulate between the aisles, making it difficult for the librarian to locate a book. Emotions also play a crucial role in determining which books we remember long after they've been filed away in the library stacks. Books connected to strong emotions are more straightforward to locate, like the joy of your wedding day or achieving a milestone in your personal journey.

My friendship with Meri and Davis was rooted in deep emotions – maybe not as intense as a marriage, but undeniably powerful. They were the first true friends I made during my overseas adventure in Uganda.

With the final lacuna in my memory seemingly filled, only the experience of my final boda ride remained – an irreparable and forever lost fragment, according to the doctors' grim prognosis. But perhaps, it's for the best – such are our brains' mysterious ways of protecting us.

Meanwhile, two of my economics professors from Wellesley, who were still teaching at the college, maintained regular communication with me. One offered to share my story with the Wellesley community, seeing it as a source of motivation. The other provided valuable recommendations for specific good books I could explore and connected me to another alum who had received a similar injury to the brain. This alum, Trisha Meili, widely known as the Central Park Jogger – she had been assaulted in Central Park while out on a run – offered me valuable guidance and motivation, assuring me that I could overcome my challenges just as she had hers. In these moments, I witnessed the truth of what one of the professors would only later tell me: friendships are never lost; they are accumulated over time.

And, of course, there were the steadfast constants.

Every day at around 6 p.m. IST, when it was early morning on the US east coast, Pallavi would unfailingly call me, and her voice would fill the room with warmth. As expected, one evening, a few minutes past six, I heard my phone buzz on my bedside table.

"Hi, Tarins," Pallavi said, her voice full of weariness. "I wish I didn't have to get out of bed to go to work today. I'm so tired."

It frustrated me to hear her complaining about her glorious life. If only she knew just how lucky she was.

"Oh shush, Palloo," I chided. I had to push myself to be civil toward her. "You have no idea how lucky you are that you can go to work at all." Only now do I realize the frustration my friend must have endured, silently holding back complaints out of respect for the difficult circumstances I was facing.

Pallavi merely sighed, "You're right. Thank you for always reminding me to look at the big picture. I know you will return to work soon and be successful at whatever you choose to do with your life because you are the most determined person I know. It's just a matter of time."

I smiled, though my mind was a hive of buzzing thoughts. *Pallavi is being such a devoted friend, but I bet she wouldn't be quite so caring if things were like they were back when we lived at 10 Stuyvesant Oval – when I used to yell at her for taking too long in the shower or for cluttering our hallway with all her shoes! When will those days return?*

"I have news!" Pallavi burst out. "I'm following your path – leaving my job and moving to the development sector. Acumen Fund just offered me a job!"

"Congratulations, Pallavi! That's amazing."

Almost instantaneously, my gaze turned inward. It felt like I was indirectly serving society from my bed at home.

"I'm so happy to hear this. You *must* take it!" Joy bubbled up inside me – not just for her landing such a coveted position, but for seeing me as I was, never once reaching for that well-worn word "inspiring" that so many others drape over my shoulders. I harbor a particular distaste for the word because of its all-too-common use with us, people with disabilities. It is often loosely tossed without understanding the person's story or circumstance. The frequent use of the word 'inspiring' for people whose challenges are visible is paternalistic in its praise. Pallavi would have been partly excused if she'd used that horrid word, but still not entirely.

"But I need your help, Tarins," Pallavi continued.

"What do you need?" Looking down at my feet propped up on the bed that day, I doubted I could be of help to anybody.

But, as Pallavi went on, it became clear that just as she stood firmly by my side, she needed to rely on me in return, just like she always had. Pallavi explained her concerns about the new job, and I offered my advice and encouragement. Despite the distance between us, we were still able to support one another. The routine we'd built meant everything to me, especially how Pallavi treated me like nothing had changed between us. Nothing had. We wouldn't let it.

Day after day, Pallavi's calls were a welcome break from the monotony of my daily routine, a chance to escape into the vivid stories of her life, one that felt like my own. I never had anything exciting to report, just the same old tales of the tedium of my daily routine. But even as I repeated these tales of woe, I found myself laughing at my own situation, sharing jokes with Pallavi, and teasing her in turn. The story of my Hindi-speaking speech therapist made it to her, of course.

"Tarins, I'm in awe of you. You are doing an incredible job dealing with your situation," Pallavi said.

"You are too kind, Palloo. But can I tell you a secret about what's making this easy?" I asked rhetorically. Without waiting for an answer, with a mischievous grin, I continued, "I have a new physical therapist who comes home for my therapy. And I can't tell you how good-looking he is."

I paused dramatically, relishing the moment.

"And even though my sense of smell is weak now, I'm pretty sure he smells like heaven, too!"

Pallavi burst into laughter.

"Oh, Tarins, I miss your ridiculousness so much!" she exclaimed. "So, your motivation to do your exercises comes from having a handsome therapist?"

I nodded, still smiling. "You know it. I never thought I'd look forward to therapy, but here we are."

Pallavi chuckled. "Okay, I have to admit, I would feel the same way! You and I are the same person."

Once again, my mind drifted to examining the subtle nuances of pity and sympathy. While sympathy was certainly more desirable than pity, what I craved above all at the time was empathy – a genuine understanding of my experiences and the ability to connect on a deeper level – a complex cognitive and emotional ability Pallavi embodies in all its glory. I longed for my friends to see the world through my eyes, to feel the emotions I felt, and to form a bond that transcended the boundaries of pity or sympathy. Through Pallavi's friendship, I felt truly seen and understood, in a way that was authentic and genuine.

It wasn't as if friendship was a one-way street, with me as the sole recipient of its benefits. One day, Pallavi's excited voice filled my ear as she recounted a chance encounter at her office with the charming

Harvard student, Ishan Sen, whom I had introduced her to in our second year of college during my summer internship in Rajasthan when she came to visit me. I had confessed to Pallavi that, had it not been for my deep feelings for Nikhil, I might have been attracted to Ishan. In response, Pallavi had grunted and shrugged, saying, "Are you kidding me, Tarins?"

But it was her excitement that day that caught my attention. It turned out that, by pure coincidence, Ishan had walked into her New York office for a meeting, four years after I had introduced them. As he was leaving, he coolly sauntered over to Pallavi to exchange numbers. Bursting with enthusiasm, I wholeheartedly granted my approval of the new man in her life and prepared Pallavi for a potential first date with Ishan.

"Let's not get carried away," she cautioned me.

For once, I had non-therapy news to share – Nikhil's impending visit to India. I confessed my fears to Pallavi. It had been months since I had seen Nikhil and it worried me whether he'd still be attracted to me. But despite my changed appearance and various limitations, I still felt like myself – in my mind, I thought in the same way and behaved similarly to how I did before the accident, save for a few disproportionate emotional outbursts I'd had.

I really wanted to feel worthy of being somebody's girlfriend. Including figuring out how to get out of my comfy baggy sweats and loose t-shirt into more alluring attire. Baggy clothes had become my uniform since my hospital days, as it was easier for my nurses to dress me in loose clothing.

After my call with Pallavi ended, I lay in bed, staring blankly at the ceiling. My parents were frantically trying to connect with as many people as they could to ensure that their daughter received the best care possible. Clothes were the last thing on their minds, as they focused on the more pressing matter at hand: my physical health.

Which is why I finally confided in Seeta Bua about my clothing dilemma. Shopping was impossible for me at the time, and home delivery wasn't prevalent in India then. My pre-accident clothes, still packed away, would be far too small to fit my now filled-out body.

"Don't worry about clothes, I will help you with that," Seeta Bua offered, her kindness a balm to my anxieties.

She kept her promise and arrived the following week with a bag of new clothes. There was even a red T-shirt dress with a collar that I could wear over trousers to conceal the imposing white brace I still have to wear on my right leg. Though the clothes were not exactly alluring, I was overjoyed because I could finally shed my tracks and regain a sense of feeling more like myself.

8
Up Close

Nikhil's flight was scheduled to land in under three hours, and I could barely conceal my excitement. The mere thought of being under the same roof as him made my heart race. In Nikhil's company, I felt whole and deserving of love.

But now, in addition to the anticipation, I felt nervous. I resisted the urge to let my thoughts spiral out of control, but the trepidation in my chest was hard to ignore. I was confident my self-consciousness about my appearance would fade with time, but in the moment, the space around me seemed to contract, and my body became everything.

It was 9 p.m., and I had tucked myself into bed for a while now, trying to calm my nerves. I didn't want my anxiety to prevent me from having a good night's sleep, which in turn would wreck my first day with Nikhil. Yet, my mind flitted from one thought to another, and I was awake when, finally, I heard the sound of the key in the lock. I lifted my head, and saw my night nurse sitting wide awake on a stool in front of my bed, ready to assist me if needed.

"Go back to sleep," she whispered to me in Hindi.

I grunted and buried my head under the covers. I knew my parents would not think it appropriate for me to be visited by Nikhil in my bedroom late at night. Even though my father was socially liberal, he and Mama have always presented a united front in all things relating to raising their children – not to mention that my nurse, too, would have been scandalized at the arrival of a young man into my bedroom at this late hour. I had not just lost my physical independence but had become shackled in other subtler, ways too. Having to rely on my family and caregivers for support also meant paying lip-service to their ideas of what was acceptable. It made me realize how much I had taken my freedom for granted. I took a deep breath, pushing away the quicksand of comparisons, and made a conscious choice to count my blessings. *Tomorrow, I will finally see Nikhil again.* I closed my eyes and drifted off to sleep.

"Rise and shine, Tarini, today is a special day for you!" Mama said as she raised the blinds the next morning.

The thought of Nikhil's presence made me want to jump out of bed and fly into his arms, but I couldn't actually start my day until I was helped out of bed and into my wheelchair for my morning routine. I could see it was Mama at my service today.

"Where is Sandhya?" I asked Mama, feeling a wave of disappointment as my hope of looking my best started slipping away. Sandhya was more than just a caregiver to me; she had become my friend. Although I had a continuous stream of family, family friends, and a few childhood friends visiting me, I was also walking profoundly different paths from them, leading to an overwhelming sense of isolation. While Himali visited regularly, she couldn't assist with personal care. Sandhya could and did – she was a lifesaver.

"She should be here any minute. What's the matter, Tarini? Tell me what you need – I'm here for you."

I sighed, knowing that though she meant well, there was no way Mama could comprehend the mix of emotions I felt about seeing Nikhil after so long. My relationship with each parent was so different. My father offered me shelter and supported my life choices, without laying out the path ahead. He had an almost supernatural ability to read my emotional state, even before it surfaced in my own consciousness. My mother's fiery and fierce love wound closer still, weaving itself into the daily minutiae of my being. It was both more demanding and more intricate in nature, resulting in cycles of closeness and friction. The intensity, high in my teenage years, had abated as I went out into the world and took charge of my own life. Now, we were sort of negotiating that terrain again, and it was all made more complex by an unshakable truth: she was (and is) my constant.

Ten minutes passed, and there was still no sign of Sandhya. I decided to take matters into my own hands.

"Do you remember, before my accident, I used to wear black eyeliner every morning?" I asked Mama, frowning as I stared at my reflection in the mirror. My eyes appeared recessed, with the skin around them showing signs of weariness, and it seemed as though they could use a touch of eyeliner to gain defining lines and restore their vitality.

"Yes, of course, I do. Would you like me to put it on for you?"

"Can you please help me with that, Mama?"

Soon, I was ready, but was still quite a bundle of nerves. I couldn't wait to see Nikhil again. After what seemed like an eternity, Mama wheeled me into the living room, where I spotted Sandhya seated on a wicker stool by the door. She must have entered the house, found my bedroom door locked, and we must have missed her knocking. Upon seeing us, Sandhya immediately sprang to her feet. Within a second, my eyes wandered to the other person waiting in the room. Nikhil, in the flesh.

"Nikhil," I said softly, with my heart in my throat.

"Hey, babes," Nikhil said, sounding both excited and apprehensive.

There he stood – hazel eyes misty, frame solid, lips full – my man.

"I've missed you so much," he said, approaching me and taking my hand.

I quickly turned to check if Mama was hovering behind me and was pleased to see that she had taken her cue and left us alone.

"Come here," I said, summoning him closer. "I love you, Nikhil." I felt my eyes moistening.

Nikhil stood up and looked at me with an expression I couldn't quite read.

"Babes, you know how the two of us can get overly sentimental with each other. I'm here for two weeks, so we have plenty of time for that, but let's not get too emotional on day one and try to have fun too. I am craving authentic Indian food!"

Love him, I did, but at the moment, I bristled at how Nikhil had shut me up. I would have rolled my eyes and rolled them again, if not for my cursed facial muscles. But this was not a moment for irritation – he had flown from the US to be with me. *Calm down, Nikhil's continued partnership is proof of his love for you.'*

As I reflect on that moment, it amazes me how, instead of displaying fragility, I was already back to being myself – strong-willed and assertive. But the irritation was all in my head.

My mother appeared just then with the good news that she had postponed my morning therapy sessions to the afternoon. "This way, you two can spend uninterrupted time with each other."

Sometimes, I underestimate my mother.

But then, Nikhil intervened.

"Thanks, Aunty, but I am looking forward to going with Tarini to her therapies."

A heavy silence hung in the air as my mother's eyes darted from me to Nikhil.

"It may be a better idea to let Tarini get used to your presence here first," she said finally. "You can start going with her from tomorrow so that her mind is fully focused on her therapies today."

I stared at Mama, my lip trembling. Why was she speaking as though I wasn't in the room? And how about asking me what I wanted? I fought to hold back tears of frustration and helplessness.

I could sense Nikhil's discomfort with Mama's hovering presence.

"Sure, whatever works best," he murmured.

My mother now insists her proactive parenting style was necessary in the early stages of my recovery, but the truth is, even as I gained strength, her hovering persisted. It was pure instinct; she just couldn't stop herself. When one thinks about it, faulting a mother for this is impossible. However, such truths are often only realized with hindsight. At the moment, it was getting on my nerves!

Later that day, Nikhil's eyes softened as he watched me struggle through my home rehab exercises. I could feel the weight of his unflinching support and his quiet strength.

Recovering from trauma is not a solo journey, but a collective effort of those who refuse to let you give up on yourself. Progress is not always linear, but with the right support, some form of progress is always possible.

But at that moment, Nikhil's presence beside me was also a stark reminder of how far I had to go before I could start living again. Truly living. His presence beside me did make me feel that all was right with the world – but not quite. Our once fluid connection now felt strangely measured – five years of spontaneity replaced by a closely monitored stilted existence. Still, his presence brought a quietude that had eluded me since the time we were last together, before my accident.

With Nikhil by my side, I descended the ramp to my driveway, each step a struggle. "You got this, babes – good job!" he said, his words lighting the path ahead as I focused on transferring my weight to my weak right leg.

Nikhil looked at my feet.

"If you understand the logic behind why it's hard for you to get your left foot ahead of your right, it will probably help you focus your mind on correcting your gait."

A few more small steps later, I paused, turning my head to face Nikhil.

"You know me too well," I said. "Knowing the logic will help. But first, how do you know all these things?"

Nikhil smirked.

"What do you think I do after you go to bed at night? I do TBI research. And then, of course, I talk to my mom." He dug his hands into his pockets with a playful and sheepish expression. Nikhil spoke to his mother every day – he was quite openly a momma's boy. I had always found it quite endearing.

When he launched into an explanation of the reasons for my poor gait, I found myself captivated by the way his hazel eyes shone with compassion and intelligence. His light brown hair was tousled and wild as if he had been running his hands through it. Two wispy strands of natural blond hair stood upright just above his forehead. I couldn't resist the urge to reach out and touch his hair, drawing him closer to me.

"Be careful, Tarini – you'll lose your balance!" Nikhil said, stepping closer and extending his arms instinctively.

The next day, I summoned Nikhil to my room to help answer the unresolved questions weighing heavily on my mind. He perched on the leather couch while I lay on my bed, my body a constant battleground of discomfort. Despite my desire to present myself as a regular girlfriend and not a patient, I couldn't ignore the relief of lying down. The bed felt like a sanctuary, a haven amid the constant torment my body was in. Every muscle in my right arm and leg felt like it was straining against invisible shackles. The agony of adjusting to my new reality was a heavy weight on my chest, a relentless ache that only grew more pronounced each time I met other people.

I stretched out my right arm beside me, grateful for the temporary relief provided by the hand splint that Nikhil helped me strap on. The hypertonicity of my right arm muscles was my primary source of discomfort, but now, the hand splint's straps were keeping my hand open without the constant and exhausting effort to resist the mysterious force tugging it shut.

My absence from the world for three months felt, and continues to feel, like a black box, a mystery that confounds me. I needed answers to so many questions. What had transpired during those months? How had my friends reacted to the news of my accident? Who was with my brother when he found out? How did he cope? When did my parents and Nikhil arrive in Uganda, and what were their reactions upon seeing my lifeless body?

Despite the bazillion self-absorbed questions, there was one that stood apart from the rest, one for which I needed an answer above all else.

"Please tell me who else was on the scooter with me? I really need to know. I remember I always traveled with a friend."

Nikhil squirmed in his chair, and the sound of the shifting leather heightened my unease. I knew him too well to be fooled by his attempt to buy time.

"I would tell you, but your father said he wanted to be the one to tell you, so I think it's best to wait," he said.

Looking back, it seems clear as day what everybody was concealing from me. Yet, at that moment, I could not even imagine the non-existence of the only person in the world who might be on the same rocky journey as me. I longed for a companion who would know exactly what I was going through.

Just at that moment, in his trademark fashion, Papa poked his head in through the crack in my door, grinning playfully.

"Hi, Papa," I said. "Come in. We need to talk to you."

"Oh?" he said, as he shuffled into my room. "What is it?"

"Uncle," Nikhil began, "Tarini wants to know who was on the boda with her, and I told her we'd wait till you came since you said you wanted to be here to have this conversation with her."

"Pom, I don't want you to think too much about this, okay? Promise your Papa first."

"*Uff*, yes, yes, Papa. I promise to only think of it a natural amount, as anyone in my position would," I said with a loud sigh. "Now just tell me, so I know whether I can reach out to anybody, because both of us are probably going through the same ordeal."

"Oh, Pom, I know you are going through a very tough time, but I have to tell you something not very nice . . ." Papa paused and took a deep breath. "It was your friend Sujal on the boda with you. Do you remember Sujal?" He paused to study my face and quickly added, "Unfortunately, he didn't make it. Sujal is not with us anymore."

Yes, I did remember the name as one belonging to a friend, but didn't have a very sharp sense of what Sujal was like, or the nature of our interactions – just that we'd had plenty of fun. Still, I had just learned that a friend had died. Upon seeing me biting my lower lip, my eyes widening in shock, Papa offered me more information. He clearly thought it was time I knew even though I hadn't inquired about the particulars.

"Sujal was sitting behind you on the motorbike. A speeding SUV, we think it was, crashed into your boda-boda from behind, throwing you and your friend off the bike. Both of you fell with your heads hitting the ground. With no helmets on, you both experienced traumas to your heads. Sujal had obviously felt the impact of the SUV along with the impact of the ground and endured greater bodily injuries along with brain trauma. His case was too severe, and he passed away right there in the hospital in Kampala."

I sat there, blinking rapidly, at a loss for how to react. Stray facts about Sujal started coming back to me – who he was, what he was doing in Kampala – but not my feelings toward him. Memories, as we know, are of many types, among them semantic and episodic memory. Semantic memory involves general knowledge and facts about the world, while episodic memory pertains to personal experiences, events, and associated emotions. Both are components of long-term memory, which in my case, has remained intact.

The details of the six-week friendship I had shared with Sujal were lost in the fog of my short-term memory, still struggling to fully recover after the accident. I could merely grieve in theory at this tragedy, which sounded more like a movie than real life. However, I had some facts and somehow a sense of the person Sujal had been – gifted, idealistic, fun-loving – and felt a deep sense of regret that the world had lost someone special. I felt deep gratitude toward him for his last good deed. It felt strange, knowing that I could never properly thank him for saving my life.

"Oh my god," I finally said. "Sujal was going to be a doctor. He'd planned to devote his life to saving others ... how could this happen?" My mind raced with questions, and I blurted out the one that troubled me most. "And what about the SUV driver? Didn't they stop to take us to the hospital?"

"The SUV never stopped. It was a hit-and-run. We know about the good work Sujal was doing." Papa clasped his hands together, knuckles whitening. "We met his parents there," he said. "It is tragic. But please don't think too much about this, Pom."

It didn't seem fair. Sujal had been doing noble work. Until then, I will admit that in my naïveté, I had thought that eventually, all good deeds are repaid in kind. How could Sujal ever be repaid for all the good he had done in his life if his "eventually" had already passed?

Like he was reading my thoughts, Papa said, "Yes, Sujal's position behind you took most of the impact. But, Pom, you promised not to overthink this. This is not your fault; don't blame yourself. If you have any more questions, ask us, and we will do our best to answer them. I have given you enough information for now."

On a lazy Saturday afternoon, Nikhil came up with an enticing suggestion. "Let's take a stroll in the park," he said, referring to the sprawling, forest-like green space near my home. My nurse joined us to push my wheelchair, freeing Nikhil to walk beside me. We made our way through the lush greenery, the gentle breeze caressing my cheeks. I felt alive and at peace.

The tranquility was short-lived. While relaxing on a bench, Nikhil reminded me, in a low voice, that he would soon be leaving. I was caught off-guard when it suddenly hit me – I had only three days left with him. Between battling daily struggles, time had slipped away. Amid the chaos, I found sanctuary in Nikhil's company.

I remained silent, staring at the ants scurrying on the dirt path. My lack of independence meant I had no say in when we would see each other next.

Nikhil pulled my wheelchair closer to him and took my hand in his. A lone tear escaped from the corner of my eye. I blinked it away.

He reassured me with warm, comforting words. His hand was soft in mine as he leaned in for a kiss, and for a moment, everything else faded away.

As we pulled apart, I realized Nikhil had thought ahead, timing his departure to overlap with my brother's arrival. The thought of having someone else to lean on after Nikhil had left was small comfort, but it was something.

I promised myself that I would try to find happiness in other places too, not rely solely on Nikhil for my joy. I couldn't be *that* girl – the one who lets her happiness hinge on her partner. But it wasn't easy to be independent where Nikhil was concerned. We had been together since we were eighteen, and I felt Nikhil was an extension of myself. Our lives were so interwoven that even most of our friendships were shared. Gazing into Nikhil's hazel eyes on that park bench, I remember feeling a great sadness at the unpredictability of life and its potential for altering relationships.

A day or so later, as I was scrolling through photos on my laptop, Rasoo poked his head into my room to announce his arrival. After a fair amount of squealing with happiness, I returned to what I was doing. I was keen to create a collage with photos of my family and friends to hang on my wall. As I scrolled through the memories stored on my laptop, I stumbled upon a photo of Rasoo and me as toddlers, fast asleep and hugging each other tightly. In the picture, he looked like a cherub with an overgrown fringe veiling the top of his forehead.

My mind drifted back to our childhood when we would escape into our own little world, seeking refuge from the mundanity of family dinner outings. We would bring along our favorite books – Sweet Valley Kids for me and Noddy for Rasoo – and spend hours lost in their pages. But more often than not, we'd pretend to be the different characters we had created. Eventually, sleep came knocking, and we curled up under a navy blue blanket, our short arms wrapped tightly around one another. At the end of the evening, our parents would load us into the car.

Another snapshot captured us sitting at the dining table in our school uniforms, with half-eaten bananas and mugs of plain milk in front of us. Our mother had had a few of her dance students over for class, and she'd reminded us to finish our neglected breakfast. We were not keen to be around those students, many of whom were in our school and we saw on the bus daily. I chuckled at the memory of Mama's well-intentioned but embarrassing speech, in front of them, on not wasting food in a country where so many children go hungry.

After quickly downing our milk, Rasoo and I ran upstairs and tossed our bananas out from a balcony overlooking a banana tree in our aunt's front yard. We harbored a particular aversion to bananas likely stemming from Mama's daily ritual of coaxing the yellow fruit past our reluctant lips. We then turned on the TV and cranked up the volume to watch *WWF Raw is War*, relishing the forbidden violence that we were forbidden from watching.

When I was a teenager, Dhaval, who would later introduce me to Nikhil, was my boyfriend for a while. He loved watching and playing soccer, as did Rasoo. I asked my brother to teach me the basics of the sport, and some soccer terminology that I could use to impress Dhaval.

"Didi, you're such a freak," Rasoo had said, groaning at my antics. "But fine, tell him that Rooney's bicycle kick in the Manchester derby last week was awesome."

Now I beamed at grown-up Rasoo's face, which I still consider cherubic.

"Thanks for coming home to visit me," I said, "when you could have been frolicking with your friends – that too for the last time as college students." He was here on his final spring break, a few months before he graduated.

Later that day, just before my evening walking routine, Rasoo disappeared upstairs to "unpack". But I knew he was just giving Nikhil and me space before Nikhil's departure.

"I don't think Rasoo will be able to make me walk the way you do – so effortlessly," I said outside as I practiced. "He's a baby."

"Don't be silly," Nikhil said. "He is a twenty-one-year-old man. Take it from me – he won't let you fall."

As if on cue, Rasoo appeared.

"C'mon, Didi, stop opening out your feet before you take a step," he commanded, his voice firm but gentle. Rasoo had quickly become an expert on my gait pattern. He knew what was out of my control and what I could work on.

As we walked together, I felt a sense of camaraderie that I hadn't felt with anyone else since my life had changed. Since birth, Rasoo had seen my messy, vulnerable, and unpolished self, whereas Nikhil had met me as my more complete self, making it jarring when he was forced to cross the line between romance and caregiving. Rasoo's presence made exercise time feel like a bonding experience, not a chore. Plus, after spending almost every waking hour with one or both of my parents, I was relieved to have some time away from them.

In the months that followed, life around me continued its forward march, seemingly oblivious to my absence. Each missed event stung like an open sore, a reminder of the new identity forced upon me. When Rasoo graduated from Yale, I stayed home. The support of two aunts – Seeta Bua [father's sister] and Mallu Masi [mother's sister], one from each side of the family – who sacrificed their responsibilities to come to spend five days each with me, stitched wings for my parents.

My heart had shriveled as I heard about the dinner my brother and his friends had planned for themselves and their families at Barcelona, a tapas restaurant in New Haven. It had been eight long months since I had been out and about in social company, and the mere idea of it felt like a distant dream.

Watching the Yale University commencement ceremony unfold on my laptop screen, I was thrilled to see Rasoo bouncing along amid a sea of black regalia. Yet, as is the case while living with injuries and illnesses, my gaze quickly turned inward yet again. I found myself juggling an odd blend of emotions – pride and desolation. The three members of my immediate family, most of my close friends, and Nikhil were all oceans away in the US. I felt my sense of isolation deepening.

Rasoo returned with my parents, and his mere presence lightened the air. He'd perch on my bed's edge, and I could breathe easier, letting half-baked thoughts tumble out. But I had already started dreading his departure to Mumbai when his consulting job began.

My brother was quick to resume his role as taskmaster, as he took charge of helping me with my therapy homework.

"Come on, Didi, focus on your gait. Keep your feet straight," Rasoo commanded during my evening practice. His logical instructions made it hard not to follow his lead. He even took it upon himself to help me with my right-hand exercises, all while keeping the mood light with playful banter. He transformed picking up and dropping colored blocks in their designated spot, which I then had to pick back up, into a slightly less tiresome task.

Then there was the dreaded speech therapy.

"Open your articulators," Rasoo would remind me, coaxing me to practice rolling my Rs and performing facial exercises. Speech therapy homework felt like having trouble with a first-grader's homework. Looking back, it appears illogical that I found speech therapy more bothersome than my other therapies. After all, learning to walk is a skill a first-grader would have mastered a long time ago. Alas, this remains one of those elusive mysteries that I will likely never know the answer to.

One afternoon, while Rasoo was upstairs, I sat alone in my room, mindlessly scrolling through my Facebook news feed. The images of friends and acquaintances drifted by, barely registering. They felt distant as if from a world I no longer belonged to. Pictures of that one lukewarm friend slurping ice cream while picnicking in Central Park, or that close pal at an art gallery with colleagues, twisted something inside me. Yet, I somehow pulled myself back from falling into the bottomless pit of self-pity. I had to remind myself that at twenty-four, my story was just beginning.

I returned from the hospital wrapped in a strange cocoon of certainty. The threads of my future felt firm in my grasp, and I was convinced that sheer will and therapy would bend recovery to my desires like a blacksmith shapes steel. But as days bled into weeks, that cocoon began unraveling, leaving me teetering between resolve and despair. The simplest acts – rising from bed, dressing, eating, even the private dignity of using the bathroom – all required helping hands. My mother, father, brother, Nikhil, friends, nurses, cook, driver – everyone who crossed my path – became a caregiver in some form. Despite all the hard work and the relentless schedule I followed, I still couldn't feed myself. A nurse stood beside me at meals, lifting each spoonful. My weakened muscles meant every movement from bed to wheelchair, couch to bathroom, needed another's strength. My world had shrunk to a space where survival hinged on others' kindness.

Seated on my bed one day, I tried to twirl the soft new growth that had manifested on my once-bald scalp. The short strands slipped through my fingers, but the gesture sparked something in me – what good were all my past victories if I surrendered now? I couldn't let myself sink.

I squared my shoulders and straightened my posture. I resolved to find a way to occupy myself beyond the endless cycle of therapy.

That thought alone felt like a small spark in the darkness. And then it hit me – why not go ahead with my plans to apply to business school? Why let the accident derail my life? Sure, it would be a year or two later than I'd originally intended, but so what? I could apply now and start next year, once I'd fully recovered.

I called out to my father and soon enough, he poked his head into my room.

"Papa!" I called out, beckoning him to come closer. "I have to tell you something important."

"What is it, Pom?"

With conviction in my voice, I announced, "I want to apply to business schools this year."

Papa strode to my bed and cupped my cheeks in his palms. His voice was soft as he spoke, his eyes shining with pride. "What an excellent idea, Pom. You still have at least half a year before you will need to get your applications in. Plenty of time to figure out all the details." He bellowed for Mama to join us, wanting to share the news. "If anyone can do it, it's my Pom," he declared after he filled her in on my decision.

Being a "daddy's girl" all my life, his faith in me opened worlds of possibility. The mere thought of having a man as wise as my father believing in my potential to be accepted by the world's top universities sent a surge of adrenaline through my veins. Mama, too, was delighted and supportive. My parents' unquestioning confidence in me became the catalyst propelling me forward.

My heart was already set on business school long before my accident. I had taken the GMAT test toward the end of my New York days, and had prepared a list of schools to apply to. Now, in this altered landscape, even gathering my thoughts felt daunting. True, I was unemployed; but instead my days overflowed with therapy sessions and exercises. On top of that, a steady stream of family and old friends visited me regularly, and it didn't seem right to tell them not to come. Amid all of this, I guarded my peace: nightly calls with Nikhil and Pallavi restored my spirit.

As I pushed forward with my plan, I couldn't shake the unsettling feeling that the accident had affected not just my motor skills but also my cognitive abilities. Math, a subject that had always eluded me, now had me baffled, even with the most basic arithmetic problems that my father had me practice in the evenings. Adding to my worries was the glaring six-month gap on my resumé. I feared that being upfront about my injury on my resumé would hurt my chances of getting into a top university. Anxious calls to Nikhil and Pallavi followed, but their reassurances rang hollow. *Do they think determination is a substitute for a functioning brain?* I wondered. My head spun.

On a sweltering June day in 2011, sitting on the couch, I called out to our cook, Gopi, requesting him to bring my laptop to me. Then, just as I opened my laptop, my parents burst through the living room door, both slightly out of breath.

"I took longer upstairs than I thought I would, *nyari*," Mama said, with a hint of apology. "But you were seated and safe, right?"

I had always preferred the upstairs part of our house. It had housed the only TV in the house, it was where the room my brother and I shared in our childhood was located, as was my father's desktop computer on which we were allowed to play games when he wasn't working. A lot had changed since the nineties – everyone had laptops on which they could watch movies if they wanted, and my parents had even gone out of their way to install a new flat-screen TV in my room. But I missed my old room upstairs. I yearned for my old life, a life where staircases didn't feel like mountains. A life just out of reach ...

This despondent train of thought was abruptly abandoned when Papa spoke.

"We have big news for you," he said. He reminded me that he had been appointed at Yale to teach during the fall semester for three years.

I nodded, intrigued.

"Well," he continued, pausing to study my face, "we weren't sure if you were ready to travel, but we just got a letter from Dr. Patir, authorizing you to fly. So we can all move to New Haven for the fall semester." Dr. Patir was the Max Hospital neurosurgeon who was overseeing my case.

My jaw dropped as Papa delivered the news. The only thought in my mind was that I would be moving closer to Nikhil and Pallavi. It felt like a dream come true.

Yale had offered to cover me as a dependent with full medical insurance, including rehab, even though I was technically an adult. The university also promised to assign a medical coordinator to assist my parents in identifying appropriate medical professionals.

My head was buzzing. The school of management at Yale University was my top choice among the ten schools I was planning to apply to. It focused on non-profit management *and* it had a loan forgiveness program for those working to serve society, either in the public sector or at a non-profit. That meant that once I graduated – if I got in, of course – my loans would be forgiven.

I relayed all this to my father, who beamed at my excitement, but cautioned me to hold my horses and "take things one step at a time".

I continued as if I hadn't heard him.

"Devika and Joerose," I said, naming two friends from school, "are currently enrolled at Yale SOM [School of Management]. Maybe I can sit in on a few of their classes to see if I can handle the academic rigor of graduate school."

Papa adjusted his glasses.

"Good idea, Pom," he said. We'll plan for all that."

He also suggested I contact Susan Davis at BRAC.

Later, I sat with my laptop, entangled in a web of thoughts, ready to start composing the email to Susan. I glanced at the keyboard's width, wishing I had learned to type properly with both hands when I had the chance. Instead, I had relied solely on my index fingers. Now, unaccustomed to using the fingers of my left hand, I was finding it cumbersome to cover the keyboard with my one working hand. I positioned my left fingers on the ASDF keys as I'd been told to do all along, but found reaching for the keys on the right side of the keyboard made typing painfully laborious. But with each fumbling keystroke, I was determined to improve. With practice, I knew I could learn to type more quickly, even if it was with my non-dominant hand. I began typing.

As I wrote, I couldn't shake the feeling that what I was doing was wrong. It had been almost eight months since I last spoke to Susan Davis, and the thought of asking her for anything, let alone a job, felt indecent. I knew that it would be a gamble for her to take me on, and I couldn't expect someone as smart as the CEO of BRAC USA to take a risk on a near stranger like me. But I also knew that I had to try.

Dear Susan,

I would like to thank you for all the concern and support you have shown over the last few months. My parents have told me that you came to the hospital to see me. That really means a lot to me.

I moved from the hospital back home two months ago after five-and-a-half months there, and now I am in the loving care of my parents. I am doing fine, and well in general, but I still can't walk and I am in a wheelchair, and my right arm doesn't move much.

But all these things are gradually improving because I have intensive physiotherapy every day . . .

I have been working hard to recapitulate my memory of Uganda, and now I remember a lot, especially the amazing field trips I went on with Mozammel.

I really enjoyed my time working for BRAC, it was exactly what I had wanted to do. I remember starting to work with you on a project. I vaguely remember it being about livelihood intervention, but the memory is hazy at best. Can you please remind me what it was about and what I was doing?

I am moving to the US with my family this August, as my father teaches at Yale in the fall semester. I am going to continue physiotherapy there and begin my applications for business school. Since New Haven is pretty close to New York, I would love to have the opportunity to meet you if possible!

I hope you are doing well and thank you for your caring support.

I lowered the laptop screen and signaled my nurse to help me into my wheelchair. Sandhya emerged from the shadows, a silent but watchful presence. I suddenly wanted to move to my room myself – a stone's throw away from the living room where I was at present. What would have taken me less than a minute now took as long as ten. Sighing, I wiggled my behind on the seat of the couch the best I could. The memory, from an earlier life, of the fleeting moments that existed between desire and action were still vivid in my mind, although that was all it was now – a memory. I now viewed my life and the world through two distinct lenses – through my non-disabled past, and my current "othered" state, where simple pleasures felt worlds away.

My family and Nikhil urged me to live in the present and stop comparing myself to my past self. But how could I not? I was still me, just trapped in a body that refused to bend to my will. As Sandhya helped me into bed, I tried to quieten my overactive mind. Then, she returned with something glinting in her hand. I squinted to see that it was my steel bedpan. A rude reminder that my present still reigned supreme.

9

America, My New Normal

The loud thumps of suitcases being moved, the rush of scurrying feet, Mama's voice calling out instructions to Gopi – they were the sounds of a household preparing for a flight later that night. To my relief, my mother had taken care of my packing. In record time, my bags were ready, waiting in the corner of my room, except for my laptop and hand splint, which would go in my carry-on.

I reached for my laptop one last time to call Nikhil. Hope flickered through me as I thought about moving to the US – the strain of long distance would ease, no more wrestling with expensive flights and impossible time zones. I would see him more often. Every fiber in my being longed to run toward Nikhil. Who knows, I thought, maybe the world-class therapy I would supposedly receive in the US would allow me to do that. But could things ever be as they once were? That beautiful past of ours, which I was so reluctant to let go of – could it be restored?

Lately, I had been feeling a strange sense of foreboding whenever I saw an incoming Skype call from him. His love was like a balm. His presence in my life brought a vestige of normalcy to it. But I sometimes wondered: Why would he stay? In return for the fragile comfort of normalcy, I had given Nikhil an ocean of complexity to manage. My slurred speech on the phone was a constant reminder of the obstacles hindering our plans for a lifetime of togetherness. I needed constant reassurance because I had begun to feel the world saw me as "damaged".

Our interactions had also become limited and stilted. I wrote to Nikhil on topics ranging from my dinner menus and my exercise routine, but deeper discussions left me increasingly on edge. We had been intellectual partners once, but now, the gap between our levels of mental acuity seemed too wide to bridge. I'd type notes beforehand about the Arab Spring, drone policies, healthcare reform – but connecting dots, crafting arguments, finding that natural eloquence that flowed so easily for him – it all felt just beyond reach.

I pushed these thoughts away as the four of us prepared to leave for the airport. Despite securing his desired job as a consultant at the Indian office of a top international development consulting firm, Rasoo had chosen to delay his start date and help us settle into New Haven. He wanted to be with us during this crucial early stage after head trauma. Fortunately, his new employers were gracious enough to allow him to start work when he returned to India with the rest of us in the winter. He had found a part-time job in New Haven, working at an online publication, focused on global affairs, based out of Yale.

Papa was dressed in his customary navy blazer and beige pants, the epitome of the professional at work. Regardless of his destination, he always dresses in "office" attire. My brother and I tease him mercilessly about his dress sense, but he brushes it off and proceeds with his day in office wear.

At the airport, I sat motionless in my wheelchair, watching as my brother heaved our suitcases onto the conveyor belt for check-in. As my parents conversed with the ticketing agent, I saw Papa's forehead furrow and Mama's eyes widen. I could not make sense of their exchange – the counter and the piece of paper they were gesturing toward were beyond my view. Mama held her hands upright in front of her chest with palms facing outward, and the agent stepped back in a surrendering gesture.

As an onlooker with no means to assist my family during this moment of stress, I felt a deep pang of helplessness. I quickly looked away.

The problem I had seen unfold, whatever it was, got sorted. I saw my brother ambling toward me, waving his hands.

"*Didi*, our bags have been checked-in. Should we head toward security while Papa and Mama finish up?" I reached out to touch his hand, and he placed it gently on my shoulder.

I was so glad he was with me. He always seemed to know what I needed. Right now, I needed movement. Freedom.

He nodded, adjusting the strap of his cerulean-blue Eastpak backpack. Then, with a firm grip on the handles of my wheelchair, he propelled me forward, weaving through the bustling crowd of travelers.

It was 2011, and in India, motorized wheelchairs were still a rarity, if they existed at all. The broken pavement and potholed roads in Indian cities are far from conducive to easy mobility of any kind. But my family and I did not, or could not, dwell on this fact for long. The novelty of my altered reality made it difficult for me and my family to grasp any concept of my independence just yet.

Standing rigid, his face bereft of emotion, the guard at the security check instructed me to rise from my wheelchair and "simply walk" through the security checkpoint. The security check, and the entire plane boarding procedure, proved to be labyrinthine – I had to explain what kind of injury I had that prevented me from rising and taking a few steps past the metal detector. Airport check-ins for people with disabilities are even more daunting in a society that often treats disability as an anomaly. These sorts of experiences lead to a vicious cycle of people with disabilities staying indoors to protect themselves, further perpetuating society's lack of exposure and understanding.

Later, in mid-air, I felt as fragile as a soap bubble as I made my way to the airplane washroom, my quad-cane in hand, and Mama close behind in case I stumbled. The tiny washroom felt even smaller when Mama had to help me rise from the seat, which was way too low for me.

Mama returned to sit down only once I was buckled up in my seat. I looked past my slumbering brother and gazed out of the window at the crystalline blue sky dotted with fluffy white clouds. For a moment, I let myself believe that life was beautiful.

Then, out of nowhere, a sharp pain jolted through my right leg, causing me to wince. The sensation spread quickly, a light fire burning up from my shin to my thigh. I placed my left hand on my throbbing thigh, trying to conceal my discomfort. *Relax, it'll pass. I have physical disabilities and am stuck in a plane for sixteen hours – of course, my leg will feel some discomfort.* My knuckles turned white as I clenched the seat's handle.

But then, I caught sight of my brother, deep in sleep, and grunting and snoring with gusto. I chuckled softly, welcoming the amusing distraction. Glancing over at my parents, I saw my father, who appeared entranced by the bright, flowing outfits of two Bollywood actresses shimmying across the screen in front of him, and my mother, staring off into the dark aisle, her thoughts entirely her own. Life *is* beautiful, I reminded myself.

Hours later, I took a deep breath as the plane touched down at John F. Kennedy International Airport.

The August breeze kissed our faces as we left the airport. Once buckled in, Papa called out his usual "We're off!" and we set off on the two-hour drive to New Haven. My heart leapt at each familiar sight – the EZPass lanes, Dunkin' signs, Manhattan's glass towers reflecting sea and sky. I felt like a child discovering magic again.

An hour later, my father stopped the car to get us new US SIM cards. I beamed and asked him to request a Massachusetts number for me, one beginning with 781, and as similar as possible to my previous number, 781-801-5047. You could tell how eager I was to emulate the carefree existence that had once been mine. I sat squirming in the back seat of the car, waiting to see what my father would come back with. Sure enough, he arrived, waving my blue LG flip phone in his right hand.

"Be happy, Pom." I rolled down my window to wait as he rummaged in his breast pocket for a slip of paper. "Your new number is 781-801-5932, only a difference of three digits." I smiled.

Nikhil and I were texting back and forth on the drive to New Haven. Giddy with excitement, I had to caution myself against getting carried away.

Once again, despite my having taken Tylenol three hours earlier, the persistent throbbing in my leg deflated me, even threatening to steal away the thrill of discovering my new home in a sleek building, 360 State Street in New Haven. Though I did marvel at the cozy sofas in the lobby and the abundant amenities for residents, all accessible by wheelchair, these luxurious comforts could not distract me from the pain in my right leg, now transformed into a dull ache.

To add insult to injury, my younger brother was given his own apartment on a higher floor, when it was me, the older sibling, who'd previously lived independently in New York, and even Uganda. *I should be guiding Rasoo, showing him the* way, *not the other way round.*

The real shock came when I learned that Mama would share my small room to watch over me and assist me with my bathroom needs during the night. My lip trembled. This was no way to live. I would be robbed of the minimal freedom I'd looked forward to, unable to have late-night conversations with Nikhil or turn off the lights at my discretion. I felt trapped, suffocated under Mama's watchful gaze. But the truth was, I was not capable of living alone in a room. This reality would have dawned on me sooner or later and I would have eventually asked for my mother's presence at my side.

Only later did it cross my mind how difficult it must have been for *her* to be separated from her husband at night to care for her grown daughter. The impact of a traumatic event extends beyond the survivor, reaching the caregiver in a multitude of ways, too. But at that moment, I was too focused on coming to terms with the upheaval in my life to consider the challenges it imposed on hers.

Upon seeing me downcast and witnessing my vanished cheer, Rasoo put down the kitchenware he was unpacking for our mother and rushed over to plop himself down on the couch beside me.

"Don't worry, Didi, you can hang out in my apartment during the day and just come to your room to sleep at night. We will make your life as independent as possible."

My heart bloomed with gratitude. I would now have "my" own apartment to hang in with Nikhil when he visited. The broken shreds of my life were being glued together, at least for now. I called Nikhil on my new navy-blue LG flip phone. After taking a year off after my accident, he had returned to Stanford Law School to restart his first year.

"Welcome back, babes!" Nikhil exclaimed when he heard my voice. He promised to visit me over the upcoming Labor Day weekend, just a couple of weeks away. A mutual friend had offered to host him during his stay. The universe seemed to finally align in our favor. Nikhil would be beside me soon, but not all the time, sparing him from witnessing the unflattering parts of my dependence. Two more weeks.

Meanwhile, life continued to move forward. On my first weekend back, Pallavi came to visit from New York, and her mere presence filled the room with light. In her company, life felt normal: the sun continued to rise in the east and set in the west. She was in a happy place. As I'd suspected, Ishan had called her after they'd exchanged numbers, and their first date had led to several more, until they were official. Seeing my best friend in love was truly delightful, and I felt a warm glow at having helped bring this couple together.

Even more momentous was my meeting with Meri. Her visit to New Haven marked the first time we met face-to-face since I'd regained consciousness. The moment Meri walked in through the door, she wrapped her arms around me in a tight hug.

Once she settled in, I unleashed the torrent of never-ending questions swirling in my mind. What had she gone through during the harrowing ordeal of the accident? How had she coped?

"What was the sequence of events to get me to the ER? "What was it like for you and Davis?" I asked, the words finally spilling out. "Tell me everything."

Meri's expression softened with memory.

"It was awful," she said, quietly. "When you left, so did I. I just couldn't make sense of my life in Kampala without you." Her words opened a window I hadn't looked through before. Meri didn't answer all my questions directly, but she gave me something deeper – her truth, her piece of our shared story. More than anything, her words brought a sense of clarity and connection. They not only helped me piece together parts of my story but also helped me realize my story wasn't mine alone – it was ours.

Then Hurricane Sandy battered New York, closing Meri's flight path home for a bit. In New Haven, removed from the true damage, we just laughed at how chaos seemed to chase us. After she left, I settled back into my measured days of therapy and recovery.

Unlike in Delhi, it was a relief to have all three therapies – physical, occupational, and speech – under one roof. My family dutifully took turns escorting me, three times a week, to Gaylord Hospital in Wallingford, a nearby suburb. I hit it off quickly with my therapists, making therapy less of a grind and more of an opportunity for building relationships.

Sue, my physical therapist, was an affable woman with curly auburn hair. She timed my slow walking in the parallel bars, encouraging me to quicken my pace while holding one parallel bar with my left hand for help with steadiness. My occupational therapist, Toni, was a no-nonsense older woman with short gray hair, piercing blue eyes, and a kind, caring demeanor. She worked her magic by teaching me a technique that would enable me to put on my bra largely using only one hand – a godsent trick I practiced repeatedly until it became second nature.

Rob, another occupational therapist, was a friendly man in his forties who engaged with his patients on their own terms. He laughed and joked with me, gently guiding my right hand, and helping me grip a pen and form letters. This was to help me become right-handed once more. But writing with my once dominant hand proved to be a titanic effort, for it refused to execute the commands my conscious mind gave it. Now a decade on, my right hand and arm remain frozen in time, spectators rather than participants in my daily life. But as luck would have it, I've come of age in an era where typing is the norm, not writing by hand. And so I spent hours mastering one-handed typing – still slow, but faster than my parents!

Rebecca and Meaghan, my speech therapists, were skilled professionals who encouraged me to work on adding expression to my otherwise monotonous speech. She coached me on techniques for emphasizing certain words in a sentence – adjusting the pitch or pausing before speaking a word for added impact.

Each therapist had a unique way of pushing me to work hard.

In stark contrast to the heavy load of patients seen by therapists in India, the pace was slower at my hospital in the sleepy town of Wallingford. However, I was surprised, and felt quite proud, to discover that the amount of attention I had received from my therapists at the bustling Max Hospital in Delhi was on par with that offered by my Gaylord therapists. I attributed this apparent dichotomy to the warmth of my Indian culture that created space for even the most overworked therapist to provide the level of attention necessary for recovery from serious injury or illness. There is some truth in the adage: distance makes the heart grow fonder.

After a satisfying packed lunch of leafy greens drizzled with balsamic vinaigrette, partaken in the beautiful hospital courtyard dotted with trees bearing yellow flowers, the family member accompanying me would drive me home. Given my inclination to share my life experiences, the longing to call Nikhil and discuss my therapy accomplishment of the day was irresistible.

"Nikhil! Today I walked up a ramp with my quad cane, with Sue just lightly holding my shoulder!"

Much later, I understood how hard it was for another person to fully appreciate the significance of small triumphs that people often take for granted. Yet, not once did Nikhil disappoint.

"Wow! That's amazing. I always knew that if anyone can beat this, *you* can."

Then Mama – who had dedicated herself fully to my care for the second time in her life – would gently lower me down on the couch in our living room with my laptop nestled on my lap. With time, most of my hazy memories had resurfaced, and with them, a narrative began to emerge – a narrative that would soon weave its way through the five essays my Yale SOM application required.

I never questioned the validity of my predefined life path, even though it had been irrevocably altered. I never asked whether I should let this altered trajectory steer me toward a new, more fitting aspiration. Should I craft a new identity? *Could I?* While I accepted that identity was fluid, I couldn't imagine not holding on to the identity I had once constructed for myself, for I had lived as that person for at least a decade.

I knew why I wanted to go back to studying. I wanted to learn the skills to help people lacking the means, opportunities, abilities, or motivation to pursue a decent and fulfilling life. I won't deny that I enjoy my creature comforts, but I'm not driven by the need to make vast sums of money. My parents had played a significant role in shaping this mindset. Despite never having pursued extravagant wealth themselves, they always seemed content, always seemed to have enough.

All of this was part of a plan that I had yet to formulate.

My final Yale essay, the longest and most daunting of them all, centered around the complexities of leadership in today's interconnected world. The topic explored my experiences that demonstrated an understanding of organizations, markets, and the intricate relationship between business and society. This last essay was the one setting off tiny sparks in my mind, threatening to explode into an inferno. To tackle this challenge, I would need Nikhil's help to remember certain key experiences during my time at both Morgan Stanley and BRAC – experiences that undoubtedly reflected my character. He was my lifeline, preventing the past version of myself from vanishing.

The concept of identity has always intrigued me, particularly the idea that it is not a fixed state but rather a fluid and ever-changing one. Even after my accident, while I felt like the same person, it had surely changed me in ways I still can't fully articulate. I cling to the idea that while the essence of who we are remains constant, our circumstances, and the passage of time, have the power to mold us into something different – maybe even something better – if we let them.

A prominent American philosopher, Irving Copi, grapples with the intricate issue of changing identity. He does so by presenting two separate, seemingly contradictory claims, each of which, when examined on its own, holds a ring of truth.[6]

The first claim posits that when something or someone undergoes a transformation, they are no longer the same as they were before. The second claim, however, introduces a paradox, arguing that although a change seems to have taken place, if you carefully examine the entity in question before and after the change, you can't actually pinpoint it as the same thing that has changed. The transformation is so complete that the original entity appears lost, making it nearly impossible to recognize any change.

Together, these two claims illustrate the enigmatic nature of identity over time. Whether identity stays the same over time is still unclear. But, if Copi's second claim leads to a completely new identity, it goes against the idea that identity can remain consistent as time passes.

Regardless of whether my identity changed, my desire to further my education never did. While toiling on my Yale essays, I eagerly awaited the familiar sounds indicating my brother's return from work. I strained to hear his footsteps on the hallway carpet, the jingling of his keys, and the swing of his leather bag, brushing his trousers. Those sounds in the hallway would be followed by the click of the unlocking door, and my brother would appear, returning from a full day of work.

On one such day, Rasoo walked into the apartment, waved at Mama, poured himself a glass of cold water, and settled down at the opposite end of the couch.

The distance on the couch between my brother and me seemed infinite at that moment. It would have been so simple to spring up and skip over to hug my brother whose company I had been longing for all day. The memory of effortlessly rising from a seated position was still as clear as the cloudless sky. What was impeding me from jumping up? I wiggled my toes. Not a scratch on my legs. What was it then? Was it a simple lack of desire? Firing neurons, damaged motor cortex and nerve pathways felt like nothing more than intriguing jargon.

I remembered how to run and to gesture with my right hand while speaking – at least in my mind's eye. The absence of any visible evidence of serious injury fueled my determination, more than just once, to defy the limitations of human biology and show the world what I was capable of. I stirred in my seat and flexed the muscles behind my formerly trim belly in preparation to rise from the sofa. Alas, in vain.

After a while, I signaled to my brother, and he had to help me stand up, having straightened out my wheelchair for me. Mama called out from the open kitchen, where she was chopping vegetables, with a wide smile, "Rasesh, tell your sister what we have decided about the wheelchair."

Rasoo's face lit up.

"You'll like this, Didi! Tomorrow, we are going to get you a new power wheelchair with which you can roam around on your own." He paused, waiting for my anticipation to build, and then added with a grin, "That way, you can go wherever you want when Nikhil is here and after." I was thrilled. "Okay, now let's go down for your exercise," my brother said, steering me toward the door.

Due to its proximity to the university, many Yale students and faculty tend to reside at 360 State, the building where we lived. Several students were seated in groups at the various study tables in the sixth-floor common room, where I was to practice my walking. I was quite pleased when a young man with disheveled brown hair and a muscular build, observing me struggling to get up from the wheelchair, offered to help. At the same time, he glanced at my brother, who had taken a step back. Rasoo rolled his eyes at me and flashed me a quick, wry smile, signaling that he had noticed my willingness to accept help from this good-looking guy. He intervened, explaining that he was deliberately not helping me; the idea was that I should get better at helping myself. The cute guy backed away, palms up, after flashing a quick thumbs up to my brother.

Leaning heavily on my quad-cane, I kept my eyes on the students, closely observing the dynamism in their lives. Only when an impatient Rasoo gestured at me to get a move on did I lift my right foot and take one big step forward, followed by a minuscule one with my left. With a sigh, I prepared myself to try again. However, before I could even lift my left foot again, Rasoo's stern voice came from behind me with a string of instructions. Out of nowhere, his voice then took on a gentler tone.

"I'm right here. I won't let you fall."

I quickly realized Rasoo wasn't a mere prop when he accompanied me to Gaylord. Rather, he was all ears when Sue, Toni, Rob, and Rebecca gave me specific instructions and rationales to help with my therapies at home. Rasoo repeated their instructions to me, and with time, he developed an empirical expertise. He truly became a "super-doc" to me.

Anticipating the arrival of my school friends, Devika and Joerose, I couldn't help but fidget in my seat. Both are my friends from my school days – Devika from Shri Ram School in Delhi and Joerose from MUWCI, in Pune. One from Delhi like me and the other from dreamy Kerala. Both of them were students at Yale SOM now, and I was eagerly looking forward to hearing what advice they had for me. Seated on my new red power wheelchair, I was granted a new lease on life, thrilled at the prospect of spending time away from my parents' loving, but protective, and at times, overly watchful gaze.

With great oomph, I told Mama that I was heading off with my friends. Ah, the sweet taste of freedom. With my head held high, I led my friends to the common room, where we settled down with our steaming cups of complimentary coffee.

My friends' eyes flickered as I spoke. Though my thoughts ran clear and sharp, the words that emerged were slow, and fragmented. I projected confidence I hadn't yet found, knowing my mind and voice now moved to different rhythms. Devika and Joerose promised to take me to their classes, offering me a glimpse into a day in the life of a graduate school student. The relief I felt was akin to the first blast of air conditioning on a scorching June day in Delhi. My shoulders loosened as the weight of uncertainty lifted .

I was finding my way back – not to some new version of me, but to myself, the only self I had ever truly known.

Soon, Nikhil would arrive soon, and for once, I had news beyond therapy milestones to share.

Joerose and I met up that week for the planned day at SOM.

"We'll sit in on two of my elective classes. You might like Game Theory. It won't be too unfamiliar since you're an econ major." She tucked away a strand of long dark brown hair that had escaped from her blue claw clip as she turned to brief me. Joerose was being a darling, but she could not possibly understand the limited abilities of my brain, and just how long it took me to process complex material. I struggled to grasp my father's carefully thought-out explanations of the straightforward math problems he had assigned me. I, myself, was reluctant to accept these cognitive limitations, let alone explain them to others. All I could do was hope that the innumerable hours I'd dedicated to solving Sudoku puzzles had made me sharper.

"After we attend two classes, I can help you do a mock job interview and grill you about your work at Morgan Stanley to jog your memory." She paused, her eyes scanning my face for any sign of hesitation, before continuing, "And you don't have to worry about anything, because it's only me!" I beamed with gratitude, feeling closer to cracking my Yale SOM application.

I whizzed down Whitney Avenue, with Joerose struggling to keep pace. We made a sharp left turn onto Prospect Street, now Sachem Street, where I breezed into an austere-looking gray building at number 135.

"Welcome to Yale SOM and the Hall of Mirrors, Tarini!" Joerose exclaimed with a flourish.

In a room plastered with mirrors, groups of students sat on chairs pulled close together, discussing what sounded like an econ problem set unlike any I'd ever heard. A swarm of students rushed past me, up the stairs, on their way to class.

What I would give to trade places with Devika, Joerose, and these other students, living my dream. I sat up straighter and strengthened my resolve – I, too, would one day blend into this crowd. We took the elevator down one level to get to class. I glimpsed a slight smile hovering on the edges of Joerose's lips as she watched me look around, my mouth agape. She gestured toward the classroom behind me.

"Tarini, the classroom for my Game Theory class is behind you. Turn around and let's go in so I can introduce you to the professor before class. And relax, you'll be great," she assured me, obviously, having seen me biting my lip.

Sitting mute, observing the class, I listened to the professor's lecture, riddled with obscure jargon. I scanned the room to find the other students nodding along. Suddenly, I understood just how out of my depth I was. I noticed the walls were painted a monotonous shade of beige, making everything feel duller. I remember feeling physically uncomfortable, shifting in my wheelchair seat, desperately seeking a more comfortable position.

"Fully solvable by backward reasoning. . ."

"Reverse ultimate game . . ."

"Mixed strategy . . ."

"Preference profiles . . ."

My head felt light. I clenched my teeth as the lingering pain in my right leg shot up to my thigh. I knew Joerose was smart, but I had no idea she was swimming with this level of tide.

At the end of the school day, I breathed a sigh of relief. After the class, Joerose had grilled me on my Morgan Stanley days, and I had scraped together some experiences that might be useful for my Yale essays. Now, it was Devika's turn to take over.

With an infectious smile, she bounded up and hugged me, and introduced me to her circle of friends, creating a tangible, welcoming atmosphere. Their easy chatter and playful banter helped me feel a sense of belonging. To my delight, one of Devika's friends even suggested we meet up for coffee over the weekend. We settled on meeting at Cafe Bru, the cozy cafe beneath my apartment building. I could already picture us sitting at one of the small tables, sipping coffee and chatting about our lives. Would this young woman, named Priya, be my first new friend since the accident?

I felt whole again, inching closer to the self I knew, the confident, outgoing person who could make friends wherever she went. Until now, in my five years of adulthood – before the accident, that is – forming new friendships had proven remarkably effortless. This was largely because NYC life in one's early twenties and the expat life in East Africa are hotbeds for social connections and don't represent the typical adult office life. The two solitary years of my post-accident life, predominantly spent in my parents' company, would have been more of a shock to the system had my recovery from trauma permitted me to remain clear-headed and fully present. It behooves me to extend a celestial thanks to the stars that I wasn't.

I headed home, brimming with happiness, eager to share the day's developments with my family. In my excitement, I didn't notice the pain in my right leg. The path ahead of me appeared clear, and with the support I had, I felt confident that any remaining obstacles could be overcome.

But at night, the pain resurfaced, and I cried out to Mama, who rushed to my side. She took one look at my face and knew something was very wrong. Mama asked me to describe my pain to her, her fingers working their way up and down, massaging my leg.

"Have none of the painkillers we've given you worked?"

I turned on my pillow to meet Mama's eyes. "Not one painkiller has worked, Mama," I whispered. "The pain is there 24/7. It ebbs and flows, but never leaves. I can't find the right words to describe it."

"That's strange, especially because you never have any problem expressing yourself," Mama said, her voice laced with worry. "While you think, let me fetch you the cold pack."

I closed my eyes, trying to focus on the sensations in my leg. It was like a vice grip, squeezing and releasing at sporadic intervals, but not quite. The pain felt like a language with no words – elusive and indescribable.

As Mama left the room and I lay still in agony, my mind wandered. I couldn't help but reflect on humans' innate desire to help others, just like I'd witnessed earlier that day. Then a cynical voice chastised me for my naïveté – *can humans truly be altruistic?* I couldn't help scrunching my eyebrows as I reflected on this. *Could a deep-seated desire for praise help explain my desire to be of service to people with needs greater than my own?* I didn't think so. Lying there in the dark, a faint sliver of light filtered through the door left ajar, accentuating the surrounding darkness. Restless, I began fidgeting with the bedsheets.

People are inherently social creatures, naturally inclined to help one another, I reasoned. The warmth of their acts extends beyond the recipient. And in helping others, they, or we, find something too – not enough to dim the giver's kindness, but a quiet glow of connection.

Despite these comforting thoughts, there was no end to the pulsating pain in my leg.

Nightmarish thoughts invaded my mind. I thought I saw the contorted face of a terrorist. I pictured myself in my wheelchair, attempting to lift my right arm to display my struggles to this evildoer. I imagined myself, in an act of vulnerability, requesting this man – clad in black, brandishing a black flag bearing the emblem of his terrorist outfit in one hand and a rifle in the other – to assist me in retrieving my fallen Kindle. Instead of offering his help, he responded by tossing his head back in laughter, cruelly mimicking the limited movements of my arm.

My eyes flickered open. On the ceiling, eerie shadows loomed ominously. Shivering, I drew my red comforter over me. Wincing, I bent and straightened my leg, hoping to relieve the pain. I craved movement, the dissipation of pain, the return of my life.

I was certain even the terrorist would, in due time, feel a tug of compassion and extend a helping hand to me. *How could he not?* My need was so visceral, impossible to ignore. But then I wondered, would this person even be able to empathize with the needs of another? I envisioned the terrorist scoffing and kicking my Kindle across the rugged terrain. My feverish thought processes led me to conclude that there would always exist people who, regrettably, would not feel inclined to show me empathy or extend support.

Fortunately, my mother walked in with the cold pack, which she placed below my right heel, and kissed my forehead before climbing into the bed we shared.

"Go to sleep, *nyari*. I'm right here – I'll wake up if you need anything."

I continued to quietly writhe in pain, waiting for sleep to envelop me and snatch me away from the realities of this world. A peculiar sensation under my foot caught my attention – something warm and lumpy – the "cold" pack, which, now, was anything but. Sighing, I reached for my flip phone, charging on the bedside table beside me to check the time. 3.27 a.m.

The pain had melted into a blunt tingle by the time I opened my eyes the next morning. It was a special day – Susan Davis, the CEO of my former organization, who I'd last met in Uganda, was taking the time to visit me. It seemed reason enough to pause my routine, but my obsessive nature wouldn't allow it. Instead, I had planned for Susan to come in the late afternoon after I completed my rehab and put in a day's work on my SOM application.

Susan arrived, brimming in equal measure with kindness and admiration.

"I saw great potential in you when you worked for us," she said. "BRAC would be lucky to have you work for us again if you ever decide to, and when you feel the time is right," Susan added.

I closed my eyes briefly, overwhelmed by her kindness.

"Under my guidance, you can start working for BRAC remotely from wherever you are after submitting your Yale application," Susan said. She promised to write me a glowing letter of recommendation. "And, of course, BRAC will also be flexible with your therapy needs," she added, smiling at Mama, who was in the kitchen, preparing chai for Susan.

While I was fumbling for words to express my gratitude, Mama appeared with a tray of chai and goodies. Papa joined us, both parents offered their thanks, but she just waved it away as she rose to catch her train. I sat in the warmth she'd left behind, yesterday's fears dissolving in the afterglow of simple, boundless kindness.

10
Between Two Worlds

My phone buzzed.

"Hi, Nicky! Are you downstairs?"

"I'll be there in five minutes, according to Google Maps."

For a split second, I was consumed by a burning desire for a smartphone. All the young people seemed to have one now. But I still wasn't sure it'd be easy to use with one hand.

"Sweet! Going downstairs to wait for you in the lobby."

I zipped up my makeup bag and set it by the mirror, smiling at the thought of the upcoming two days.

Without pausing to exchange pleasantries with the kind concierge, José, like I usually did, I raced to the front door of my building. In the blink of an eye, I was at the entrance, ready for Nikhil. Goodness. Just the thought. Meeting on his home turf felt closer to reality. This was the country where our relationship had taken root and blossomed. Here, I felt more alive than ever.

Yet, it wasn't like all my anxieties about the new dynamics of our relationship had faded. Even here, I resented my injuries for making me feel like a teenager sneaking into her father's study to call her boyfriend, away from her parents' watchful gaze. Something as natural and commonplace as dressing up for Nikhil had felt awkward and stilted.

"Mama, can you please put eyeliner on for me?" I had said in my sweetest voice, earlier that evening. My mother, having already told me I looked lovely and shouldn't "overdo" it, had looked disapproving.

"The problem with you," she had said, "is that you stay fixated on your beliefs. Nikhil already finds you beautiful, because you are. But okay, if you insist, I can put some kajal on for you." I immediately directed her to where she would find my Mac eyeliner pencil, which Pallavi had recommended three years ago. It'd become my daily fix since. I rarely ever stood in front of the mirror now, as the face I saw before me was still an unfamiliar one, and it made me flinch. Still, there I stood, with Mama standing guard beside me.

After I told her I wanted to be left alone in front of the mirror a while longer, she quietly walked out. I'd childishly peered out of the door to check if the coast was clear before rummaging through my makeup bag for my chili-red Mac lipstick.

I waited for Nikhil, my heart fluttering. Did he understand that my mind hadn't regressed, even if it sometimes seemed like it had? Could he see that my core was still intact? Then, I felt a hand on my shoulder.

My heart turned cartwheels.

"Nicky! You're actually here!" I said, my words tripping over each other.

Nikhil dropped his backpack on the floor, his eyes twinkling, his form tanned and more muscular than I remembered. He bent down to wrap his arms around me, took my face in his hands, and kissed me, long and slow. We stayed still for a time after the kiss, foreheads touching, his warmth against my skin making the moment solid, real. I gazed into his eyes before pulling his face back down, for another kiss. This freedom to love openly, unselfconsciously, in an apartment lobby felt like I had been handed a gift-wrapped slice of heaven. The trauma I had been through, both physical and psychological, eviscerated any desire for sexual intimacy, leaving in its place a simpler, more elemental hunger: the need for sharing vulnerability, trust, and companionship – for a heart beating in time with mine. The kiss was a tangible expression of our emotional connection.

"I've waited for this moment for longer than you know. I love you, babes," Nikhil said, picking up his bag.

All my concerns vanished into the ether.

We spent the weekend in our own little world, lost in each other's company. We lounged on the terrace, soaking up the sunshine and each other's laughter. Or we huddled around my laptop in Rasoo's apartment, brainstorming ideas for my Yale essay.

Ever my ally, my brother quietly left his apartment after exchanging a few words with Nikhil to give the two of us space. In the evenings, Nikhil went off to spend the night at a friend's place.

Time seemed to slip by. The Labor Day weekend was over before we knew it. It was time for Nikhil to leave.

"Keep me updated on your Yale SOM application status. I know you'll do great." With that, he planted a soft kiss on my lips and rushed to catch an Uber to the airport.

As his taillights disappeared from view, it felt as though my entire world was melting away. The demands of law school and the six-hour coast-to-coast flight meant I would see Nikhil for just one more weekend, if his schedule permitted, before heading home to India.

The remaining month of the fall semester hummed along to a familiar tune. Mornings devoted to rehabilitation at Gaylord and working on my application essays. Afternoons spent in the convivial company of my brother, who routinely became my all-round therapist, and evenings unwinding with my family. Joerose, Devika, and Gautam – another school friend now doing his PhD at Yale – would all often drop in, too. Gradually, the bitter cold swept across the East Coast and we packed our bags to return to Delhi since my father taught at Yale for just one semester a year.

Truth be told, India was no longer my comfort zone. After spending time in America, it grated on me that my home country was a land so blind to the dignity of people with disabilities. Yet, one eventually settled into a feeling of calm. It would happen every time I returned to India. I had to leave my power wheelchair locked away in the US, not just because of the widespread lack of accessibility in India and the lack of curb cuts, or small ramps built into sidewalks, but also because the two countries function on different voltages and plug types, rendering electrical appliances designed for one country useless in the other. Thankfully, my old school friends in Delhi helped me feel at home, so I didn't long for my power wheelchair as much as I'd expected.

Himali made frequent visits, while Sahil and Manak hunted tirelessly for the elusive wheelchair-accessible eateries that served authentic North Indian food to satisfy my craving for the rich, luscious flavors of home. Graciously, they took it upon themselves to open up a social life for me, scoping out the difficult terrain of the restaurants we chose, ensuring it wouldn't be too difficult to manage with my wheelchair. I played my part by scouring menus until I zeroed in on one that met my high standards. Nikhil's love for good food had seeped into me, awakening a deeper appreciation for subtle flavors and making me a more adventurous eater. Before I met him, food was just fuel for me, but now, I view it as an integral part of life's pleasures. But, I wasn't only pursuing life's "pleasures". For five to seven hours daily, I would work remotely for BRAC, work I had begun doing soon after submitting my Yale application.

Though not the magic bullet I had dreamed of, American rehab taught me to work within my limits while still reaching for independence – a freedom not envisioned for those with disabilities in India. Here, I coached my therapists, rather than the other way around, on the single-hand technique for fastening a bra, with minimum assistance from the other hand, to teach to other patients. While both countries aimed for the same recovery, America taught life skills alongside rehab. With time and endless practice, my walking reached a certain level, and my physical therapist in the US directed her focus to improve the quality of my life – she connected me with a "wheelchair clinic" that would add a coffee cup holder to my wheelchair for outings with friends. At home, I had made my own rule: no wheelchair-use allowed indoors. I believed this would help rewire my brain to view walking as part of living, rather than just physical therapy. While I walk painfully slowly, the short distances and absence of crowds make a big difference. The movement also helps quiet the never-banished chronic pain in my right leg – a pain that still baffles my doctors – making not using the wheelchair indoors is a no-brainer for me.

I still needed someone to shadow me to prevent me from losing my balance and falling. Yet, I continued to inch along, aching for transformational change.

One March morning in 2012, in Delhi, I sat on the edge of my bed, shivering with nervous anticipation, awaiting the verdict on my Yale School of Management application I'd submitted during the winter. *Would I? Wouldn't I?* My sweaty palms left damp imprints on my maroon cotton pajamas as I reached for my laptop with trembling fingers. With the sudden realization that my fate – my dreams, hopes, ambitions, and future – hinged on the contents of a single email, my anxiety intensified. Despite my shaky hands, I mustered the courage to log into my Gmail account and saw it – a new unread message from the Yale School of Management. My heart racing, I clicked to open the email and held my breath as the text appeared on the screen.

Dear Tarini,

Congratulations on your admission to the Yale School of Management Class of 2014! ...

I didn't read the rest of the email for the rest of the day.

Woozy ecstasy.

Within seconds, however, the omnipresent heaviness of self-doubt descended on my being.

A mistake. Fake news. Not possible.

My mind flashed back to the chilly late-November day in New Haven when I arrived at the Admissions Office on Hillhouse Avenue for an in-person interview, dressed in business casual attire. Mama's careful hand had pressed every wrinkle out of my shirt. As the interview progressed, I remember the two senior admissions officers exchanging a look that I interpreted as confusion over my speech. How could they have seen hidden potential in me when they were used to interviewing the brightest, most articulate students in the world? But clearly, they had.

I quickly relayed the news to my parents, and the joy that lit up their faces remains indescribable to this day.

"Three Yalies in one family!" my mother said, beaming with pride. Yale was not just any prestigious college for us, it has a special resonance because of the family's association with the place and the frequent comings and goings.

"Why three?" Papa interjected. "You were a non-resident fellow at Yale, teaching dance. We are now a family of Yalies!"

Cupping my cheeks in his palm, my father bent his head in my direction, and said, "I could never have accomplished what you have, Pom." Mama firmly asked him to step aside so that she could hug me.

I had dedicated myself to my Yale application to prove to myself, and to the world, that I was the same person as before, that my identity was whole, and that my intelligence was intact. I hoped that the university's reputation would serve as proof that I hadn't lost my abilities, or at least those abilities I most valued.

To me, being alive and present meant that my being must be whole, and if I couldn't be entirely whole, then at least the abilities that shaped who I am had to be intact. That is why I was certain my future ambitions would have to mirror the ones from my past. In all honesty, I didn't stop to consider how much my life had changed after the accident or whether I should reimagine my path forward. It sounds very brave, but sometimes, it's easier to keep going with the flow than to confront the fear of vulnerability and failure. No, I didn't stop to think if those ambitions were still realistic or even possible. Maybe I avoided asking myself questions because I was afraid I had no answers, so I just kept pushing forward.

Foolish or not, one can only live, experience, and ruminate based on the available information. The brain, the most complex organ, stumps doctors, making it difficult for them to predict the duration of a patient's recovery or determine their lasting limitations. In my case, they explained that, with consistent effort, my brain would slowly but steadily heal itself. With little to do except for what came most naturally to me, I continued to push forward. The steady flame of hope within me acted as a guide, urging me onward.

In the preface to his 1945 book, *Man's Search for Meaning*, Viktor Frankl warns his students about success. Having experienced the horrors of the concentration camp at Auschwitz, Frankl had planned to publish his book under a pseudonym at first, not wanting to benefit from any success it might achieve. His purpose was simple – to convey to readers that life can have meaning even in the most dire circumstances. Despite this intention, *Man's Search for Meaning* achieved widespread success, a legacy that persists today.

Frankl's warning to his students was clear: "Don't aim at success." He believed that the harder one chased after success as the target, the more elusive it became. Instead, Frankl urged his students to commit themselves to a cause greater than themselves or surrender to someone else, to find success as an unintended side effect. Frankl argued that happiness and success could not be pursued but had to ensue.

He advised his students to listen to their conscience and carry out their responsibilities to the best of their knowledge and abilities. Frankl believed that in the long run, success would follow those who didn't chase it, precisely because they had forgotten to think of it.

It wasn't "success" *I* was aiming for either – what I wanted to keep alive, instead, was the tenacity with which I pursued my "self", the striving so core to who I am and who I could become. In truth, I knew that the intelligent people at Yale didn't admit individuals based solely on their potential. With first-hand experience of my limitations, I had no illusions that I had achieved some great pinnacle of success. I had been transparent with my interviewers about my injury, and the associated impact of my limitations. Perhaps it was my authenticity with the staff interviewing me that helped my admission, or maybe transforming potential into actuality is what Yale prides itself in. Still, these will remain mere conjectures.

I had indeed shoveled the path to Yale, clearing it for myself, but the road ahead was daunting. I didn't know if I had what it took to absorb the theoretical and quantitative knowledge in the classes, collaborate effectively in teams, or deliver compelling presentations.

Would anyone understand my speech? Could I make new friends? I had no answers – just swirling wisps of doubt tinged with a somewhat misplaced yet uplifting sense of confidence.

During that summer, I was granted permission to audit a course on the political economy of India's development at a university in Delhi – a chance to help me prepare for my return to academia. The subject matter was intriguing, and I could grasp most of the professor's lectures. But there were also moments when I struggled – especially when the professor moved rapidly from discussing one topic to another. At such moments, I was left staring into space, trying to process it all. What remained in my toolbox was my own effort, and I would keep trying until it no longer served me.

Over the next eight years, we would go back and forth between India and the US. Both countries felt like home, each country offering unique merits for me that the other lacked. In the US, I experienced life under the Americans with Disabilities Act of 1990, or the ADA, as it's popularly known, which provides accessibility to public services and requires employers to make reasonable accommodations for persons with disabilities. This experience was poles apart from the uncompromising limitations to my autonomy in India. Yet, as a member of a family of means and networks in India, I have always enjoyed – and continue to benefit from luxuries rarely found in the US: access to a domestic worker to help me around the house, and a car and driver at my disposal.

I faced, and continue to face, moral dilemmas. The luxury of having a cook and a driver, which is not an option for me in the United States, highlights the systemic undervaluation of informal labor. I can't shake the deep sense of guilt that comes with having access to domestic workers in India, especially because, as a development sector professional, I understand all too well that their availability stems from being underpaid and exploited. In America, I don't feel this same guilt because everyone who assists me is paid a decent living wage. But India is where I am from and where I spend much of my time, and I genuinely need more help here than in America. Most countries in the developing world aren't designed in a way that enables a person with disabilities to function independently, whereas in America, I can just hop onto, or more accurately, roll into a public bus, and head for grocery shopping to meet a friend for coffee, or even to the post office to buy stamps when needed. All independently.

This glaring disparity isn't lost on my parents. They address it by ensuring the people we employ are paid higher wages than what is typically offered, and treat them with kindness and respect. Yet, I can't seem to get over the feeling that I'm part of a system that fundamentally exploits the poor.

Shortly after our return from the US, with nowhere much to go, and not too many people to see, I retreated to the quiet comfort of my room to battle with my thoughts alone. With time, a scant few of my childhood friends remained in Delhi, with most either studying or working overseas. Before long, my father poked his head in through the crack in the door I had unknowingly left ajar. Upon noticing me quieter than usual and seeing my eyes downcast, he entered. Papa and I discussed the dilemmas that occasionally tormented me. He listened to the challenges I experienced in my daily life in India.

"Don't view your life as fragile or vulnerable here compared to the US, Pom," he urged. "It's just different from life in the US, and you have to adapt, like people do when they depend on a translator in a foreign country." My father wanted me to shift my perspective, like turning a kaleidoscope to reveal an entirely new pattern.

That is all well and good for people in my gem-studded shoes. I felt, and continue to feel, the acute need of the millions of Indians with locomotor disabilities who cannot afford such luxuries, those who undoubtedly remain trapped inside their houses, if they possess a home at all. *Someone needs to affect change in their lives. I have the wherewithal, both in resources and aptitude, to have applied to a prestigious university in the US*, I thought with a heavy heart as I sat up straighter.

The trouble at the heart of it all was that I didn't feel empowered to implement change, which was exactly why I wanted that business school degree. I needed the skills and expertise to actually bring meaningful change to the lives of those who couldn't help themselves. Business school would offer me the chance to refine my leadership and strategic thinking in the work I already cared so deeply about. I saw the MBA as a crucible merging my background in international development with a mastery of finance, operations, and organizational management. This fusion, I believed, would forge the tools I needed to sculpt the kind of meaningful change I wanted to create in the world. Beyond skills and expertise, I also needed a platform to enact positive change in people's lives. In a world where the MBA held near-mythical status – that so-called "MBA Premium" everyone whispered about – earning the degree felt less like a choice and more like a passport to legitimacy, a key that could unlock doors to the platform I yearned to build.

"Don't be so hard on yourself, you have been working to improve the lives of poor people ever since you left Morgan Stanley – if not even before, during your college internships," Nikhil said on the phone when I shared my feelings with him.

I was still working for poor people, through my work with BRAC. But the approach was markedly different from my experiences in Uganda. There, I would see women farmers toiling in their fields, their faces corrugated under the blazing sun. Sitting in India, Susan had me working on various projects related to organizational development and miscellaneous poverty alleviation strategies for BRAC. At present, Susan tasked me with independently working on a report for BRAC USA, focusing on knowledge management, and recommending strategies to enhance their knowledge-sharing practices. About a year on, she would transition me back to working on agricultural development, this time focusing on raising funds through proposal writing. The welfare of smallholder farmers would become my niche focus once more. But it still was remote work.

One weekend, as the morning light streamed in through the parted curtains, I lay in bed, mulling over my desire to contribute to meaningful change. Amid this quiet moment, it struck me that at the very least, I could use the power of the written word to advocate for legislation promoting the use of helmets on two-wheelers to prevent disability and death.

By now, physical therapy had helped me build back some muscle strength, allowing me to sit up without assistance, and occupational therapy enabled me to dress myself. Mama stood guard while I walked to the living room, my mind set on shaping my thoughts into words. I envisioned my article being published in the *Indian Express*, a leading voice in Indian media, hoping to stir up public support for legislation on helmet use. In those days, back in 2012, pillion riders didn't need to wear helmets in most Indian states. With youthful idealism, I believed that my harrowing experience would awaken others to the dangers of non-compliance. I brushed away the thin veil of dust from my laptop screen, my eyes drifting to the window where the money plant's emerald leaves danced in the afternoon light.

With Nikhil assisting me from early brainstorming to the final edit, I felt emboldened to weave together a compelling narrative. The article transcended mere statistics and research findings, becoming a deeply personal meditation on road safety and its consequences. I wrote:

> You would think that given that my accident happened in 2010, I would have completely recovered by now. I wish that were true. My bodily injuries have indeed healed, but the part of my brain that was injured will remain so. The boda driver suffered only bodily injuries that naturally healed; he was saved from a head injury because of his helmet. I had a brain injury because I chose to look pretty that day. I have learnt my lesson. I had a year of looking very pretty indeed with my head completely shaved for head surgery. I do not enjoy telling this tale. I am doing so because I believe I experienced this horror for a reason: to save others' lives.

Reading these lines now feels like opening a letter from my younger self – her earnestness makes me smile and ache all at once. I see how far my craft has come and how I've learned to weave words with greater nuance and skill. But what touches me is that burning sincerity blazing through every sentence. I can still feel how desperately that earlier version of me wanted her words to light fires in others' hearts, to spark the kind of change she knew the world needed. That pure earnestness still echoes, even if I would compose the article differently now.

A few weeks later, in June 2012, the *Indian Express* published my article.[7] The article was titled, "Because Accidents Don't Only Happen to Others". It was a momentous occasion, the first time my words would appear in the public domain. I was even awarded an honorarium for my contribution. Perhaps it was my deep-seated desire to contribute to social causes, or maybe it was the validation from a prestigious university that empowered me, but I knew I had taken a small yet significant step forward. No longer would I be a silent citizen, sitting on the sidelines. It would take another six years for the law mandating helmets for pillion riders to be enacted in Delhi. However, I understood that change is a slow process, and every bit of effort counts.

11

"Highly Educated Woman"

I lay on my bed in the oppressive fury of the Delhi summer of 2012, exhausted after a day of therapy, when I saw a new email from Nikhil in my inbox. I perked up at once. With feet stretched out and the window open, I opened the email, preparing to savor it leisurely.

"Miss you babes, and especially our fun life!"

Reading these words now – so innocuous, even tender on their surface – I felt growing dread. It was as if I'd been stung by a wasp. Did Nikhil not see that I longed for the return of our "fun life" just as much as that he did, if not more? Was he not aware of how heavily it weighed on me that he was sharing in my misfortune? I had voiced my gratitude to him for staying by my side innumerable times, which he always dismissed as "senti[mental] talk." *Stop it, Tarini, you're overthinking, as usual. Don't be such a drama queen.*

Previously, if Nikhil or anyone else said something hurtful, my immediate instinct would have been to confront them. However, I noticed a change within myself. Now, more often than not, I discovered that I was more inclined to defer to others' opinions instead of engaging in immediate confrontation.

I simply replied to another mundane topic he'd raised in his email, but not before passing a snide comment: "But you definitely won't be seeing that fun life that soon." Then, I focused on channeling my emotions into writing a second opinion piece I had been outlining, encouraged by the publication of my first. Having already proven my ability to write with authority on one topic, I wondered, why not write another? However, my weakened eye muscles posed a challenge. With a stopwatch in hand, Rasoo informed me that reading now took me three times as long as it had previously. (To gauge my original reading speed, we simply used my brother's reading speed as a proxy.) Determined to overcome this hurdle, I chose a topic on which I possessed considerable firsthand empirical knowledge, believing it would lend credibility to my article. I decided to focus on the lack of accessibility for people with disabilities in India – for example, the absence of ramps and elevators in public buildings, inaccessible toilets, inaccessible sidewalks with no curb cuts, inaccessible public transport, inaccessible ATMs, discrimination at large. I intended to urge the government to enforce existing laws such as the 1995 Person with Disabilities Act. I chose a conversational writing style hoping to engage my readers more directly.

With my keyboard as my gateway, I completed the first draft in record time, relatively speaking, and promptly shared it with Nikhil for him to work his magic. Again, I received an email from him that jolted me.

> I'll look this over and let you know over the next couple [of] days. On a quick read, I liked some of the points, but a lot of the language is a bit too silly for me to be in a real newspaper …
>
> Even though an Op-Ed should reflect the personality of the author and be conversational, doesn't mean it should be so informal or seem like it was written by a young girl … [when you are] a highly educated woman …

> Show your Wellesley chops by bringing out more policy-like arguments.

I could feel the restrained frustration behind his words. The wasp sting burned afresh. Despite being doubly stung – by his hurtful words and his pointed critique – love's stubborn grip on my heart made me desperate to impress him. I had hoped he'd edit my article until it shone, but deep down, I knew that what I'd been searching for wasn't a shortcut at all, but the warmth of his validation.

I found myself confronting him about his words – how his suggestion that my writing failed to reflect the voice of a "highly educated woman", had stung. Yet, in a bid to avoid conflict, I hurriedly bandaged the wound with words of conciliation:

> What was brutal was 'you should bring out the voice of a highly educated girl and that doesn't come across.' Thanks though for all your criticism, you are the only person who gives me any and all of it is constructive. It's brutal because your point is that through this article I don't sound very educated. I know you do it with only good intentions so no worries.

At the same time, I tried to process his criticism of my work. Rereading our exchange and the opinion piece I had crafted, I realized with horror how cringeworthy my writing was. It felt as if I was looking in a funhouse mirror that had not only distorted my appearance but also twisted my thoughts. Far from coming across as a "highly educated woman", I sounded like a fifth-grader who'd been allowed to join the grown-ups' dinner table but had failed to impress with her maturity. I sat gaping at the line I had opened my article with:

Delhi government, oh, please, please help me be an India-bhakt again!

My brain felt sluggish and out of control. The words on the page reflected the chaos in my brain as it struggled with a new task, one that forced it to confront its limitations head-on, and I was embarrassed to have bared them for Nikhil to see. Doubt crept in as I wondered if his stinging feedback was justified and if I was being oversensitive in my reaction. Searching for answers, my eyes wandered to the ceiling as if it held the key to unlocking my inner turmoil – as if somewhere up there was the truth of who I was becoming.

Nikhil's critiques continued. Despite our recent conversations about my views on Indian laws and my attempts at writing for national newspapers, he voiced a concern during that same scorching summer of 2012. Nikhil's words came through the phone one evening, measured but pointed.

"I've noticed that we don't have the kind of discussions we used to have – about politics, about what's happening in the world. Don't you miss how we'd analyze things together, debate ideas?"

It was true, our post-accident conversations were generally light, uplifting, and life-affirming. We would reminisce about old times, share stories and laughter, or update each other on the mundane details of our daily lives. While he acknowledged the difficulties I was dealing with, it seemed like he felt compelled to bring up the shift in our intellectual rapport.

Despite my hurt, I did understand what Nikhil was going through. I scrutinized and reflected on every change in Nikhil's voice, word choice, and manner. True, he'd stayed by my side and conducted himself with grace – but this wasn't the future he'd chosen. Perhaps his patience was wearing thin as my progress inched along, too slow to promise a return to what we'd been.

But at that moment, my mind froze, like an elevator caught between floors. Part of me wondered why I needed to keep proving my intelligence, especially to Nikhil, who knew the entire story. My difficulties with crafting well-structured opinion pieces, language, and conversation arose from the specific injuries in my brain. Over time, there would be some improvements, even if some difficulties would persist. Looking back today, there have been great improvements. Was it even remotely constructive to put such pressure on me, especially when I was far from sunk in apathy and working every day to improve myself?

Through all of this, a part of me recognized how Nikhil and my worlds were drifting apart, and the difference between how he and my family viewed my recovery. While my family was committed to helping me live my best possible life, Nikhil appeared to be pulling away – as if searching for an exit before his own life stalled. Or perhaps, accepting my cognitive limitations was a task too far. Was he just trying to "will" back the person I'd been?

However, rather than accepting the possibility of a looming disconnect, I chose to draw comfort from Nikhil's untiring love and support since my injury. And to ready myself for the uphill task of reclaiming my intellectual rigor .

With the benefit of hindsight, I realize that I was being too hard on myself by trying to keep pace with Nikhil's thoughts, but in that time of great turmoil, I lacked the necessary self-awareness to accept this truth.

During a phone conversation, Nikhil would casually ask for my thoughts on the kind of topics I once loved to discuss.

"What do you think would have been the impact on emerging stock markets if Romney had won instead of Obama?" he might ask. The answer invited one to dwell on the complex relationship between cause and effect, short-term versus long-term consequences, and competing global interests. Where I would once have enjoyed untangling such complexities, I now felt myself drowning in them. Caught off guard by such a question, I would stumble and entangle myself further as I tried to embody my former self.

Our conversations would inevitably devolve into fraught exchanges, with Nikhil irritated by the workings of my brain. He'd press me to let logic guide my thinking, while I struggled to meet his expectations. I was forever trying to live up to his unspoken standards, convinced I could answer his questions intelligently. Our interactions began to fill me with dread, often leaving me wrestling with an even weightier question than our compatibility – the question of my identity.

Who was I if I could no longer engage in intelligent discourse, what remained of my self-image? Who was I if not whip-smart anymore? Would I have to construct an entirely new identity? Could I? Did I want to? The deepest confusion lay in how intact my inner world felt – I had the same vivid thoughts and feelings as before. Could Nikhil not see that?

It wasn't until I had been through several humbling interactions with Nikhil that I began to see things differently. My strength had shifted: no longer in lightning-quick mental acuity but in my patience, empathy, and a strengthened capacity to connect with others. I realized that we all carry a unique set of qualities that shift and change over time, and it's in those quiet changes that we come to truly understand the core of who we are.

While I was dealing with the complications of my relationship with Nikhil, I was also grappling with a difficult decision about my future. Hope possesses the power to work wonders. It instills within us the belief, however illusory, in a glorious tomorrow. In the beginning, I had naïvely clung to the hope of a full recovery within one year of my accident on that October evening in 2010. It was this hope that had carried me to where I was now, in the summer of 2012, with an acceptance letter from Yale University in hand – an application I completed amid grueling rehabilitation, relearning how to walk, talk, and manage my personal care, all while coming to terms with my changed reality. I'd once believed that worldly wisdom always overshadowed optimism, yet I now realize that sometimes it's better to embrace the naïve optimism of a fool.

For much of the last two years, I had indeed been a fool for clinging to the belief that recovery from a head injury was just a matter of time. I was living in a bubble, blissfully unaware of the gravity of my condition. It wasn't until much later that I realized that recovery from a head injury is not a linear journey with a predictable endpoint, but rather a journey that lasts a lifetime, with painfully slow and sometimes invisible progress.

A year after my accident, a growing sense of urgency motivated me to reclaim my life by immediately applying to business school even though it was still early in what would be a long recovery. I believed I'd have returned to my "normal", unscarred self by 2012, so I poured my heart and soul into my MBA application.

However, as the fall of 2012 neared, I knew I wouldn't go to New Haven as a student. I still needed focused therapy to improve the clarity of my speech, and considerable self-motivation to improve my walking and mobility in my right arm and hand. Then there was the time and effort required to address my cognitive limitations, which made fast-paced, complex lectures a challenge. The thought of trying to absorb all the new, knotty concepts while still battling the scars in my brain made my head spin. Enrolling at Yale now would mean my energy would be swallowed by the rigors of academics and the much-hyped social scene of business school, leaving little room for the tedious but essential grind of rehabilitation – the kind that yields the best results early on.

So I put off crafting a new vision for my future and reluctantly prepared myself to decline my admission offer to Yale University. Although I knew this was the logical, sensible path, I felt something within me shrivel.

My parents recognized the difficulty of my decision but understood it was the wisest choice. The pain of seeing their child giving up on a dream was etched on their faces. Failing at something I had put my heart and mind into was inconceivable to me, but I was certain that enrolling at Yale would inevitably lead to me failing out. *Nothing would be worse for the self-confidence I've only just partly reclaimed.*

I wasn't ready for another assault on my identity – the danger of being branded as a failure. It felt safer to decline my admission and redirect my energy to my ongoing therapy and self-improvement. I positioned myself in front of my laptop, summoning the courage to compose the dreaded email.

Upon conveying my decision to the admissions officer via email, I received a reply within the hour, stating that they wouldn't even consider the option of allowing me to decline: *"We respect your decision to focus on your health, but we are prepared to hold your seat for you. Come to us whenever you are ready."*

Fixed on the laptop screen, my eyes welled up, and my heart filled with renewed hope. As I called out to my parents, they rushed over and wrapped their arms around me. They'd somehow sensed what had transpired.

"See!" Papa exclaimed once I explained what had happened. His voice brimmed with pride and joy. "Like I've always said, things that you give your all to have a way of working out. Today, more than ever, I am very proud to call myself a Yalie," he said, wearing a broad smile on his bespectacled face.

Mama leaned close to me from across the aisle in the plane as we headed to Yale that fall of 2012. Her eyes were full of tender concern.

"How are you feeling, *nyari*? Is there anything I can do to help?"

I shook my head.

"I wish there was, Mama, but my right thigh and shin are still throbbing. I guess I'll have to wait for this turbulence to stop and then ask you to walk up and down the aisle with me. That should help ease some pain, if only temporarily."

Half asleep, my brother grunted in the window seat beside me. I smiled at the little fellow's unflagging devotion to his sister. Even in his groggy state, he stayed awake long enough to make sure I was comfortable, with various options for entertainment within my reach. He carried the weight of sibling loyalty on his small shoulders with remarkable ease.

Papa stopped by my seat on his way to the toilet to check on me. Without a minute's delay, Mama filled him in on my predicament.

"I wish there was something we could do," he said. "We've tried everything the doctors have recommended."

And then, as always, there was a word of encouragement for me.

"You are going through far too much, Pom, but I know you will conquer this. You're a champion."

I glanced up at Papa and mustered a small smile before waving him away. It was true, we had exhausted every conventional intervention suggested by my doctors, both at Yale and in India. We had consulted with a pain management specialist and had even dabbled in the world of alternative medicine with acupuncture. During our time back home, my parents had arranged for me to be treated by the most well-regarded acupuncturist in Delhi on the advice of several doctors and well-wishers. I had been hopeful about the healing powers of this ancient practice.

I remember the acupuncturist, a middle-aged man with thinning, wispy hair, a shiny bald crown jutting out like a mountain peak in the center, and an air of inflated self-importance. I was shocked when he poked thirteen to fifteen needles into my flesh without offering any explanation whatsoever. He bid me adieu in a voice tinged with arrogance, sucked in his protruding belly, and waltzed over to attend to the next patient. My questions remained unanswered. Despite my disillusionment, I returned for about a dozen more sessions, driven by my desperate need for relief.

During our last session, the acupuncturist instructed me to lie still and reflect on the success of the last two months of treatment. Instead of rolling my eyes, I closed them, attempting to keep my skepticism in check. When I reopened my eyes, I saw the acupuncturist strutting around the room like a rooster, crowing about how I was "as good as new." That's when I noticed he was holding a piece of paper, which he thrust in my direction like a trophy. It was a "certificate of healing". I raised my eyebrows. What was this all about? The pain in my right leg felt like it always had – a constant, throbbing ache like I was repeatedly being torched. But the acupuncturist winked and gave me a thumbs up.

"I am happy to inform you that you are now pain-free."

I remember sighing inwardly and making a solemn vow – I would refrain from voicing the searing ache in my entire right leg to anyone except when necessary, as no words of sympathy or medication would ease the pain. The mere mention of pain was counterproductive – it drew my attention to the excruciating sensation, intensifying my discomfort in a cruel and relentless cycle. Besides, acknowledging my pain out loud only evokes pity in others, their sympathetic glances cutting deeper than the agony itself, transforming my private discomfort into public spectacle. Amid the chaos of my circumstances, I clung fiercely to the only aspect of my life I could control – my willpower. Steering my willpower is a breeze compared to agreeing to budge from my stance. I'm like a stubborn mule and about as flexible as a metal ruler.

We quickly settled in, as usual, into our apartment for the semester at 360 State Street in New Haven. Two to three days later I was still contending with the after-effects of the long flight. The throbbing ache in my right leg had kept me up most of the previous night, and I felt like a zombie trying to rouse myself from the dead. Nikhil had given me some helpful life improvement tips the day before, urging me to find fast, one-handed typing techniques on the internet, and even suggested I audit some courses at the community college to prepare myself for enrolling at Yale next year.

Despite the evidence of his care, I was still plagued with anxiety before any long conversation with him, and also by the general direction of our relationship. I feared I was constantly walking on eggshells to avoid being the shriveled version of myself that he seemed to see. And there had been a new pattern of behavior for me to process. Our conversations had begun to decrease in frequency. Almost out of the blue, Nikhil's schedule seemed to fill up with important study group meetings he wasn't able to extricate himself from. It left me feeling worse than ever. Yet, I avoided a flash point. Our lives had been intertwined for the past seven years, my entire adult existence, and I couldn't imagine it any other way.

I focused on the task at hand. The video tutorial on one-handed typing I was watching was finally nearing its end. Momentarily, I gazed out the window above my desk, overlooking the State Street train station. Fresh-faced students, clad in crisp button-down shirts, tucked into tailored trousers, were disembarking from the train that had just pulled in from New York City. Putting myself in the students' shoes, I felt a wave of comfort wash over me as I imagined myself returning to the serene tree-lined streets of New Haven, a welcome escape from the frantic energy of the big city. But in the next moment, the comfort was replaced by a pang of envy. *Will I ever lead a regular life like those students again?*

Baby steps, Tarini, baby steps, I reminded myself. *Let's learn to type faster using all the fingers of your working hand first; you can dream of NYC afterward.*

I'd never been aware of the existence of a technique called One-Handed QWERTY, which allows the fingers of one hand to cover the entire keyboard. It involved placing the fingers of my left hand in the middle of the keyboard, on the FGHJ keys instead of the traditional ASDF keys on the far right. Intrigued, I spent the entire day familiarizing myself with this new technique. After demonstrating my newfound superpower to Rasoo, I settled into the couch, brimming with confidence. My eyes fell on my flip phone. Of course, I knew I had to call Nikhil next.

"Hi babes, good you called because I've been missing you and just being together . . ." Nikhil said, his voice, trailing off. I pictured him sitting in his room in Palo Alto, his shoulders slumping as he spoke. "How was PT today? Anything exciting to report?"

My heart began to pound. I felt something catch in my throat, a mild panic setting in. *What if I never fully recover? It isn't right that I should feel pressured to achieve something completely out of my control. Calm down, Tarini. Act mature.*

"Nikhil, the purpose of this phone call is to update you on some progress I have made, not to talk about the progress I haven't, which is what the subject of this conversation will be if we talk about PT,"

I said, my voice shaking slightly. "And besides, you are as up-to-date as my family on the progress of my recovery."

"Don't get mad ... I was just checking. You know how much I care," Nikhil said, his voice slow and deliberate. "Okay, I'll talk to you later. David has organized a study group and I need to go."

Unsure of what I was feeling, there was nothing to do but let the tears flow. It was clear to me – something beyond my control was amiss. Apart from a few spats, we hadn't encountered any significant disagreements in our relationship. I didn't know how to process these unfamiliar emotions. It was true that I had provoked this particular row, but that doesn't diminish the empathy I feel for the twenty-six-year-old I was then, navigating a relationship shaped more by long absences, rather than shared moments, trying to come to terms with the shifts in my partner's attitude. Yet, looking back, my heart softens toward Nikhil, too – we were both young souls, trapped by circumstance.

I heard the jangling of the door's security chain and looked up to see my parents walking in from dinner out with a professor friend. Seeing my tear-streaked face, my mother rushed over to me, and asked, "What's the matter, Tarini?"

Papa dropped the car keys on the kitchen counter and took a few steps in my direction, worry lines appearing between his eyebrows.

"Don't worry, nothing happened; just some Nikhil stuff that I will sort out myself. Good night," I called out, on my way to my room.

But there was no sanctuary from the whirlpool of thoughts that collided with each other, jostling for dominance. I whimpered into my pillow. *How much longer would Nikhil continue to hold on to nothing? Why doesn't he have the courage to walk away graciously? I am just lucky that he doesn't know what a catch he is – he probably thinks he'll never find another girl after me.*

Sighing, I wished I could switch my brain off for the night. I imagined rubbing a genie's lamp to reveal all the answers that remained hidden from me. The thoughts weren't passive. I was an active participant in contending with them, if not in creating them. *Clearly, I am an echo chamber without Nikhil, with voices reverberating in my head. Has my desire to recover fast, which others call my "determination", distorted his perception by giving him false hopes for our planned future together? Well, my "determination" is not working. Chances are that I have lifelong disabilities.* My eyes flickered open. *I probably can't ever be a mother, given how long it takes me to just care for myself, and I know how much Nikhil wants to have kids.* I lay motionless, devoid of meaning, feeling robbed of a planned future identity.

The next thing I knew, the morning rays were filtering in through the cracks in my blinds. My thoughts from the previous night had crystallized, and I was filled with love for the love of my life, who had stood by me during these most traumatizing years .

I knew what I had to do.

12

Semicolon or Full Stop?

As I waited for Nikhil's arrival that weekend, my eyes remained glued to my phone, waiting for the familiar buzz. But instead, the doorbell rang. I heard Nikhil's voice greeting Mama, and pleasantries being exchanged.

Pausing in the bathroom, I took a moment to compose myself, smoothing down my hair, and applying a fresh coat of lip balm. Then, with my heart beating in double time, I rolled over to the living room to meet Nikhil. He wrapped his arms around me, planting a kiss on my temple. But mindful of my mother's presence, I gently pulled away and sat at a distance on the couch. Nikhil, meanwhile, brushed his hair back and leaned into the sofa, stealing quick, furtive glances in my direction.

"It's super awkward to be seeing each other here. I expected you to message me five minutes before getting here so I could meet you in the lobby like last time," I murmured, my usually flat voice suddenly taking on a playful but accusatory lilt. It looked like the prosody exercises in speech therapy were beginning to bear fruit …

Nikhil leaned forward, his hands clasped together in front of him.

"I wanted to surprise you," he said, with a sheepish grin. "Don't worry, it's chill. I wanted to say hi to your parents, too, because anyway, we will be together all weekend."

I longed for more intimacy than was appropriate or permissible with my mother at striking distance.

"Let's go out to the deck," I suggested.

Once downstairs, Nikhil held the door to the deck open, allowing my power wheelchair to sail through. We stood in the wide open space, which served as a walking track around a patch of green. With the cool fall breeze brushing our skin, it felt good to be alive, and as we approached one another, our eyes met. Noticing that the only other people on the deck were students, Nikhil bent down till our faces were level before I felt the touch of his soft, full lips. My skin tingled with delight as they gently brushed against my neck. The taste of the salt in the breeze wafting in from the Atlantic Ocean behind me brought me to my senses. I pulled away. A flicker of confusion danced in Nikhil's eyes.

Whirling around, I beckoned him to follow me to the enclosure where the swimming pool, was.

"Come here; we need to talk." I parked myself beside a deck chair with an unused dry towel draped on it and motioned for Nikhil to take a seat. I felt surprisingly clear-headed.

"What's going on, babes?" Nikhil asked, clearly lost to what was coming.

I wasn't sure what was coming either.

The words just rolled off my tongue.

"There is absolutely no doubt that the two of us will love each other forever," I started. "It's only because of my deep love for you that I see how unfair it is that you have to deal with my limitations when you didn't exactly sign up for this." I paused to catch my breath. "I don't want to be an obligation."

Small wrinkles formed around Nikhil's eyes.

"I don't understand."

I waited for my tears to fall, for uncontrolled sobbing to commence, for my unquenched pain to grow unbearable, but nothing came. Instead, I felt like a placid lake, almost inexplicably calm and unhurried. I knew what I was doing was right, even though it would cause short-term misery. Letting go of my partnership with Nikhil would preserve the beauty and vibrancy of our relationship forever. It was like some celestial force was guiding me.

"Nikhil," I said, my voice barely above a whisper. "Open your eyes. It has been about two years since my accident, and things are still not back to how they were before. You need to lead a full life, which you won't be able to do with me as your partner. This is not what you signed up for – it'd be different if you had."

Nikhil's gaze fixed on the vacant space in front of him, his face blank, his eyes welling up with tears.

"You *will* recover, I am certain of it. And I'm willing to stay by your side even if you remain in a wheelchair indefinitely or walk with a slight limp or whatever. None of that is important. The only thing that we need is for you to become fully independent."

I placed my hand lightly on Nikhil's leg.

"I totally get that," I said. "But, lately, I've been consumed by all this, our situation." I hesitated briefly upon seeing flickering confusion across Nikhil's features, before continuing. "If my recovery continues at this pace, you'll miss the chance of finding a partner during your law school years by staying in a defunct relationship."

"Babes, what you are doing is very commendable, but I *know* for a fact that I will never find another partner. I think you know that too," Nikhil said as a lone tear slipped down his cheek.

"Just you wait. Some lucky woman will snap you up. And anyway, if I am able to recover enough to function independently, we can always get back together."

With nothing left unsaid, Nikhil put his hand over mine, and we looked into each other's eyes. My love for Nikhil was infinite, and I couldn't wrap my head around what I had just done.

"I know this is crazy of me, but can we kiss each other one last time? A goodbye kiss?"

Nikhil's silence enveloped me.

"I don't want to say yes, but I can't imagine not kissing my babes ever again. Come here," Nikhil said, after a brief pause, pulling my torso to his. Lost in his arms, I leaned in and gently pressed my lips to his. The kiss was bittersweet and tender. Moments from the last seven years, too many to count, flashed behind my closed eyelids. I had witnessed how much could change in the snap of a finger. I still couldn't fathom the enormity of what I had done.

With no weekend to share any longer, Nikhil bid me a hasty farewell and went off to his friend's apartment for the night.

What becomes of us when we lose a part of our identity? Do we cling to resentment, find solace in denial, or try with all our might to move on? The answer is as unique as the individual asking the question and perhaps it is in our response that we define ourselves. Maybe identity is not a puzzle solved overnight, but rather a journey of collecting different pieces, losing some along the way, and ultimately creating a mosaic of all the people we've been.

My daily routine kept me aloof for most of the next day until I reached for my phone to message Nikhil in the late afternoon. While some of us have the power to keep our inner worlds to ourselves, I didn't know how to belong to myself and, truth be told, continue to have trouble resisting over-sharing. Broken images of our shared dreams and memories weighed on me as my mind struggled to piece back the shards of my scattered identity. Who was I without Nikhil? Who could I be without him? Had we even decided anything about staying present in each other's lives after I decided to set him free?

Struggling to find the pieces of myself untouched by Nikhil and the pieces he didn't take with him, deafening loneliness thundered around me. As a tidal wave of contradictory thoughts and questions surged through my mind, I found myself reaching for my phone, hoping to see a message from Nikhil. I longed to find clues in his words, seeking his perspective on the boundaries that, technically, *I* had drawn. I stared at the blank screen. My eyes welled up as I imagined being soothed by Nikhil's arms tightly wrapped around me. Not ready for my internal world to be crippled, I hugged my pillow close to my eyes, weirdly comforted by its dampness.

My need for us to still be part of each other's lives left me hollow and bereft, but somehow, I didn't once question whether I'd done the right thing. Sometimes, the hardest paths are the ones we know, bone-deep, we must walk.

I was intent on enabling him to not feel tied to me, not because of any virtue in me, but because I, too, longed to be free from the weight of what I believed was Nikhil's expectation of me. Tragic as it is, I was the only one who could set myself – and him – free.

In the two years since my world capsized, I'd become fluent in the language of unsaid things. Though I had been dazed and confused by Nikhil's sudden criticisms – over phone calls and emails, the pieces slowly began aligning. Over our long separations, and on the few occasions we met, weighed down by circumstances neither of us could control, I'd sensed Nikhil's frustration, even when not overtly expressed. I believe I caught glimpses of his unspoken frustration. Behind his words lay a desire for a carefree mid-twenties lifestyle similar to his peers – free from worry, full of spontaneous adventures, and lazy Sunday mornings with his partner. Though he had the right to leave, he seemed to lack the courage to do so. He would have found it hard to live with himself after walking away from me, of being the one to deepen my wounds. How could I fault him for such gentle hesitation?

Yet, there were moments when I felt overcome by the shattering of a dream: all the whispered plans, the lifetime of togetherness Nikhil and I had sketched for ourselves over seven precious years. In quieter moments, my mind would circle back to the same painful questions: why he hadn't simply asked for a pause in the relationship to sort out where we stood after seven years, instead of channeling his restlessness and dissatisfaction into what felt like pointed criticism of my intellectual prowess. But even then, I found myself making excuses, smoothing over the cracks in our foundation. Wet tissues littered my bedside table. I grabbed another to dab my eyes. I told myself I was ready to overlook his flaws to keep our friendship alive. Ultimately, it was simple: I just wanted Nikhil to remain in my world, in whatever way he could.

As the day unfolded in quiet rhythms, I became less emotional and more reflective. Our togetherness had been magical, but even the most magical things can shatter before a typhoon. Nikhil's unwavering loyalty to me had been a thing of beauty. But as the dust settled, it became clear that our foundation was not strong enough to hold us together. It was time to accept what my mind had known but refused to name and step forward into the unknown.

Finally, hearing my phone vibrate on my bedside table, I patted my eyes, collected my thoughts, and sat upright in bed. With a deep breath, I reached out to grab the phone. As my fingers trembled over the screen, I knew what lay ahead: the familiar, draining task of reading between his lines, of searching for meaning in every carefully chosen word. With a quick touch, the message appeared before me.

Sorry for not responding sooner, babes – went to the hospital with Chethan. Left my phone at his apartment. Let's talk soon?

My eyes continued to scan the text, unsure if I was missing something. Were we acting as though nothing had changed? Could we? *Had* anything changed? Were we back at square one? What did I truly want? My mind swirled. Change is exhausting, but so is stagnation. With that thought, I pushed my shoulders back, my resolve crystallizing. No, I wouldn't go back to square one. I, too, didn't want such a partnership. Yet, I couldn't fathom simply erasing a core part of my identity for no fault of ours. Confident that Nikhil, like me, wouldn't want to part ways completely, I picked up my phone and composed a well-thought-out response. Then, I pushed off to my happy place – Cafe Bru.

My wounded heart found temporary solace in the steaming cappuccino and joyful chatter around me. I perked up further when I spotted Papa walking home from his office, his silhouette gradually becoming more visible as he drew nearer. He strode up to me, his hand gripping the back of my chair.

"I have news I've been waiting to share with you," he said. "I received an offer this morning, appointing me to the board of the IMF as an executive director for three years."

My mouth fell open.

"That's amazing, Papa. Congratulations!" I exclaimed. But then a thought struck me. "The IMF is headquartered in DC," I began. As if on cue, my thoughts did an about-turn. "You mean I will get to use my power wheelchair for longer?" The thought of roaming with friends freely beyond just the fall semester seemed too good to be true. Not to mention that working in the same time zone as my BRAC colleagues would simplify my life, and maybe even open doors to a fuller professional life.

Though my heart was soaring, a part of me couldn't help imagining how thrilling this news would have been if Nikhil and I were still together. I shook the thought away, letting Papa's words fill the present moment instead.

But Papa has an uncanny knack for sensing my worries, often even before I know them myself.

"Pom, is everything okay with Nikhil?" he inquired, his voice warm and concerned. "You know you can talk to me anytime. But I also want you to know that my colleague's wife is a counselor, and he's offered her services if we ever feel the need." He studied me for a moment while I absently toyed with the hem of my shirt. "Sometimes," he continued softly, "you know, it might help to speak with a professional about your challenges, especially about issues you feel are too difficult to share with us."

As I gazed up at my father, I couldn't help but feel really, really lucky to have him in my life. While thoughts of starting mental health therapy and telling my parents what had happened with Nikhil had crossed my mind, I chose to set them aside for the time being. At this very moment, I just wanted to focus on Papa's exciting news.

"What does Mama think about this move?" I asked, to keep him on-topic.

"Mama has agreed to move to DC, though she would ideally like to be in Delhi to be closer to your Nani and Nana [mother's parents]," he said. "We want you to get world-class therapy in DC. We'd also like you to be examined by the world's top neurologists who are aware of the latest discoveries in brain science, which I know you're reading about."

My heartbeat drummed in my chest as I glanced down at the book by the Canadian psychiatrist Norman Doidge, open on my

Kindle, and then back at Papa. I wanted to wrap my arms around my parents with my entire being. There are no words to describe the enormity of what I was feeling.

My parents have always lived by their conviction that success lies at the crossroads of luck and hard work. Napoleon Bonaparte once said, "Ability is of little account without opportunity," and here were my parents, laboring daily – Papa at the office, and Mama at home – to create opportunities for the lives they had brought into the world. Like all parents, they must have dreamed that their hard work and sacrifices would transform into joy and success for their children. I desperately wanted to reassure them this dream would come true, but my quivering chin betrayed the doubts I couldn't hide from Papa. *I have caused my parents much hardship, which they have borne with quiet dignity. They have uprooted themselves from their home and loved ones, all for my sake.*

And then, another, more soothing thought flickered through my mind. I straightened my posture and picked up my mug to savor the last few sips of my coffee. Papa's appointment as an executive director of the IMF brought to mind the community of friends my parents had in DC from when they'd lived there thirty years ago as newlyweds. *There's no reason to worry. My parents will be just fine.*

13
Wheels in Motion

All I had to do was roll out to the bus stop behind our apartment block in Washington, DC, catch the bus driver's eye, and wait for them to lower the ramp. Once I was on board, they'd secure my wheelchair using straps and hooks to prevent it from sliding with the movement of the bus. And then the bus would be off and away. I'd simply tug on the blue ribbons overhead to indicate my stop. It was a living demonstration of the Americans with Disabilities Act, or the ADA, in action. Indeed, a scene I had seen play out on repeat for other people as a commuter in New York. But to know how empowering a facility like this is for a person with disabilities, you have to be one.

In other ways too, DC opened up new worlds. With places like the supermarket chain, Whole Foods, and Sweetgreen, a chain of restaurants serving salads, next door to our apartment in downtown DC, I could browse shelves or make impromptu lunch plans at leisure. Accessible public transportation made it easy to venture into neighboring Georgetown for jazz shows at Blues Alley or movies at AMC with the new friends I had begun making.

And I had an office to go to, too. After my last meeting with Susan Davis in New Haven, when she offered me a role at BRAC

USA whenever I was ready, I kept those embers burning. When I learned about our move to DC, I reached out to her, saying I was available and interested in a job. Susan was quick to act on this. My move to DC ushered in a new chapter, with a new position at BRAC. As a program advisor for the agriculture program at the BRAC USA office in New York City, I worked remotely from DC. My primary responsibility was to help craft fundraising proposals. While BRAC USA didn't have an office in DC, Susan tapped into her network, introducing me to several key figures in the global development community with offices in striking distance to me. I began to work from one of these offices. After three years of feeling professionally adrift, I was finally heading to an office again, something I hadn't done since Kampala.

Although I had the flexibility to prioritize my well-being with thrice-weekly visits to the National Rehabilitation Hospital (NRH), where we began consulting doctors soon after we arrived in DC, I found it hard to forgo my office routine. Each day, in under fifteen minutes, I zipped from home to the office on my power wheelchair to do the work that brought me deep fulfillment. All this whispered promises of *freedom* – a freedom tied to mobility and the kindness of thoughtful people – not to mention, the freedom derived from one's own hard-earned paycheck. With my power wheelchair and equal access, I relished the autonomy to live life on my own terms, day after day.

The word "freedom" will always shine for me, wrapped in the warm glow of twinkle lights.

With my organization's support, I slipped back into the life of a young professional as smoothly as a figure skater gliding across the ice. All I needed was for its leader to understand that speed and speech were my primary limitations, from the perspective of a desk job, and to make the necessary accommodations. Susan Davis was that leader. At BRAC USA, our primary mission was to raise funds for the organization's poverty alleviation programs in various countries. Although I worked independently from Washington, DC, technology enabled me to collaborate closely, albeit remotely, with my colleagues in New York City, the UK, Bangladesh, Uganda, Sierra Leone, and Liberia. In my new office, surrounded by other young professionals, friendships came naturally and I was welcomed as a peer – in the US, disability didn't seem to carry the same stigma. Looking in the mirror was no longer so alienating.

"I wish we had ten of you." The weight of Susan's words, uttered not just once but several times, settled in my soul, and I was mesmerized by her remarkable leadership. She truly embodied the organization's values: "*a world free of all forms of exploitation and discrimination, where everyone has the opportunity to realize their potential.*"

One day in 2014, a year after our move, Susan was in DC for work and paid me a visit at home. I suggested taking her to see the office I worked out of. As we made our way there, she marveled at my independence.

"Let's see how fast you can go!" she exclaimed with a playful grin.

She didn't have to ask me twice. Gripping the joystick of my wheelchair, I zoomed down the sidewalk on New Hampshire Avenue to show off my prowess and speed. Beaming with delight, I finally whirled around to face Susan, who had quickened her pace to join me.

"Unbelievable!" she said.

After giving her a tour of my office setup, I walked her to the nearest subway station. On our way, all of a sudden, I sensed her growing quiet, more somber.

"Tarini, that was a really fun day, but now I want to discuss your Yale SOM deferral. What did you think and how did you feel after auditing that accounting class at GW last year?"

I sighed as the memory of that dreadful accounting class at George Washington University resurfaced. Upon moving to DC, before resuming my work for BRAC, we discovered that our apartment was conveniently located on the same block as GW's business school. Papa and I discussed various approaches I could take to determine if I felt ready to pursue my MBA as yet. With my father assigning me math problems to solve, we had already witnessed the impact of the TBI on my quantitative skills, which weren't exceptional even before the accident. We concluded that auditing a quantitative business school course was the way to go. Despite my apprehension, the class I chose was accounting – filled with dreaded numbers. Armed with my Yale admit letter, Papa managed to get permission from George Washington University to allow me to audit a class.

Looking back, I must admit that I hadn't absorbed a single morsel of what was taught during those classes. Instead, I found myself entranced by people-watching. My eyes paused on a serious-looking, attractive grad student with chestnut-brown hair, fiddling with her pen as she focused on the professor's words. *This could be me.* I sat there imagining countless opportunities ahead for such a capable-seeming woman as the professor continued his lecture. It wasn't until I blinked and refocused on the PowerPoint slide that the professor had directed the class's attention to that I snapped back to reality.

I remember being unable to process the whirlwind of new information that came at me like a discus ball – fragments of knowledge spinning at a furious pace. And if I'm being honest, part of me just didn't believe I could scale the odds stacked against me.

On top of all of that, the profound upheavals in my life – shouldering the unfamiliar weight of a disabled identity in the full bloom of adulthood and breaking up with Nikhil – had made me long for comfort. The comfort-seeking continues to this day. I had even put off thinking about the possibility of conquering the looming Yale SOM mountain until some unspecified future date. My existence in ordinary three-dimensional space became a thing of the past, as I now found myself inhabiting a novel place in spacetime. I moved slower, spoke slower, thought slower, and worked slower. The world around me had slowed down too, thanks to my loved ones adapting to my speed. There was no going back, just an acceptance of my evolving identity, a process that would take time, tears, and a world of patience.

In response to her question, I told Susan about the self-confidence I had only just regained through my work, and that I didn't think it wise to enroll at a top-tier business school where I was certain my fragile self-confidence would be shattered.

Susan's forehead creased as I voiced my thoughts, but she never once pooh-poohed anything I said. Acknowledging that I was the best judge of my capabilities, she simply said, "Given that I have seen your work, I have full confidence you will be successful at Yale."

I didn't know until then that I needed to hear these words to feel a weight lift off my shoulders.

Susan had always seen more talent and potential in me than I could see in myself. Her investment in me touched me deeply – the way she went above and beyond the call of duty to help me realize my full potential. But I also knew she couldn't fully comprehend the cognitive struggles I was up against.

With a hug, she descended the escalator into the Foggy Bottom metro station.

My time in DC was marked not only by my re-entry into the workforce and the blossoming of new friendships but also by countless therapy sessions at the National Rehabilitation Hospital (NRH) and an unrelenting stream of doctors' appointments.

My first encounter with the NRH occurred shortly after our move to DC. My parents encouraged me to take a break from work to attend NRH's intensive therapy program, also known as the Day Program. The long hours of the Day Program left me mortified – not just physically drained but emotionally exposed. I even shed private tears behind closed doors. At first, I felt I had no choice but to follow my parents' wishes. Taking a step back, I realized that what they were asking of me was far from outlandish; it was, in fact, for my own good. After all, world-class rehabilitation had been the driving force behind my parents' relocation to DC.

I persevered through the daily grind of physical, occupational, speech, and cognitive therapies. The cognitive exercises felt simplistic and embarrassing, as if designed for children. Once, when asked to solve an exceptionally juvenile puzzle, I lifted my chin and announced, "I was recently admitted to Yale University for a Master's degree." After the cognitive therapist expressed sufficient awe and wonder, she pleaded with me to get on with the sessions, assuring me they would benefit me in the long run.

At NRH, I was under the care of two renowned neurologists specializing in TBI, pain management, and neurological rehabilitation: Dr. Michael Yochelson and Dr. Heechin Chae. Dr. Yochelson, who also happened to be the head of the NRH, was the first of my many doctors to inform me gently, during a visit with my mother that "in limbs with spasticity,[8] it is commonly observed that a complete restoration to one's pre-existing function is unlikely."

That day was the first time, three years since the accident, that any doctor had discussed the possibility of regaining my pre-accident state. As time passed, I became deeply grateful to Dr. Yochelson, but at that moment, his jarring statement left me feeling trapped in that room. I wanted out.

I could feel my heart pounding. My mind raced. What else wouldn't return to its pre-accident state? What else were the doctors concealing from me, possibly to spare my feelings? My tense expression made Dr. Yochelson curious. When I revealed my doubts to him, he assured me that dishonesty is against the Hippocratic Oath.

I was in turmoil. If Dr. Yochelson couldn't help me solve the mysteries of my brain, I wasn't sure who could. The air grew thick with uncertainty, and I glanced at my mother, who came to stand beside me, her hand gripping my shoulder. I gently brushed it aside; today was not a day I needed to be treated like a child.

The other doctor, Dr. Chae, became a regular presence in my life. During my frequent appointments with him, he patiently unraveled the complex mechanics of the human brain in layperson's terms. Dr. Chae had a way of weaving metaphors and idioms into his explanations, like a skilled storyteller, painting pictures with words.

Dr. Chae was responsible for injecting Botox into the overactive muscles of my right arm and leg, a painful but necessary procedure to help reduce muscle spasticity, which I needed twice yearly. To this day, I receive a minimum of fifteen injections in my arm twice a year as an ongoing necessity. Without Botox, my right hand becomes stiff and unyielding, like a tightly coiled spring, always ready to curl, but never able to relax.

During one of my visits with Dr. Chae, he told me, "Imagine there is a traffic jam in your brain, and the neuron vehicles are trying to find the best detour to get them to their desired destination in the most efficient manner possible. That traffic jam represents the damaged pathways in your brain. While that jam won't ever clear, the clever neuron vehicles will work to find the best alternate route to their destination."

I couldn't help but smile at this vivid imagery. But my amusement was short-lived. A sensation akin to a blaze of fire tore through my right leg. I clenched my jaw, resigned to the pain, which had been ever-present for four years now. All I wished for at that moment – during those months – was to understand *why*.

Dr. Chae clarified that the problem lay not in my leg, but in my brain. He quickly followed up by assuring me that he didn't mean that my *pain* wasn't real, but that the problem is in my damaged central nervous system. Due to the inability of my central nervous system to rectify the cause of my acute pain, my brain continues firing shots of warning, resulting in the once-acute pain reincarnating as chronic pain.

I remembered having read about chronic pain referred to as "learned pain".[9] I could finally begin to wrap my head around this round-the-clock discomfort. Despite Dr. Chae describing chronicity as "difficult to treat", a thin layer of calm settled over me – I felt I had scored a small victory by finally uncovering a solitary, mysterious element of the human brain.

Chronic pain is an intensely individual experience and cannot be separated from the point of view of the individual expressing and communicating the pain. In determining what's at the root of the perception of human experience, we cannot separate experiences caused by the brain and those caused by the mind's interactions with the world. Rather, experiences are formed by the intermingling of both of these systems. The intersection of human biology, medicine, philosophy, and phenomenology intrigues me like no other – mysterious, elegant, and yet undeniably distressing.

I returned home that day feeling like a child who'd stumbled upon a volume of existential philosophy. One negative thought after another swirling in my mind, I began to drown in a sea of self-pity.

My pain will last forever. I won't ever experience companionship again. Nobody has the answers. The human brain is unknowable.

Staring into the abyss, I felt myself being pulled in, but I soon gathered my composure, realizing that the void was of my own making. Taking a deep breath, I dialed Pallavi's number and poured out my thoughts to her, holding back nothing except tears. Pallavi listened intently, offering comfort and advice, and I was glad for how seen and understood I felt.

Though weighed down by sorrow and creeping despair, I couldn't help but smile a little. Thank goodness for friends who allow you to reveal your whole self without hesitation – the kind who speak the truth, even when it stings.

Pallavi continues to be one of my most empathic of friends – she didn't just witness my struggles from a distance, she walked beside me through the shadows, seeing the world through my eyes. True friends don't just feel your pain – they shoulder it with you, step by step.

On a sunny weekend in late spring, when I heard that the cherry blossom trees would be in full bloom, I felt inspired to orchestrate a little sunset expedition to the Tidal Basin with my new DC friends, Sidra and Rósant, who lived in an apartment one floor below mine. A married couple, a few years older than me, Sidra is of Pakistani origin, while Rósant is Icelandic. They had long since left home, and, like me, seemed to view the world as their oyster. I was enticed by the idea of a pink sky fusing with cherry blossoms, and I wanted to post a photograph on social media so that others could see what a spectacular life I lived.

I ached for my life to seem magnificent, hoping that if I could believe it to be so, I might finally begin to feel it too. Instagram became my canvas for crafting this illusion, veiling the less desirable aspects of living – like the round-the-clock pain in my right leg.

Social media helped catalyze an ability that I still possess – the remarkable human freedom of imagining the world other than what it is.

The art of healing, I discovered, lies less in our wounds themselves, than in how we carry them. I faced a choice: I could retreat into my room, letting pain become my world, or I could learn to accept that this unwelcome sensation in my right leg was a part of my story – as unfair as it was – and continue forward. With the blueprint, hammer, and nails in our possession, we are the architects of our fates – exactly why I planned this Saturday outing with my friends on a spring day. Like an architect, working not with steel and stone but with moments, and meanings, I planned to construct something beautiful – a memory that could bring joy and beauty to my life despite the pain that threatened to overshadow it and also strengthen the delicate foundations of a budding friendship.

On the same day as the evening picnic, I called my friend Isabel to plan a morning visit to the Smithsonian American Art Museum to see a Georgia O'Keeffe exhibition. Isabel, a striking German woman, worked in urban development at the World Bank in Washington, DC. My brother first met her through a mutual friend when he traveled to Kenya, and later, he introduced us in DC, convinced we would hit it off. Soon, it became delightfully unclear which of us had grown closer to her.

We were kindred spirits, sharing a deep appreciation for the arts and finding joy in life's quiet moments and lively social gatherings. During one of our early walks, I confided in her about feeling adrift without a companion, and she shared a similar, vulnerable experience. Over the years, we would continue to share the ins and outs of our lives, and I often invited her over for my mother's home-cooked Indian meals. Somewhere along the way, she became like a sister to me.

Isabel's decision to trust me reassured me that despite everything I was going through, I was still somebody others felt they could turn to: someone capable of building and sustaining lasting friendships. It made me wonder if I was the only one holding back the natural flow of my life into new, uncharted territory.

The morning sky outside my window beckoned, a vast canvas painted with an undulating pattern of soft white clouds that allowed the warm light to filter through – a perfect day for an adventure in the city with friends. By this time, I had long since built enough confidence to navigate the bus system on my own. I opted for the bus instead of the subway because, as I've noticed, subway systems tend to have a significant crevice between the platform and the train where my wheelchair had gotten trapped on two distinct occasions. I was lucky my brother was there to lift and pull me into the subway compartment before the doors closed.

Even in a country like the USA, where the ADA has been established for years, this glaring gap remains all too visible. The ADA was codified in 1990 to prohibit discrimination against individuals with disabilities in all areas of public life. Washington, DC, the nation's capital and a symbol of the country's well-oiled machinery, is also known as one of the most wheelchair-accessible cities in the world, and yet there's always room for improvement. For now, the bus system is a reliable, but slower, alternative.

I spotted Isabel hurrying toward me. She bent down to hug me and we made our way to the museum.

The mere sight of the building had me entranced. My eyes were locked on the majestic marble pillars that stood guard at the entrance of the Smithsonian, and Isabel had to prod me to go inside. Banners showcasing the Georgia O'Keeffe exhibition – the reason for our visit – adorned the wall. My eyes lingered on the artist's rendition of a vibrant red flower on one of the banners, and I noticed Isabel doing the same. Bright with optimism and shared understanding, we stood there for a moment, taking it all in, before heading toward the exhibition.

I rolled into the gallery, and stopping before the first painting, I marveled at the artist's skill in applying oil paints to create a smooth texture and dynamism in her art. The wooden floor creaked under my wheelchair as I passed a smattering of blue and red flowers. Standing before an abstract work, Isabel beckoned me over, her eyes wide in wonder.

As I approached her, I suddenly felt sharp pain coursing through my leg. My head reeled with the sudden twinge. Two young women, with infants held close on their hips, sauntered past me, gesturing at the paintings, speaking to each other in loud whispers. Pain has a way of isolating. No one – not the people who stood right beside me at the gallery, Isabel included – is truly aware of my lived reality, especially not at that moment. *Maybe if I just behave like it doesn't exist at all, it won't.*

I rolled up to Isabel with a sunny face.

After I absorbed her thoughtful analysis of the painting, *Only One*, we agreed to explore the rest of the exhibition at our own pace. But how does one ignore a disc of flames spinning under your skin?

I looked at the next painting – one in a series of abstract charcoal drawings of flowers. Georgia O'Keeffe appeared to be trying to depict the essence of an object, rather than just its physical features. Instead of getting lost in her vision, my gaze turned inward, to the sharp teeth of the monsters gnawing at my inner thigh. I placed my left palm on my right thigh, my fingers curling tightly around it, in a fruitless attempt to squash the pain.

When I finally looked back up, the charcoal-black shape before me slowly resolved into a flower emerging from the abstraction. My eyes drifted to the plaque with Georgia O'Keefe's words on why she paints flowers.

> When you take a flower in your hand and really look at it, it's your world for the moment. Most people in the city rush around so they have no time to look at a flower. I want them to see it whether they want to or not.

My attention was drawn to the space between myself and the sketch. Despite being surrounded by soul-stirring art and in the company of a close friend, my mind inexplicably drifted to thoughts of Nikhil. Now, with time, I have noticed my pain intensifies when my mind is occupied by a heavy dose of negativity – grief, anger, frustration, paranoia. Beneath my cheerful demeanor simmered a tumultuous sea of emotions. Conflicting thoughts crisscrossed my mind as it traversed, perhaps for the hundredth time, over the terrain of our relationship and parting. *Why couldn't Nikhil see the living, breathing essence underneath my exterior?*

I had a sinking feeling that Nikhil had orchestrated our break-up like a maestro, ensuring that I would be the one to draw the final curtain. *Craftsmanship masterfully executed by Nikhil, for which I can never fault him.* The hints, the nudges – whether subconsciously or not, felt like they'd been there all along, harmonizing into a truth I could no longer ignore: he wasn't fulfilled, not in the way our love demanded and I needed him to be. I couldn't even fault him; his quiet orchestration had been gentle, almost kind. Still, my mind churned. *Does this mean that Nikhil's love was never unconditional?*

A pit formed in my stomach.

Staying with me would have profoundly reshaped Nikhil's life, just as my limitations had reshaped mine. Yet, the questions gnawed at me: *Why didn't he feel a void in his life from my absence? Would he be pining for me if I still looked like that woman, the one who turned heads on the dance floor?* My eyes traced a path from my changed body to the quad cane standing proudly beside me. My eyelids grew heavy and I felt something inside me shrivel.

O'Keeffe's work stirred something deep within me. As the flower before me came into sharper focus, I began peeling open my own concept of fairness: how could I expect unconditional love from Nikhil when I was still struggling to accept and embrace the exposed essence of my being? I was only just starting to inhabit this new identity, with all its edges and limitations. *But shouldn't Nikhil want to walk beside me through the darkest valleys, if he truly loved me the way he said he did?*

"Enough," I scolded myself. If there was even the faintest possibility of something or someone offering me freedom from these constraints, wouldn't I jump at the chance of leading an unencumbered life? It was me, I was the one keeping Nikhil from that freedom. And it had to be me who had to let him go. My deep love for him remained pure. But it was only my respect for his graceful handling of our impossible situation that had led me to compose the last sentence of our story.

Love, after all, is like a braid, intricately woven with respect, trust, and affection. But our situation had become something different, something difficult for outsiders to grasp. Each of these three strands still existed, still intact, but now they coiled around something else – an unshakeable core of everlasting friendship. Our "braid" wasn't gone, it was just different. More intricate, perhaps, even more beautiful in its own way. As my mind lingered on the notion of friendship, Isabel's presence beside me pulled me back to the fascinating sights and sounds of the museum.

"You're going to have to tell me what you find so breathtaking about this charcoal sketch over coffee in that gorgeous courtyard outside," Isabel said, rousing me from my reverie. She must have seen the look on my face, for she continued, "You aren't your usual chatterbox self today; you seem lost in thought. I won't pressure you, but you know I'm here if you want to talk."

14

Between Data and Hope

A month later, in the summer of 2013, Nikhil secured a summer internship in DC. We would now get the opportunity to discover how possible it was for the two of us to "hang out" only as friends. The first time we met, we went for brunch at a popular neighborhood spot in Foggy Bottom called "Founding Farmers". After a scrumptious meal, we headed to Kramer Books in Dupont Circle to browse. As we walked and talked, I realized that hanging out as friends wasn't quite as heart-wrenching as I had imagined.

On the way, I stopped to watch a pigeon fly up to perch on the dry spout of a fountain. The sun bathed the bird in its warm glow as it stretched its wings, its beak shimmering. Below, its companion looked up, seemingly captivated by the elegant display.

"Babesauce! Hurry up, why have you stopped?" Nikhil called out when he realized I wasn't beside him. I couldn't help feeling a hint of satisfaction that the nickname he had given me had stuck, as after seven years, that name had become a part of me. "Stop daydreaming!" he exclaimed, his tone tinged with exasperation.

I quickly collected myself and snapped back to reality.

Nikhil's internship was at a law firm in DC – his first foray into the "big bad" corporate world. It hadn't been easy for him to set aside his aspirations to help those with structurally unequal access to legal services in favor of chasing the almighty dollar, even for just three months. He had reassured himself that it was simply another experience to add to his growing repertoire. Meanwhile, I had patted myself on my back, perhaps prematurely, for shaping my former partner's perspective. We shared a vision of working for a sense of purpose rather than for money, even as we recognized that these values could be given wings because of our privilege.

As we wandered through Foggy Bottom and up to Dupont Circle, I realized that it'd been nearly ten months since we'd "officially" parted ways. Despite that, we continued to carry echoes of our former intimacy: the same terms of endearment, familiar warm exchanges. With our shared future now slipping out of reach, the inescapable reality of a more strongly-etched separation loomed large. Observing the all-too-familiar spring in Nikhil's step, I was instantly overwhelmed with a profound sense of happiness and relief, knowing we had made it through without bitterness. After all, I knew every layer of him. The only ingredient fading between us was romantic love – a small price to pay for preserving the bedrock of our friendship.

Glancing at Nikhil in his purple flannel shirt, I felt a familiar ache rising.

Maybe if I pretended long enough and no one knew that I still harbored the deepest feelings for him, my feelings would eventually fade. My wish for my feelings to dissipate was strong, but a fervent wish was all it was. I found bittersweet comfort knowing that Damascus would be ours alone. We were lucky to have shared those precious moments in its ancient streets before war rewrote its story. It was magic he couldn't recreate with anyone else – not for a while, at least.

Perhaps there's wisdom in how greater losses can reframe our smaller ones, casting them in a gentler light. Through its hard-earned lessons, life has taught me that although we cannot orchestrate the winds that blow through our lives, we can choose how to set our sails. Yet the ease of setting the sails is a privilege reserved for calmer waters – only when the storm has passed can we truly see the shape of what we've weathered.

Nikhil fidgeted, shifting from one foot to the other, his eyes avoiding mine.

"Tarini," he said, summoning the courage to meet my gaze. "I want to be upfront with you and not delay telling you something any longer than I have."

My heart skipped a beat. My thoughts started racing. *No, it can't be what I'm thinking. Calm down, Tarini. Take a deep breath. You always jump to the worst possible conclusions.* Aloud, I could only muster an "Mmm, okay . . ." Then, pulling a sentence together, I spoke with my voice barely above a whisper. "Can we go back to the fountain? There are benches there in case you want to sit."

Rather than sitting by the fountain, we wandered for a few minutes.

"So . . ." he began, followed by an inordinately long pause.

"I've started seeing a girl named Layla. She's in my class at SLS," Nikhil said, finally. Then, the minute the words left his mouth, he quickly reached over to stroke my arm.

It seemed like a million flocks of pigeons had been let loose in my head, so loud was the cacophony of my thoughts. *Relax. Don't speak just yet. Take a second to process this.*

One minute the screeching pigeons were clawing at each other most unnervingly; the next minute they pulled a Houdini, and I breathed a heavy sigh of relief.

This was good. There was a chance Nikhil would get to live the life he'd envisioned for himself – just not with me – and he wouldn't subconsciously, blame me for holding him back.

I reminded myself that I should be happy for him. If I measured up to the person I thought I was, then joy should come naturally.

I'll figure this out later. For the time being, just smile, and pretend.

Except that I'm generally useless at pretending. Unable to summon a smile as wide as I'd hoped, I could just manage the beginnings of a half-smile.

"That's awesome, Nikhil. I'm so happy for you," I said, my voice sounding flat to my own ears. "See! I told you another woman would swoop you up in no time." I paused, taking a deep breath before asking, "So, Layla? Is she white? Hispanic? Actually, wait, first tell me, is she cute?" My eyes lit up, and my lips curved into what I hoped was a mischievous grin as I tried to mask the bittersweet emotions swirling beneath.

My playfulness was lost on Nikhil. His casual swagger now missing, he seemed to be carefully weighing his words before speaking.

"She's quite pretty, but don't worry, nowhere near as cute as you. Let's see where it goes. She *is* white . . ."

My heart quietly hummed a joyful ètude. *Nikhil definitely can't replace me, not with how complete I make him by connecting him with his Indian roots, and how much we've been through together.*

He glanced at his watch.

"Why don't we check out Kramer Books another time? I told your mom I would get you back in time for your exercises."

"First, show me a photo of Layla," I pleaded, my voice rising in urgency.

"I'll show it to you later. I don't want to be late," he replied.

I glanced over Nikhil's shoulder at the red awning of Kramer Books, under which sat a handful of people, some sipping on mugs of coffee, a few with a selection of books spread out across the tables in front of them, still others picking on their salads. This was where I longed to be, among them, quietly soaking in the hum of life.

Instead, I had been dealt the blow that I could soon be replaced, and in the midst of it, my mundane exercise routine awaited.

Upon entering the courtyard of my building fifteen minutes later, I found myself chewing on my lower lip, feeling a twinge of apprehension. I waited for Nikhil to bid me a hasty goodbye. After all, he would surely be desperate to escape the discomfort of being around me. But to my surprise, he sank his hands deeper into his pockets and lowered himself onto the bench beneath the crabapple tree, its lavender blossoms painting the spring air with their fullness.

"I'm looking forward to seeing how far you've come with your walking,' Nikhil said, finally breaking the silence. There was no mistaking the warmth and sincerity in his voice.

A moment later, Rasoo appeared. Unconsciously, he took charge, his physical therapist instincts kicking in. After exchanging a quick hello with Nikhil, he barked out commands to me, his tone stern but caring.

"C'mon, Didi, don't drag your left foot, and try to put it ahead of your right one."

I took a step forward, my weak right side trembling under my weight. Nikhil's eyes followed my every move, his face lighting up when my left foot finally landed ahead of my right. The warmth of the gentle breeze on my skin echoed the feeling that enveloped my heart. Though I had tried to skate past the creeping jealousy, I now understood that I couldn't keep gliding forever without eventually bumping into it. It was frustrating to imagine another woman enjoying my former partner's virtues: his caring nature, razor-sharp intellect, panoptic curiosity, and undeniable cool. Consumed by an emotion I'd never before experienced, I felt possessive of Nikhil.

It was supposed to be me soaking up all the goodness of Nikhil's traits. Me. Me, me, me! If only I hadn't broken up with him, maybe it could have worked ...

One day, out of nowhere, I learned I would soon have a most unexpected visitor in Washington, DC. It was Davis, my Ugandan guardian angel.

My accident, occurring just when I'd begun a new journey to find meaning in my life, had damaged – though not fully revoked – my faith in the laws of the universe. Hearing that Davis had applied and been admitted to a community college in the United States rekindled my faith in the universe rewarding those who go out of their way to help others.

Back in Kampala, the barbershop, the CD business, and his expat friends had guzzled up all of Davis's waking hours. Stimulated by this wild, fun-loving, generous bunch of do-gooders out in his home country, Davis was also bewildered by us. He would glance at us expats over his mug of beer, his brows knitted, wondering how all of us who worked in the development sector led such happy-go-lucky, bar-hopping, youthful lives.

Davis would shrug away his curiosity and take a swig of his beer instead. "Muzungus are wealthy people who lead luxurious lifestyles," he'd concluded later while explaining how he'd resolved his puzzlement.

In the wake of my accident, my friends of a mere six weeks had displayed an extraordinary depth of kindness. Even as I lay in the sterile, fluorescent-lit ICU, Davis and Meri refused to leave my side, spending every night in the hospital on the off-chance they were needed. The intensity of their devotion, especially for someone they had known for only a short while, and who couldn't even acknowledge their presence, is both enigmatic and profoundly moving.

By following his instincts when the lifequake struck, Davis claims he did nothing out of the ordinary, but this doesn't fool me. He could have easily maintained his distance, tending to his own life while offering occasional support. Instead, he actively *chose* to show up for me repeatedly, day after day, exhibiting a fierce loyalty, when nothing bound him to me and my family.

Life is an inventory of choices that reveal our true characters. Davis's actions during that difficult time revealed a depth of character that continues to humble us.

After my accident, Davis's lifestyle, too, had been disrupted in a flash – with my and Meri's departure, gone were the raucous late nights with newcomer expats. But, quite as quickly, forward momentum rescued him. He found a partner in a Ugandan woman and was inspired to take control of his life, building a foundation for a solid future. Davis was now adulting hard.

At twenty-seven, he became a father to a baby boy in 2014. A year later, he gained admission to Malcolm X Community College in Chicago and was financially supported by a US government grant. All he needed was the will to keep going.

My accident, it turned out, had also played a critical role in shaping his future career path. Even as a child, he'd felt a need to help those who could not help themselves. While in the hospital with me, he found himself humbled by the devotion of medical professionals. Witnessing the undivided attention and round-the-clock care the neurosurgeon and the ICU doctors offered me and Sujal ignited his own desire to help others in dire need. He gained a fresh perspective on the inner workings of the healthcare system and wished to be part of it himself. But without even a basic school-leaving certificate, this dream seemed out of reach. His admission to a community college opened the door to a dream he'd held close to his heart: to one day, contribute to society by becoming a practicing nurse and helping those unable to help themselves.

Despite vastly differing degrees of privilege, and now, abilities too, Davis and I had come to share a friendship so deep that when he flew to the US to enroll in community college, he knew he had to find a way to visit me in DC. The extreme moments we'd shared, from lighthearted gaiety to an almost deathly silence, have bound us together for eternity – distance, borders, time difference, differing life paths no bar.

The sound of the doorbell instantly lifted my spirits. I heard Mama cry out in glee as she welcomed Davis in.

I sat up on the couch, my mouth agape as he walked in.

"Davis! Come to me," I hollered, extending an arm toward him.

"Miss Tarini!" Davis exclaimed as he rushed to me, eyes wide in seeming disbelief. "Wow, wow, wow, you are a miracle, my friend."

"Look who's talking," I said, chuckling, pulling him into a hug. "I've planned a fun day in the city for us," I said. "I have a feeling you'll love the Air and Space Museum."

Davis's face broke out into a wide grin.

"I wouldn't expect anything less. You planned all our outings in Kampala. Remember the Goat Race?"

Laughing, we exited the apartment and headed to the bus stop located just behind my apartment. I was eager to show him the wonders of the ADA and how it had opened up my life. It wasn't until after the accident, especially once I returned to India from the States, that it struck me just how much I had taken my unfettered access to life outside the walls of my room for granted. The ADA serves as a passport to a world of expanded access. The barriers to public transportation, buildings, spaces, businesses, education, and employment have been redrawn, if not eliminated, to enable smoother navigation. Davis watched with a raised eyebrow as the bus driver lowered the wheelchair lift and I rolled onto it. Once lifted into the bus, I settled into place while the driver secured my wheelchair. Davis sat attentively beside me.

"This is amazing, Tarini," he said, a sparkle in his eye.

As the driver fastened my wheelchair to the bus with a click, my mind drifted to the last time Davis and I had journeyed together. We'd sat cheek-by-jowl on a boda-boda with the wind whipping our faces on the unpaved roads on the outskirts of Kampala. A smile played on my lips, thinking of the contrasts.

We returned to my apartment in the early evening after a delightful day at the museum and the surrounding area. I'd promised Davis a delicious home-cooked Indian dinner.

"Hey! Do you remember you promised to cook a chicken curry for me in Kampala?" Davis said, his voice taking on a mock accusatory tone.

"What a clever, roundabout way to ask me if I'm fulfilling that promise I'd made to you in another lifetime!" Perhaps Davis didn't fully understand why cooking a meal was an uphill task for me now. Since the accident, even simple tasks like chopping vegetables take me three to four times longer than it did for my mother. She would be the one preparing the meal that evening."

"I wish I could cook for you, Davis," I said, with a hint of apology. Then, I jerked my right arm up to help him see the problem for himself. "But as you can see, my right hand doesn't function."

"You do know that onions are the base ingredient in chicken curry, right? Just imagine how long chopping onions and cooking with one hand would take," I added with a groan. "My poor balance makes it that much harder. Standing at the stove to do everything necessary for that long would be uncomfortable and tiresome." I tried to avoid giving too much information, but I wanted Davis to understand the reasons for my imperfect hospitality.

Davis grew somber.

"You know I'm not serious, right?" he said, smacking his forehead with his palm. "I wasn't actually expecting you to cook for me."

He sounded earnest, but I have my doubts. All I know is I still owe Davis a spicy Indian chicken curry.

Davis's visit was a delightful interlude in my life, otherwise dominated by work, therapies, and doctors' visits. My parents, being my trusted gatekeepers, had never, not once, let the yarn of hope roll out through fortune's narrowing door. They were on a quest to find something, anything that could transform their daughter's life into something brighter, something fuller. My folks had pursued an entire landscape of treatments both ancient and modern for me – from the precise science of allopathy to the restorative and intensive rhythms of rehabilitation, from whispered prayers to the persistence of acupuncture and homeopathy.

It had been Papa's idea, a few months into our move to DC, to seek out neurologists at the National Institutes of Health (NIH), the primary agency of the United States government, leading biomedical and public health research. NIH is renowned for its groundbreaking research successes, such as unraveling the complex world of neuronal connections, which it did in 2011,[10] to provide a basis for new neuronal models that have the potential to repair damaged neuronal networks. In 2012,[11] NIH scientists identified a promising new HIV antibody called 10E8, offering hope for preventing lethal infections.

Aware of the waiting game that science involves, my parents kept a cool head and merely considered it an optimal strategy to have more experts weigh in on my case to help us decide the best way to proceed. I was not so level-headed. I couldn't stop hoping, wishing, waiting for someone to throw me a life vest to save me from the shipwreck my life had become. For me, living a good life is not about fulfilling others' expectations; it's about the freedom to live on your own terms, free from judgment. NIH seemed like the team of lifeguards who could help me stay afloat.

Dr. Yochelson and Dr. Chae put their heads together and referred me to Dr. Christian Shenouda, a supervisory research clinician at the Center of Neuroscience and Regenerative Medicine (CNRM). The CNRM was a partnership between the NIH and the Department of Defense, mandated by the US Congress to research TBIs in both military personnel and civilians.

After receiving a stack of my medical reports, which Papa had neatly organized and labeled before emailing them to the doctor, Dr. Shenouda determined that I met the criteria for being included in a particular research study examining the natural history of TBIs.

The research study, named Protocol 10-CC-0118, was a study of the history of TBIs with multidisciplinary assessments, including physical assessments, neuropsychological examination, and imaging biomarkers. With no two brains being identical, scientists have to rely on a large sample of individuals at different stages of recovery from differing TBIs to get closer to understanding the likely condition at a particular stage of recovery.

I would provide the NIH researchers with data on my status, determined by multidisciplinary assessments three years post-TBI. Both the NIH clinicians and my family shared the same goal – to deepen their understanding of the human brain. But in truth, what my family wished for was merely an improved understanding of their Tarini's brain.

An unapologetic dork, I was thrilled about participating in a research study at NIH, where I would, indirectly, benefit society simply by being. However, it hurt my head when I learned that it wasn't just a question of participating in the study for a single day, but rather four days, and six hours each day.

How long will I be asked to defer the actual act of living? Will my twenties include anything I will actually look forward to? So much for my euphoria on my eighteenth birthday, signaling the start of adulthood.

Papa entrusted me with the responsibility of investigating the NIH study further – an astute move to give me more agency over my life. While my emotions often steer the wheel, Papa's faith in my logical aptitude holds strong. It was refreshing to see him treat me like the adult I was. Stepping up, I took charge of gathering all the relevant information needed.

With Papa at the wheel on our way to NIH, my heart raced with excitement. Though I knew even NIH's chances of finding someone with an identical injury were slim to none, the mere thought of contributing to something that could have a profound impact on a national if not global scale had me practically bouncing in my car seat.

We went straight to meet with Dr. Shenouda, a well-dressed, clean-shaven white man, who appeared to be in his early forties and had a sharp twinkle in his eye. I was taken aback by his genial manner and youthful appearance, given his expansive achievements, which I had obviously googled before the appointment. Dr. Shenouda had clearly done his homework, too, seeming well-versed in the details of my background. After congratulating me not only for my admission to Yale but also for my "audacious" decision to apply in the first place, he spent an hour asking me a series of questions and chatting with me, while the nurses checked my vitals and drew blood.

"I keep myself busy, so I haven't had the time to dwell on negative thoughts," I replied to Dr. Shenouda's question about my mood. Sensing that he was trying to get a read on me, assessing my character and potential for success, I sat up straighter and added, "I prefer to not think of myself as a patient."

Dr. Shenouda nodded approvingly, jotting down some notes on his pad.

"Excellent," he said. "Staying busy and maintaining a routine often do the trick." He then turned to include my parents in the conversation. "I believe in getting to know the people who volunteer for our studies, not just treating them as data points."

Seizing a natural pause in the conversation, I leaned forward and broached the main reason I'd chosen to participate in the NIH Study.

"Dr. Shenouda, do you think the results of this study might help me decide if I can attend business school at Yale?"

A momentary silence filled the room as Dr. Shenouda slid his feet forward, using them to propel the wheeled stool he was sitting on closer to me. He held my gaze and said, "Yes, the neurocognitive assessment and your consultation with Dr. Dsurney should help you better understand your capacity to cope with the demands of graduate school," he assured me.

With that, he glanced down at the notes he had taken on my history before concluding with a thorough physical exam.

That was the last I saw of Dr. Shenouda for the next four days – four days packed with activities, including two MRIs, two occupational therapy assessments, a vocational therapy assessment, and eight hours of neurocognitive testing, with an hour-long break in between for lunch.

There was no magic here, nobody offering any scientific cures, merely one assessment after another – tests similar to those conducted at every rehab hospital I had been to. All I remember about the neurocognitive assessment is that those two-and-a-half hours each day proved to be the most infuriating part of my visit to NIH. It felt like a test designed to illuminate my deficiencies. I could sense it wasn't going well because of my slow processing.

As it turns out, I would never truly uncover how I actually performed on that test.

My father, being the caregiver in charge of email communication with my doctors, determined it would be a blow to my self-confidence to see some truths about my brain. My parents were to meet the NIH doctors about their findings in the next day or two. To this day, my father refuses to show me the report the doctors wrote on NIH's neurocognitive assessment, leaving me baffled about whether my wise father is doing something ethically questionable by concealing his adult daughter's medical report or if it's wiser to guard my mental health in the quest to better my physical health. Despite my uncertainty, I have too much faith in Papa's wisdom to put up a fight.

As far as I know, my mother shares Papa's stance on this matter, as they've always maintained a united front, keeping any disagreements behind closed doors.

Not seeing the report didn't erase my lingering impression that the neurocognitive assessment had shown that I functioned well below the average. I felt a need to talk this through with people beyond my tight-knit circle of family and friends, who would naturally tell me what I wanted to hear. The trouble with me, though, is that I've always craved the truth, no matter how bitter. I reached out to Sidra, whose judgment I valued, and set up a coffee date to hash out the tension between my reality and my dreams. I was relieved to see Rósant had also chosen to join us at our favorite neighborhood French bakery.

After listening to my tale of woe, Rósant posed a hypothetical question.

"How do you know you'll fail out of Yale?"

Sidra didn't wait for my answer before shooting off another question.

"What do you consider worse, trying and failing, or not trying at all? Isn't *not* trying the same as failing?"

I cocked my head and stared into space for a moment. Sidra had given me something to think about. Placing my empty coffee cup back on the saucer, I hugged her tight and smiled warmly at Rósant.

My parents' faces were grave as they sat down to dinner that evening. I could sense the tension in the air as my father began to speak of their conversation with Dr. Dsurney on the implication of my performance on the neuropsychological test at NIH that day. The news was not good. I braced myself as my father delivered the crushing blow: according to Dr. Dsurney, my performance on the assessment indicated that I would face significant difficulties if I pursued a graduate-level program. But that's the extent of what my parents were willing to disclose. I begged and pleaded with them to reveal every concrete detail they had of my performance on that blasted assessment. I desperately craved hard evidence – data points, metrics, percentiles, scores, rankings – anything that could definitively unveil the truth of my ability to handle the rigors of graduate school.

"You don't need to know anything more, Pom. The meeting was long and even I couldn't understand it all," Papa said. "I have given you the key takeaway."

But there was something else. Something, my father said, that had taken them by surprise. After conferring with Dr. Dsurney, Dr. Shenouda – who had clearly taken the time to understand my case – ushered my parents into his office. He shut the door behind him and in a measured, reassuring tone, said:

"While it is true that graduate school will be a challenge for Tarini, I saw something remarkable in her during our interaction. Her determination is a powerful force, and coupled with the necessary accommodations she will require, as evident from the assessment, I firmly believe it will help her overcome any obstacles she may face."

As they recounted this story, my parents looked at me with quiet pride. For the first time after what felt like forever, I felt the first fragile tendrils of possibility take root.

We stood at a crossroads: continue relying on data and evidence for life's big decisions, or trust the gut instinct of a highly reputed medical professional – someone who had looked beyond the numbers to see possibility?

Recognizing that such decisions cannot be rushed, we opted to keep both paths open during our final two-plus years in DC. We were open to further data collection while exploring various untouched avenues in our quest before taking a final call on Yale. I tried vision therapy to improve my reading speed. Ten sessions of Rolfing – an alternative therapy, involving deep tissue massage to realign the body's energy field with the earth's gravitational field – followed. If that wasn't enough, we turned to acupuncture treatment (yes, again!), while modern medicine offered electromyography (EMG) – to uncover the shadows of my chronic pain, mapping the complex dialogue between nerve and muscle.

As we explored these interventions, it became evident there was no magic bullet. Instead, they merely served as reminders of the sustained commitment required not just from me, but from my entire family.

The choice between data and hope became clear – I would choose to hold on to hope to spur my actions toward a future of possibilities.

15

New Haven, New Possibilities

Returning from the office one evening, Papa sauntered up to me after setting his briefcase beside the kitchen counter with unusual deliberation. He had a look of incandescent calm on his face I hadn't seen in months. Then came the news that would reshape our horizons. Yale beckoned once again. The university wanted my father back when his term at the IMF ended.

"Pom," he said, locking eyes with mine, "apart from that one stroke of bad luck, good things have been happening ever since." His eyes twinkled with possibility. "Think of it – New Haven is welcoming us all back. You can get your MBA, I can teach, your Mama can audit interesting classes." He paused, smile widening. "And we'll be just a train ride away from the little fellow," he said, referring to my brother, who would be starting a dual master's degree at Wharton for his MBA and the Kennedy School at Harvard for his MPA.

My feeling of euphoria at the news collided with a kernel of doubt. *Was this possible? Could I, a woman with brain damage, become a graduate student at an Ivy League school? I simply have to take this magical opportunity that has literally fallen into my lap. I know I can do it … if only it wasn't for my cognitive slowness …*

Accepting the unwanted is a delicate balance between learning to accept what life throws at us and keeping our dreams alive. This acceptance unfolds in waves – over months, years, even lifetimes – with moments that either crush our spirits or fortify our resolve.

Trying to locate the exact instant I made peace with my altered path at Yale – one without walking, skipping, and running to class – is like chasing a shadow. In my mind, I reviewed my progress – and my challenges. Yes, I could walk, but with a slow and unsteady gait, leaning on a quad cane, for short distances at home. There were instances when my balance faltered, and I found myself on the ground. The weakness in my muscles and the non-functionality of my right arm would leave me grounded when I tumbled, requiring helping hands to guide me back to my feet. Although I didn't always need someone by my side when I walked indoors or during my forty-five-minute daily walking practice, the few falls I'd had had taught me to tolerate my parents' presence by my side when needed. When speed and time are the real constraints, my trusty wheelchair is my primary mode of transport for venturing out. It's a complex equation to solve: weighing safety against quality of life.

To this day, I continue to await my daily exercise routine with idiosyncratic enthusiasm, not only for the dissipation of my chronic pain but also for the unobjectionable break it affords. My ever-expanding podcast library continues to serve as added fuel – an ear to the world beyond.

Through trial and error, I had discovered the therapeutic power of temperature for pain management. For acute pain, ice or a cold pack became my ally, its soothing cold slowing the heated rush of blood flow to reduce swelling and alleviate discomfort. But when it came to chronic pain, heat proved the gentler healer. Though heat first greets with a sting, warmth's distraction becomes a meditation. Each night, I tucked a scorching heating pad under my foot – a ritual for coaxing sleep. Throughout the day, I learned to live alongside the disquiet of my cryptic pain, but there were rare moments of inexpressible agony when I just needed a break. Come nighttime, my mind ended its six-hour vigil, and I clung to my heating pad, waiting for my attention to be redirected from the paroxysm of pain coursing up my leg.

After countless hours of physical and occupational therapies, along with mind-numbing, repetitive practice, I can now tend to my personal care unassisted unless I desire speed. Much like a puzzle, I require each element of my environment to be precisely placed within reach for me to achieve a minimum level of independence. This need for precise arrangement in both my bedroom and bathroom have transformed travel from pleasure to puzzle. Without a trained attendant's presence – a role I once thought only my mother could fill – the journey to independence posed intricate challenges. Even with help, I require essential anchors of my independence – a perfectly positioned bath bench, strategically placed grab bars. Without carefully arranged supports, even familiar rhythms of self-care become a complex negotiation with unfamiliar space.

Privilege and misfortune make for strange bedfellows. Despite being born into a privileged family, my burdens were restraining forces, preventing me from fully exercising the fruits of my privilege. My parents were always there, ready to lend a hand to help me cope with some burdens, pushing me to take responsibility for the rest on my own. So when I decided to apply to Yale SOM, recognizing the complexity of the student visa process, my father stepped in to handle it for me, understanding that juggling multiple projects would be achingly difficult for me. He saw the fire burning within me and knew that with his help, I could, and would, shoulder the weight of all that was required for the application and the goals I'd set for myself.

Although my speech gradually regained more clarity since the early days after regaining consciousness, the injury to my brain has left the muscles on the right side of my body, including those in my face, weaker than their counterparts on the left. The disruption in the brain's signals to these muscles has led to slower speech and movements, occasionally causing my words to blend into each other. Nevertheless, I am more than willing to repeat myself to make sure my words aren't lost. For the gregarious, a brief moment of repetition is a small price to pay for being heard.

My recorded voice was a stranger to me, detached from the sound I heard in my head.

One can comprehend the challenge of reduced physical speed with relative ease. Anyone can picture the frustration of typing with their non-dominant hand or navigating the world with limited mobility. But, cognitive slowness – that's a puzzling path even for me. Day to day, I moved through conversations and routines like anyone else. Yet, when faced with complex new information, my brain demands more time for full understanding. Consider how I processed a professor's case studies in class. Understanding case studies requires the brain to draw all sorts of connections to understand the larger pattern emerging, a task made slower by the disrupted pathways in my brain. If the professor spoke fast, rushing through his explanation, I became a kite drifting close to the ground, unable to catch the wind, simply watching all the other kites soar.

That's why, at the idea of Yale becoming a reality, the ever-present question came back to haunt me: how would I get through business school?

My efforts to prepare myself were forever ongoing – I audited more classes, growing my ability to absorb new information. Nevertheless, when the material ventured into more obscure territory, my brain switched off, and the professor's words seemed as elusive as my Bharatanatyam skills. The greatest hindrance was not comprehension, but the pace at which I worked.

Yet, in seeking silver linings, I found solid ground in knowing all public institutions must bend to accommodate different ways of learning, their doors held open by the ADA's mandate. Options like a half-load whispered of a path forward. With that, I began envisioning not just survival, but success on my own terms.

"With Dr. Shenouda and Susan Davis's blessings, I'm ready to enroll in the next academic year," I announced to my parents with a quiet conviction that had been many years in the making. It had been five years since I first opened my eyes, and six since those bright New York days when I had initially planned to enroll in business school.

"That's Papa's Pom!" my father exclaimed, draping his arm around my shoulder. "But, as I've always said, we need to take things step by step."

I looked at him quizzically.

"First, we should meet with the dean of Yale SOM to make sure they will allow you to complete your MBA in four years instead of two, as NIH has advised," Papa said. "And we need to address the accommodations you'll need to function on the same playing field as your peers."

I was all too aware of my limitations and I knew I'd need all the help I could get.

"In the accounting class at George Washington," I reminded my father, "I learned I would need assistance with note-taking since I can't type fast with my left hand."

My father wagged his finger at me.

"You always focus on what you can't do instead of what you can. You were in touch with the head of Yale's Office of Disabilities when you were admitted in 2012," he reminded me. "Why not write to her again? What's her name – Judy York?"

Just then, my mother walked in, carrying two large paper bags bursting with groceries.

"How do you feel about the move to Yale, Mama?" I asked, eager to hear her thoughts.

Mama balanced the grocery bags on her left arm and rested her right hand on her hip. "It would be great if everything works out," she replied, a hint of a smile playing on her lips. "But we need to carefully plan our next move. We need to be mindful of Nani and Nana's care."

I felt a pang of guilt as I realized the unintended consequences of the decision my parents had made for my benefit. My maternal grandparents, one in her late eighties and the other in his early nineties, were very dear to us, and I realized I hadn't fully considered the impact of our decision on them. I closed my eyes, feeling overwhelmed.

Papa sensed the tension in the room and tried to calm us down.

"We'll do what's best for everyone. Let's wait for more information before making any decisions."

Taking the exit for Trumbull Street, with Papa at the wheel, we pulled into New Haven to meet with the dean at the School of Management and Judy York at the Disabilities Office. Passing the familiar sights of students loitering on the New Haven Green and at the Starbucks on Temple Street quieted my jumpy nerves. 360 State was right around the corner, too.

"Will we live at 360 State again if we move here?" I asked my parents, looking up at the tall building.

"Most probably. It's conveniently located, and fully accessible for you," Papa said. "But I will also look for other, more affordable, accessible alternatives."

"Tarini, look up! Mama said, craning her neck and jamming her index finger against the rolled-down window. "There's your fancy new school," Her voice brimmed with pride.

I stared in awe at the magnificent sight of Evans Hall, its shimmering glass façade reflecting the sunlight in a blinding display of radiance, casting prismatic reflections onto the street. It was as if I was seeing a mirage, a distant dream that had finally materialized from the polished images of the university's promotional materials.

We entered the building, my parents taking turns to push my manual wheelchair. The sleek new building of the Yale School of Management felt like a futuristic dream world compared to the historic buildings of stone I was used to seeing at Yale. At the front desk, a petite woman with a neatly cropped teeny-weeny afro greeted us with a warm smile. Her navy blue dress was adorned with bright yellow flowers, a burst of color against the muted tones of the lobby. Her titanium-rimmed glasses glinted in the light as she walked us to the dean's office.

As we made our way through the bustling atrium, I felt a bit like an imposter, an outsider looking in. Students darted around us, most with cups of coffee, lost in their own worlds. Some stood in clusters, deep in animated discussion. The hum of their voices created a buzz in the air that felt electric. I longed to be one of them, to blend in seamlessly with the crowd.

I was captivated by the atrium's architecture – streams of natural light poured in through surrounding glass windows, dancing off polished surfaces, giving a sense of a modern art museum rather than a business school. If my movement hadn't been in my parents' hands, I would have lingered there in that spacious hall, watching my future unfold before me.

Lost in my thoughts, I was jolted back to reality when Kimberly, the receptionist, knocked on the dean's door and ushered us in with a smile.

A man of Indian origin, dressed in what looked like a freshly dry-cleaned suit, introduced himself as Dean Anjani Jain. His large forehead, accentuated by thinning black hair, gave him a wise and earnest appearance. With a big smile, the dean looked me in the eye and congratulated me on my admission to Yale SOM, acknowledging the uphill battle I'd faced to get here. It was heartening to know that the school's leadership recognized that I wasn't your typical MBA student. I wondered how far they would go to enable me to function as unimpeded as my peers. Would they truly accept my differences?

As Dean Jain began the meeting, he looked directly at me and categorically stated that it was his responsibility to ensure all my needs were met now that I had been accepted into the school and intended to enroll. It was refreshing to be addressed directly – a welcome change from the typical interactions with doctors and therapists in India, who spoke to my parents about me while I sat right there, as if I belonged to a different species, incapable of understanding what was being said.

In turn, I told Dean Jain about the accommodations the NIH physicians had deemed necessary: a schedule with no back-to-back classes to allow me time to process new learning, only one quantitative class a day, and a reduced course load. Dean Jain's eyes were alert behind the glasses perched on his nose. He followed up his last sentence by informing us that the school didn't have a precedent of a student taking a half-load. I placed my palm over my chest, and smiled tentatively at him. The dean paused before he spoke again – I fervently hoped he wasn't about to give up on me because of the additional work I would impose on the school.

But in the next moment, eliminating any remaining ambiguity, Dean Jain reached across the table to shake my hand and warmly welcome me to Yale SOM once more. Enabled by the provisions in the Americans with Disabilities Act, they had decided they could allow me to work toward my MBA in four years instead of the usual two. His handshake implied a reassuring certainty, and I felt a sudden rush of joy that left me feeling weightless, suspended in the air.

My heart soared on newfound wings. *My most audacious dream is becoming a reality.* I was all set to be a graduate student. After further reflection, I informed the admissions office that I would indeed enroll in 2016, confirming that it would take me twice as long, four years instead of two, to graduate with my MBA from the Yale School of Management.

It had taken six long years, but through relentless effort and the invaluable support of scores of people who cared, I found that good luck isn't just stumbled upon, it could also be created.

My family and I returned to New Delhi in the winter of 2015 to spend time with my grandparents before I started the orientation program at SOM. Stepping back into their world felt like slipping into an old sweater – the kind whose comfort deepens with time. Their slow mornings unfolded in long-established rituals, each of them settling in their trademark spots in their sunlit living room, as we waited for their faithful cook to whip up a simple breakfast of wholesome scrambled eggs, served with sun-ripened fruits. The afternoons held their own rhythm. I sat reading beside Nani, while Nana stood at his easel, absorbed in painting a bandwala with a trumpet, already playing out a tune in his imagination.

To my delight, Pallavi, now engaged to Ishan, would be married the same winter in India. It was a stroke of luck that my closest friend's wedding would coincide with my trip home.

One day, while chatting with Pallavi, she casually mentioned that she and Ishan had picked Neemrana Fort Palace as their wedding venue.

"Have you heard of it?" she asked.

My stomach knotted. How could my best friend just "steal" my dream wedding destination without even consulting me?

"I'm so excited! It's going to be perfect!" Pallavi screeched in glee, oblivious to my discomfort.

"You *know* that I've heard of Neemrana. Nikhil and I were planning to have our wedding there," I finally said, through gritted teeth.

There was a pause on the other end of the line.

"I didn't know that," Pallavi said, sounding surprised.

I took a deep breath, trying to keep my emotions in check.

"I have talked to you about it a million times before," I said, an unexpected mix of anger and sadness creeping over me.

"I don't remember," Pallavi said, her voice trailing off.

"I just wish you had cleared it with me first."

"I'm sorry," Pallavi said. "I didn't realize it was such a big deal to you."

I took a deep breath and tried to be understanding.

"It's fine," I said, my voice softer now. "I'll try to be happy for you, but it's going to be tough being there with Nikhil."

"I understand," Pallavi said. Her tone made me feel like her hand was on my shoulder, full of comfort. "And I will completely understand if you choose not to come."

I nodded, a cocktail of emotions swirling within me – anger, sadness, disappointment, joy. It was a dicey situation, and I had yet to unpack whether to be grateful for or mad at Pallavi. In the meantime my instincts kicked in – I realized I couldn't let one incident ruin our deep friendship. Deep down, a persistent inner voice chastised me for my pettiness in harboring anger toward Pallavi. A part of me understood that this anger was likely rooted in an unconscious sense of insecurity tied to noticing my friends' lives progressing in ways that mine wasn't.

"No worries, Pallavi," I assured her, "Neemrana is so close to Delhi – of course, I'll be there for your wedding," I said.

My parents winced when I told them the location Pallavi had chosen for her wedding – for different reasons.

"Neemrana is extremely inaccessible. It'll be very difficult for you to manage," they warned me. And they were right. One of them, they informed me, would need to accompany me. I loved my parents but not so much their laps.

My Norwegian friend, Maggie, from Wellesley, who was also invited to Pallavi's wedding, offered to share a room with me and help in whatever way she could. Another dear friend from MUWCI offered to ride to Neemrana with me and my father in case an extra pair of hands would help. My father would be present throughout, but with so many friends around, he could keep a low profile.

I let out a breath I hadn't known I was holding.

I looked in awe at the ancient structure of Neemrana Fort Palace, towering above us, its red sandstone and granite walls adorned with intricate carvings and latticed windows. The fort's exterior was tinged with rust and amber hues, while lush green foliage clung to its walls. My attention quickly shifted to the steep, uneven stairs leading up to the entrance, underscoring the stark reality of my exclusion from such places. The guards, wearing traditional Rajasthani garb, stood tall and proud at the entrance, their hands folded in namaste. Only now did I begin to digest the truth that I couldn't properly explore the fort in all its splendor.

Still, entranced by the history and architecture surrounding us, I stopped caring about the steep incline and jagged steps before me for just a moment. A palanquin, my trusty driver, Vinod, and a team of sturdy porters helped me navigate the countless hurdles within the fort. Maggie welcomed me into our room with a warm hug, making me feel like a queen in this stunning fortress.

After settling into our room, I climbed back into the palanquin, eager to see Pallavi. Maggie accompanied us, clearing the path ahead as we made our way. Upon catching my first glimpse of Pallavi on the eve of her wedding day, I remember being struck by the serene contentment on her face, as if nothing around her could touch her. I felt a warm fuzzy feeling in my heart, but beneath it lurked a whisper of loss, a recognition that our friendship was about to shift into something new and unknown. Among the crowd of guests were familiar faces from our New York days – friends I had once brought into Pallavi's orbit – and I gravitated toward them, hoping their company would serve as a distraction.

I was lost in conversation when I felt a tap on my shoulder. I turned to see Nikhil, carrying his signature gray and red backpack and pulling a small black stroller. We hadn't seen each other in months. Although we remained in touch, our interactions had grown less intense. The passage of time, none of it shared, had created an unspoken distance between us, and in some ways, it made things easier. Despite feeling some resentment at how quickly Nikhil had replaced me, I could now focus on how good he'd been to me after my accident, even after our separation. My longing for Nikhil as a partner on its way to fading, was now replaced by vivid memories of our time together, forever preserved like pressed flowers between pages. Both Nikhil and I now felt, and continue to feel, that our love for each other didn't vanish but may have simply shifted form.

He sat beside me at each of Pallavi's wedding functions in Neemrana, including the one where she had chosen me as one of the four wedding speakers – yes, despite my slurred, and halting speech.

> I think of Pallavi as not just my best friend, but as family, having had such a close association with her for so long – since the eleventh grade. I have always been amazed by Pallavi's ability to be as good a friend as she is to lots of people here, no matter where in the world they are based. We managed to stay in close contact with one another all through college, back in the day of flip phones, and ended up being in NYC when we graduated. Naturally, we became roommates as soon as we could ...
>
> ... At this stage, I hope for just one tiny thing – that, Pallavi, you have reconsidered your reaction to something I said to you back in 2005. You see, I had been struck by Ishan's dashing good looks and the suaveness of his way back when we met in Jaipur. And when I conveyed my thoughts to Pallavi, she said, "Are you kidding me, Tarins?!" Above all else, the key takeaway from this is: Tarini is always right!

At my best friend's wedding, I felt like a boat anchored in place, watching the world surge past carried by a swift current. From my vantage point below the raised dance floor, I had become almost invisible in the swirl of celebration – until my dear friend's keen eyes found me, and suddenly many hands were lifting me, chair and all, to where Pallavi gestured for me to join her. She spun around my chair, and I swayed my shoulders and bobbed my functioning arm to the beat. Then, with Pallavi's firm grip on my shoulders, I rose from my chair to be locked in a tight hug as I shimmied to the music the best I could. Holding her right shoulder, I leaned close to plant a kiss on her cheek and laughed when I saw Ishan, watching and snapping photos of the precious moment – a snapshot that now holds pride of place on my wall, preserving that perfect confluence of friendship, music, and motion …

It has often occurred to me that I would do well to adopt the Buddhist teaching of *mudita*, or sympathetic joy. *Mudita* is the joy you feel in others' good fortune, which may sound like the most human thing to do, but it's not that easy in practice. It requires feeling pure joy, untarnished by self-interest or comparison, irrespective of the tragedy in one's own life. As my old friends and peers from my early twenties got married, had children, and moved forward in their lives, I slowly realized I had to acknowledge that I was no longer swimming in the same current. While intellectually, I appreciate the benefits of *mudita*, its user manual isn't quite so easy to comprehend and follow. From my understanding of the concept, to truly practice *mudita* is to feel a genuine empathy without slipping into comparisons. It's to recognize that the joy of others doesn't detract from our own and that each of us is on our own unique path. It could help me conserve my friendships and live a happier life – one where comparison takes a back seat. But in the age of social media, when everyone's life is a highlight reel, avoiding comparison can be an exhausting task (trust me, I'm still at it!).

I have come to see that the serendipitous occurrence of Pallavi's wedding – and my presence in Delhi at the same time – as something more than mere chance; perhaps what Carl Jung, the Swiss analytical psychologist, called "synchronicity".[12] According to Jung, seemingly random events don't just occur by chance, but are intimately connected to the observers' inner worlds, including their thoughts, emotions, and dreams. The concept of synchronicity suggests that Pallavi and I are linked through the meaningful coincidence of her wedding date – though its full meaning remains just beyond my grasp. Jung encourages us to be mindful of the insights we can glean from such events, as they can help us learn something about our internal world. While I still can't fully comprehend the significance of this connection, I hold on to the belief that there exists an inexplicable intertwining of Pallavi's and my own "collective unconscious".[13]

16

Wings of Knowledge

My business school journey first took shape in the digital realm, through a class Facebook page where new bonds began to form. I was immediately drawn to an attractive Asian-American woman named Christine, whose virtual presence radiated a magnetic blend of warmth and self-assurance. I looked her up on Facebook, and my heart lifted when I discovered our shared Wellesley roots. I composed a message to Christine, my fingers dancing across keys with a newfound purpose. Within minutes, I received a warm reply. A smile touched the corner of my lips, the knots in my stomach loosened. *This*, I thought, *this I can still do.* My ability to make friends would stand me in good stead as I began a new chapter, in a landscape of unknowns.

Settling into our apartment at 360 State Street in New Haven, I found myself reunited with a piece of my independence – my power wheelchair. My first act of freedom was to go to G Cafe, now occupying Cafe Bru's old space, for one of life's simple pleasures still beyond my reach in India: showing up alone in my wheelchair and ordering my own coffee. Regaining the freedom to act on a whim made me feel alive again.

Though I was officially a part of the class of 2018, it would take me twice as long to graduate. I would eventually do so with the class of 2020. When I informed Student and Academic Services at SOM that attending class at 8.30 a.m. would be a challenge for me, their response came as a gentle surprise – they rewrote their usual rules, crafting a schedule that sidestepped the early 8.30 classes to accommodate the extra time I needed for personal care and the ritual of my essential daily exercise routine. Still, for my first class, starting at 10.10 a.m., I'd wake up at 7 a.m. to complete my morning routine. This routine unfolded like a well-worn script: bed exercises flowing into time on the recumbent bike in the gym, followed by the lengthy process of showering and dressing unassisted. Yet, I always made sure to carve out time to grab a coffee on my way to class – a daily reminder of my reclaimed independence.

Yale's Disabilities Office had an ingenious solution for arranging note-taking: they would offer above-market wages to students for sharing their class notes – turning a potential burden into an opportunity. Taking notes for those needing assistance would require no extra effort from the notetakers since they'd be capturing the same notes for themselves. The system showed Yale's commitment to transforming its students' disabilities into abilities. I felt seen by SOM – as not just a person with disabilities, but as an individual with the right to inhabit the classroom. The school was stitching wings for me to fly.

Despite being thankful for the help I'd be receiving, a familiar shadow of doubt crept in – the knowledge that my academic success would depend, in part, on others.

On the first day of class, my new Venezuelan classmate, Claudia, who would later become a dear friend, skipped up to me with infectious energy, her long auburn curls bouncing behind her. She introduced herself as my note-taker.

Claudia and I were paired again as members of the same "learning team" – the intimate group of eight first-years meant to tackle the core courses together. I wrestled with how to be forthcoming about my limitations, knowing they could impact our collective work if left unaddressed. Finally, gathering my courage, I met each teammate's gaze and shared my truth. To my surprise, in place of the hesitation and judgment I'd feared, I found immediate support and understanding. They didn't just offer to take on the group's in-class presentations but also offered to redistribute our collective strengths.

"We're a team," they insisted, "and this is exactly what business school is all about – how to work together, differences and all, to create something greater than ourselves."

With Claudia, I felt an instant sense of trust. To help me with note-taking, she devised an elegant solution using cloud software, allowing me to see the notes she took in real time. Although, at the time, laptops were generally not allowed in most SOM classes due to concerns about easy distraction, Yale made an exception for me. They recognized how vital it was for me to capture what I heard the professor say – alongside Claudia's notes – to improve my retention. Typing out notes for me in class also saved Claudia time from having to transcribe handwritten notes for me later.

All the pieces to optimize my classroom experience were now in place: the use of my laptop while my classmates bent over notebooks, and Claudia's note-taking support. Yet sometimes the current of the lecture moved too fast for me to catch, especially when the material was complex and ventured into unfamiliar waters. At first, the lectures on valuations in Corporate Finance flowed over my head with too swift a current. You'd think that having worked at Morgan Stanley, this topic would be second nature. But my years of analyzing metrics simply failed to translate into the deeper understanding I now needed.

The professor painted a scenario of a video rental store, explaining that it launched at a certain value, and the owners were now comparing this valuation to projected cash flows for the business. Then she casually turned to the class and hit us with rapid-fire questions: How would you estimate the value of the project? What if it's all equity? What if part of it is in debt? And how about with a fixed leverage ratio?

Watching other students' hands shoot up while others leaned back with smug, self-assured expressions offered little comfort; I was often left sitting in my own pocket of stillness, staring into space, trying to weave concepts together as the lecture raced ahead. Thoughts of failure flooded my mind, and as the class wrapped up, I occasionally left the classroom feeling defeated. Even more discouraging were the times when I thought I'd grasped the material presented, then found myself unable to explain particular lecture details to friends, even just shortly after the class ended.

When I noticed these instances becoming a trend, a family consultation brought me back to the NIH experts' advice I'd been neglecting – the time-tested practice of immediate review. It was like filling a leaky bucket with knowledge. So, I swallowed the bitter pill of tearing myself away from lively after-class conversations and dragged myself to the library, where I reviewed Claudia's notes while memories were still fresh. I remember having to consciously remind myself of the NIH experts' emphasis on repetitive training of the mind to help it form long-term memories and cement new learning, making it easier to tear myself away from more joyous activities. Common sense is not so common after all – it requires much discipline and consistency to cultivate.

During the first week of classes, one evening, nearly all my classmates were planning to go to a bar called "Elm City Social" on College Street. So was I.

Turning left to enter the bar, my eyes were immediately drawn to a woman wearing a white backless top, moving through groups of people with ease while simultaneously commanding their attention. It was Christine, my virtual friend from Wellesley, now even more vibrant in three dimensions. At orientation, I'd watched her natural leadership, and now I was intrigued. As luck would have it, she was talking to two attractive men. *Maybe this will be the night I finally get Nikhil out of my head*, I thought, grinning to myself.

Nikhil's presence in my mind had only dimmed, not disappeared. I refrained from talking out my feelings about him, believing that silence might deny them substance. I willfully ignored the thoughts that lingered in my mind, convincing myself that if nobody knew, then it wasn't real.

"No, Tarini," Pallavi had cautioned, "you should know that that's a sure-shot way of developing mental health issues." She paused, before proceeding to voice her thoughts. "Talk to me. Tell me anything. I promise my lips are sealed, and besides, I will always be on your side!" Her words struck a chord. I knew she was right. So, I opened up to her, voicing my thoughts, worries, plans, desires, and judgments of the day. But to no one other than Pallavi.

"My self-confidence would surely take a beating if I pursued a new man," I told Pallavi. By and by, I made peace with my evolving reality as I realized I was fairly possessive of the self-confidence I had worked so hard to regain while coming somewhat to terms with my injury. Having experienced a loss of self-confidence once before, I was now in a good place, and wouldn't risk losing it for a second time.

Yet, I cannot deny the quiet pull of connection, whether it manifests as a partnership or friendship. I will always keep my heart open to finding someone who sees me for who I am – and also meets my high standards.

For now, though, I found myself edging closer to Christine and the two cute men, the bar's energy swirling around us. Loud rap lyrics and hip-hop beats blared through the speakers. I could hear Drake and Lil Wayne drawling over the beat.

We walk the same path but got on different shoes,

Live in the same building but we got different views.[14]

I patted Christine on her bare back. She turned around, and on seeing me, her jaw dropped.

"Girl, you look fine!" she hollered, leaning forward to give me a kiss.

I guess my eyeliner did the trick, I thought, glancing down at my plain peach top.

"Have you met Garrett and DC yet?" she asked, pointing at the two men.

I introduced myself, practically shouting, hoping to be audible over the blaring music. But since I could barely hear myself, on my third try, I simply smiled and nodded. Disregarding my silent introduction, Garrett and DC leaned in closer, asking me to repeat my name for them.

Would I have a new identity constructed by people who didn't have a notion of my loud and gregarious pre-accident self? Was my identity devoid of my past self now? Should it be? Is that what moving on entails? What was it about fully inhabiting the present moment that unsettled me? Can an identity be crafted by someone other than oneself, like Frank Duchamp did for the urinal through his well-known "sculpture" of the inverted urinal? Duchamp had altered the urinal's identity from an object into a work of art through a simple change in perspective. Perhaps, like that mundane fixture turned masterpiece, I too, would survive.

After barely fifteen minutes in the deafening bar area, DC suggested we move to the room at the back to chat where we could actually hear one another. Soon enough, DC and I discovered we shared a striking commonality: we'd both traveled to Damascus before the Arab Spring. We reminisced about the beauty of that now-devastated city and in our nostalgia, forged an instant bond. With classmates as cosmopolitan as this, I figured fitting in should be no problem. Garrett offered to get drinks for the group.

"Sure," Christine yelled. As for me, I hoped to end the conversation by shaking my head, but Garrett appeared unconvinced, responding with a shrug and a raised eyebrow.

I hesitated and took a deep breath before speaking.

"I can't drink," I said slowly, "because of my medication." It was only a small part of the truth. The real reason was much more complicated, and not something I was ready to share with new acquaintances, and that too, at a noisy bar. How could I explain that my injury made my balance precarious and that even a little alcohol could have disastrous consequences?

My medication is meant to quell my chronic pain – a pain that has proven itself a maze with no clear exit, a labyrinthine journey of trial and error through various medications. Despite consultations with neurologist after neurologist, I still feel lost and unsure of how to dispel the interminable discomfort. The low-dose antidepressant they prescribed to combat the relentless pain – a pain that still keeps my senses and mind on high alert – is but a compass, pointing me in the correct direction but never leading me out of the maze. Five years since the chronic pain first surfaced, in 2011, I had been maneuvering through the twisting paths and, finally, stumbled upon a route that seemed to promise, if not complete freedom, then at least some relief. The choice before me was clear: to truly live life, with all its trials, or succumb to a shadow-existence defined by pain. That was an easy one. I would push past the pain until I couldn't.

As the night wore on, I glanced at my watch with a start. It was already 11.20 p.m.

Few, if any, grad students in the US live with their parents. I had promised my anxious mother I would not be out much later than 11.30 p.m. With a heavy heart, I bid everyone a hasty goodbye. Although I knew that I needed support at home for an indisputable reason, there were still moments when I felt ashamed of living with my parents, much like a child.

Even as a teenager, before I escaped to MUWCI, I had to make up stories for my parents to stay out late. I would say I was spending the night at a friend's place, as Mama always had concerns about late-night partying, both for my safety and because of her traditional mindset. Now, at twenty-nine, I needed more of my parents' support than I had at fifteen, and I didn't want to cause any unpleasantness in the house. My poor balance meant they felt safer being awake until I was safely in bed to make sure there was no risk of me losing my balance and hurting myself in the process. Depending on the severity of the fall, it could be an all-night affair.

As I waited alone in the dim glow of the streetlight, hoping the shuttle would come soon, I couldn't help but reflect on the tightrope my life had become – suspended between the intoxicating freedom of the adulthood I craved and the security I still silently relied on from my parents. It seemed like I had to choose either mental well-being or physical safety.

I felt a hand gently touch my shoulder and turned to find DC there.

"I'm here," he said, "if you need any help. Otherwise, just ignore me. I just feel better being here." His kindness, so genuine and unprompted, caught me off guard. I felt a tendril of warmth unfurl in my heart and I opened my left arm, inviting him in for a hug. If this was the effect alcohol had on DC, I wished he'd always have a drink in hand. This moment, I'd soon come to realize, was but a glimpse of who he was. We waited together outside the bar for Yale's Disability Shuttle, which finally arrived around 11.50 p.m.

My heart was pounding as the shuttle pulled into my building. Would I get an earful from Mama? Weary of the fireworks awaiting me, I had no choice but to turn my key in the lock and go in. Mama was sitting upright on the edge of the sofa, her eyebrows tightly knit and her face taut.

"Hi, Mama, why are you sitting here?" I asked, unable to hide my irritation.

"Waiting for you," Mama replied in a strained voice.

To avoid a potential argument at so late an hour, I wheeled myself to the charging point for my wheelchair.

"Well, I'm home safe. We can both go to bed now."

Mama got up to plug my wheelchair into the socket that was too low for me to reach. She remained by my side as I rose from my wheelchair.

"Thank you very much. I've been wanting to go to bed for a while now. This is not going to work if you come home at such a late hour . . ."

This was not the time to assess the merits and shortcomings of my mother's overprotective nature, and I certainly wasn't about to admit that, in times of need, her character often shone through as a godsend, eclipsing any other source of support. No, at that moment, incapable of weighing the significance of things, I rolled my eyes the best I could in response.

"Mama, you are being completely unfair," I said. I then paused, locking eyes with my mother. "It's not unusual for a grad student to come home a little late."

She stared back, waiting for me to continue. I took a breath, trying to remain calm.

"And midnight is hardly late," I added in a slightly softer voice. "You go to bed around then, anyway. What's a few minutes here and there?" I let the words hang in the air, before finishing. "I just want to remind you that I am nearly thirty years old."

I wished my father would emerge from his bedroom to back me up. After all, he had experienced a more typical student life, complete with late nights and rowdy fun. Instead, I heard loud snores emanating from his room, the door of which he'd left ajar. Had he emerged, I'm certain that his logical demeanor would have calmed us down, though he would have presented a united front with Mama.

It was Rasoo who would have unfailingly had my back, but he no longer lived with us as he was pursuing his MBA at Wharton.

My mother sighed, her shoulders slumping as if the weight of my words were taking their toll.

"This is very difficult for me," she began, in a voice that seemed on the verge of tears. "Having to alter my life at this age, leave my aged parents, and move away from my home country ..." She trailed off in search of the right words. "I would just appreciate a little respect."

"That was your choice, Mama," I shot back in a heartbeat. "One that I had appreciated. Until now."

I wanted to storm into my room and slam my door shut to unleash the frustration building inside me. Instead, I could only plod slowly, each step punctuated with the rhythmic thump of my walking stick against the floor – its echo filling the silent house. I didn't know how to – or rather, couldn't – express my anger, except peacefully, through tears. *I am already so different from my peers. I want to show them that I am like them – a regular, fun person.*

The next morning, a giant bowl of low-fat yogurt topped with a generous helping of blueberries, walnuts, golden raisins, and granola awaited me at the breakfast table. As unfair as I thought Mama had acted last night, her devotion to her family and her knack for conjuring mouth-watering blueberry parfaits daily never ceased to amaze me. I guess you could say her culinary creations gave me the opportunity for both introspection and digestion, so much so that the previous evening's altercation was swept aside.

Managing one's personhood while balancing the needs of one's primary caregivers often feels like a delicate dance, especially when the rhythms don't align. While my peers grapple with the complex choreography of raising children, "adulting" for me has its own intricate routine – learning to safeguard my independence while honoring and reciprocating my parents' care, even amid profound frustration.

At moments like these, I worry about the inherent unpredictability of life and how my family's good fortune could turn in an instant. I have witnessed the reality of sudden misfortune firsthand, and I often reflect on how dependent I am on my family, both physically and emotionally. What will my life be like without them? As the clock ticks on, something is bound to happen to my parents – all our parents.

Chewing on a spoonful of granola, my thoughts drifted to how much I've already gone through, and how my parents had coped with the outsized grief of nearly losing a child. Lost in thought at the breakfast table that day, I felt a strange, almost meditative sense of calm as I heard water flowing from the faucet. The familiar sounds of my mother pottering around in the kitchen behind me felt soothing. I need to armor myself with the hope that once propelled me forward, even if that hope had been based on ignorance. Hope is the antidote we all need in the face of uncertainty. I have to choose to believe the days ahead will be better. Nobody will deny that the sudden loss of one's abilities and loved ones is both tragic and unexpected. How we cope with tragedies cannot be planned. Each day, I remind myself: live your truth.

"Mama! Stop your bothersome pottering," I said with an affectionate lilt.

Scraping the remaining avocado off its peel, Mama looked up, and in a matter-of-fact tone said, "I have to potter. I am preparing salad for my *nyari* to take for lunch."

Okay, I'll give it to her. Her spinach and avocado salads were to die for, too.

From evenings savoring New Haven's restaurants and humming bars, to quiet afternoons in SOM's sunlit library poring over Claudia's impeccable notes and gathering with the learning team for weekly group assignments – before I could catch my breath, my first year at Yale had dissolved into memory.

The need to request help to understand class material initially made me shrink within myself. I only learned to reach out for guidance from peer tutors when I overheard familiar voices discussing *their own* peer tutors. Upon turning to see who was speaking, I discovered something surprising – it was my classmates – the very ones I'd imagined had sailed effortlessly through concepts – discussing how they worked through problems with their tutors. In that moment, something shifted: I realized reaching out wasn't surrender but rather a kind of courage, an acknowledgment of our shared human need to learn together. Why struggle in silence when someone out there is willing to lend a hand?

My accident has taught me a hard truth: we aren't meant to weather every storm alone. But internalizing that hasn't been easy. Only much later would I recognize the saboteur lurking within: internalized ableism. Internalized ableism burrows deep, a quiet poison that whispers unwanted truths about ourselves. When these toxic beliefs hold sway, they devolve into self-discrimination, making us question our own worth. My frequent need to justify my presence in those halls reflected something darker: the shadow of society's message that disability somehow lessens us; that it's a flaw to be overcome rather than simply another way of being human.

Guided by peer tutors' wisdom ever since that first quarter of business school, my grades reflected what was possible when I set pride aside and didn't hesitate to use the free tutoring service on offer. As my grades rolled in, quarter after quarter, my confidence grew.

I entered the first class of my second year with practiced confidence. But beneath the surface, I felt a shifting unease. A new chapter was beginning with the class of 2019. I knew I would have to build new connections. I worried about misconceptions – that these new faces might assume I was repeating my first year because I'd failed. I needed a crew that understood my journey and would have my back, and I, theirs. These new classmates – the class of 2019 – would be my companions for two full years. I would watch them graduate before spending my final year completing electives with the next class, the class of 2020. Questions swirled in my mind: Would my new note-taker measure up to Claudia? Would I have as formidable a learning team as my previous one? Could I find incredible friends? While DC, Garrett, Christine, Vance, Saee, Aashna, my fantastic learning team, and the rest of my remarkable first-year crew moved forward into their second year, I remained behind.

In my usual spot at the front of the room, I waited to see if anybody would join me on the first day of class. That's when Madeline, a soft-spoken, angelic-looking young woman tiptoed into the class and took the seat beside me. Little did I know then that she was not only my assigned note-taker for the year but was also a member of my learning team, just like Claudia had been. It was just another reminder of the safety net of support Yale extends to its students, providing us with a web of resources to lift us over any hurdles we may face.

My gaze caught on a newcomer as he entered the room – a handsome face with hints of South Asian descent. Upon scanning the room, he settled into the empty seat beside me in the front row.

"Andrew Mulherkar," he offered with an easy smile, "from Seattle." Just as I'd sensed, he carried the familiar duality of Indian American heritage, a blend of cultures I knew intimately. There was something disarming about Andrew's presence, an authenticity that seemed to dissolve the usual barriers between strangers.

Something in his unaffected manner drew me in, and I found myself leaning slightly forward, letting curiosity guide me.

"You mentioned that you lived in New York before business school," I started. "Which neighborhood?"

His answer – Brooklyn – pulled a smile from me, opening a door to conversation.

"I love the jazz scene there," I shared. Something shifted in his expression – surprise, changing quickly to pure delight.

"You like jazz? No way!" His voice carried a new energy. "I play the saxophone. Used to play shows in New York."

Within seconds, a treasured catalog of names flowed from my memory.

"John Coltrane, Charlie Parker, Wynton Marsalis!' I rattled off names of saxophonists whose music I had liked when my father played his records at home. They were the musicians who had shaped my understanding of the art, their names tumbling out in quick succession.

I watched Andrew's expression shift like notes in a jazz progression – from surprise to a kind of delighted disbelief – at finding a kindred spirit in business school, who could talk Bebop.

The professor's throat-clearing caught our attention as he took center stage. As class began, I felt comforted by the presence of the half-Indian saxophonist with his easy manner and shared love of jazz music. Something about him whispered of friendship to come.

My mind drifted briefly to Dhaval and Nikhil – their deep influence on my tastes and character remains intact long past their "absence", proof that our pasts remain as essential to who we are, as roots to trees.

As we packed up to leave, I felt Andrew's light tap on my shoulder.

"Later?" he mouthed, and I nodded, feeling the morning stillness dissolve into something electric and alive. The day suddenly hummed with possibility – and no, this wasn't connected to SOM's generous supply of eye candy!

T.S. Eliot's lines floated in my mind, speaking directly to the untouched promise of that morning.

The river bears no empty bottles, sandwich papers,
Silk handkerchiefs, cardboard boxes, cigarette ends
Or other testimony of summer nights . . .[15]

As I embarked on my second year at SOM, I slogged through the drudgery of coursework while still catching up on the first-year core curriculum at my own pace. But gradually, the curriculum began to offer more intriguing lessons. Numbers may have danced beyond my easy grasp, but I knew that the heart of business beats to more than just accounting and finance.

I saw my future in catalyzing change, and an MBA offered me a different kind of power: the art of inspiring teams beyond the usual "disability-related" inspiration, shaping visions into structured pathways, and turning ideas into actionable projects in the social sector. While others might excel at calculating net present values, I saw myself mastering the human equations: learning to weave individual strengths into a collective force, turning resources into lasting impact, and building bridges between vision and reality. I knew that it was not just about numbers and spreadsheets, but also about understanding the heartbeat of an organization – the hopes and dreams of its people.

Yet, beyond these practical tools, education ignites something deeper within. Each class discussion, each case study, and each group presentation stretched the boundaries of my thinking. The prospect of exploring my first elective courses, Business Ethics and Non-Market Strategy, left me with a renewed sense of excitement but still promised endless hours of work.

Amid the grind, I found joy in helping Andrew carve out his niche in the music scene at Yale – and mine with it. As his self-appointed saxophone agent, I carefully orchestrated his foray into the world of musicianship at business school. House shows at friends' apartments became our playground, and I spared no effort in creating buzz for the events with flyers, which we distributed with a curated guest list. Meanwhile, Andrew had also found his groove in an a-cappella group – the Economies of Scale – composed of four other exceptional musicians. I grew close to many of them, particularly Josh, the bass guitarist.

With each passing day, the bond between Andrew, Josh, and myself grew stronger, so much so that I affectionately dubbed them my "Sweethearts", similar to how DC, Garrett, and Vance were my class of 2018 Sweethearts.

The contrast between the isolation I had previously endured and the bustling camaraderie of my present was nothing short of heart-lifting. SOM wasn't just an education, it was a form of liberation.

17

Baptism by Fire

As the Thanksgiving of 2017 approached, excitement about the annual Harvard–Yale football game, to be held at Yale this year, filled the air. Known as "The Game", it had been held at Harvard the previous year, and as much as I had longed to join my friends in Boston, a place I knew well, I was forced to hold back, given the complex arrangements required for me to travel. In this case, it's paradoxical that my heavy yet fragile US power wheelchair was among the many formidable barriers preventing me from navigating the world freely. Far too heavy. Too heavy for even weightlifters' arms to hoist into a regular car. The only option for me to reach Boston was by the mercy of an accessible taxi; its ramp a bridge to a life I wanted to reclaim. The cruel twist? Accessible taxis charge double their ordinary brethren.

I'd cheered for Harvard at all four Games during my Wellesley years – apparently a cardinal sin that now burned in my conscience, demanding atonement. The horror! I held my breath as my friends made plans to meet at the Yale tailgate at a specific time.

Although I was full of gratitude for accessible transport services with ramps, like the Yale Disability Van and the City of New Haven's accessible taxi service, their services weren't exactly ideal for time-sensitive plans. The demand far exceeded the supply, and to complicate things, Yale's Disability Van didn't operate on weekends – just when most social plans took place. This left me at the mercy of the even more unreliable City of New Haven's accessible taxi service.

My mind drifted back to the four Harvard tailgates I had attended, where I had joined in the carefree revelry with an endless stream of alcohol fueling the fun. But I quickly pulled myself away from the slippery slope of comparison, reminding myself to stay anchored in the present moment.

I knew full well that finding my friends in the raucous, chaotic tailgate crowd while maneuvering my wheelchair would be nearly impossible. A pang of disappointment tugged at my heart as I listened to my friends' excited chatter about the upcoming plans. Noticing my crestfallen expression, Chris, my classmate, turned to me with a questioning look. After I explained my situation to him, he offered to meet me at my building and ride along in the accessible taxi so I wouldn't miss out on the day's festivities. That was the moment I knew Chris was on his way to becoming a Sweetheart. I met his focused gaze and whispered my thanks. He waved it off with a soft smile, assuring me that, from his height, he'd spot our friends in no time. In a world that often feels jaded, acts of pure kindness like this are a heartwarming reminder of the goodness around us.

True to his word, Chris arrived at my building five minutes ahead of schedule for the accessible cab. I greeted him and led the way to the porch, where we waited in the chilly air. Chris stood casually beside me, hands tucked in his pockets, exuding an easy confidence. I couldn't believe my luck – a guy with the kind of face that stops you in your tracks was accompanying me to The Game. He was the type of handsome that seeps into your bones and filled you with an almost dreamlike optimism.

"I'm so ready to see some real action at The Game today!" I said, tongue-in-cheek.

Chris raised an eyebrow.

"Oh, I'm sure you're a football expert, Tarini."

I grinned.

"Hey, I know everything there is to know about that game," and, pausing for effect, continued, "except, you know, the rules, the players, and the scoring system."

I longed for Chris to glimpse the playful spark beneath the surface – the authentic self so often eclipsed by my injury. As we traded stories, his laughter warmed the space between us. Then, running fingers through his short, wavy black hair, he glanced at his watch, and watching his eyebrows rise, realization dawned on me. Thirty minutes, and still no cab. He looked at me in concern. My heart sank. Would this newfound connection wither under the prodigious patience required to remain within my orbit? I rummaged through my bag for my phone and called the taxi service. The voice on the other end may as well have been automated – flat, disinterested, explaining that The Game had created unprecedented demand and our cab would arrive "shortly." The operator's disinterest was audible in his flat tone. I hung up, my shoulders slumping.

I watched the hour hand of my watch tick past the designated time of 9.30 a.m. and slowly advance an hour, to 10.30 a.m.

I reached for my phone, my frustration mounting as I dialed the cab company again. My growing despair caused my words to slur and trip over each other. Noticing my faltering speech, Chris quietly extended his hand, offering to talk to the cab company himself.

As I handed my phone to Chris, I felt envious of others' ability to take charge so easily. The memory of an easier life made my heart heavy, causing me to lament how difficult to befriend I had become – a person whose friendship requires extraordinary effort.

My eyes adjusted as I shifted my gaze from myself to the empty road ahead, wondering if everyone else was already at The Game. The last thing I wanted was for Chris to miss out because of me. A quiet anxiety crept in – would he resent me for this? In that moment, I acknowledged the undue weight I gave to others' opinions, driven by a deep-seated fear of being misunderstood or judged. Slowly, I've come to realize the importance of prioritizing my authentic present self, needs and all – even if this version deviates from the idealized image I have of who I once was.

I listened as Chris spoke to the taxi serviceman, his words like quiet footsteps, deliberate and certain compared to my own. His tone grew more forceful, and I could imagine the man on the other end sitting up straighter, listening with rapt attention.

Despite Chris's authoritative tone, we continued to wait in the crisp November air for another quarter of an hour. I knew from past struggles that most power wheelchairs in the West are far too heavy for even army veterans to lift, ruling out transportation without ramps. My hand instinctively found its way to Chris's shoulder, my thoughts consumed by a deep sense of loneliness as I considered telling him to go ahead in a regular taxi without me, just so he wouldn't miss the entire game.

But before I even said a word, without skipping a beat, using the same firm tone he had used with the taxi operator, he declared that he wouldn't even think about going without me.

We waited in the lobby for what felt like an eternity – two more hours before the taxi finally showed up. As we trundled along the streets teeming with crowds of students, a heavy sense of weariness washed over me. We arrived just in time to witness the Yale Bulldogs' victory over Harvard Crimson, 24–3, securing their second consecutive win in The Game. This year, the victory was a big one, as it also apparently clinched the Ivy League title for Yale, capping off a remarkable turnaround from a dismal 2016 season. We watched as screaming students rushed the field, enjoying every moment of the victory. Despite the chaos and frustration of the delay, something shifted between Chris and me. In that moment, amid the unpredictability of the night, we found a deeper connection – one forged in patience, understanding, and the shared experience of simply being present. Beyond everything else, we created a lasting memory. Amid all the merrymaking and congratulatory buzz, Chris's nobility wasn't just acknowledged by me – it was justly rewarded.

Three months later, in February 2018, Chris messaged me from an inaccessible bar he was at, called the Counter Weight Brewery in Cheshire, CT. Unprovoked, he told me the day he spent waiting for the taxi with me was the "best day of the Fall semester". His words brought a smile to my face and lifted my spirits. Chris had officially made it to my exclusive roster of Sweethearts. His reaching out from that brewery was a small but meaningful gesture, a reminder that I couldn't stop my friends from going to places that were off-limits to me, but even in the face of barriers and exclusion, connections could be forged and joy found. But, as always, far easier said than done.

Despite his front-row experience of my needs, far from avoiding me, Chris helped me navigate various challenges he was now aware I faced. Along with Andrew and Christine, we formed an unlikely alliance. That is, until my third year, when two of my other classmates, wonderful women in their own right, captured both Chris and Andrew's hearts. I feigned surprise and teased soft-spoken Andrew about managing to find a woman without me as his trusty wingwoman. It was all in good fun. I had known it was only a matter of time before Andrew and Chris would be spotted and swept off their feet.

In my third year of business school, I finally had the freedom to choose my own courses. After much deliberation, I enrolled in two seemingly contradictory classes: Strategic Management of Nonprofits and Corporate Finance. Though I expected Corporate Finance to suck the life out of me with its heavy quantitative nature, to my surprise, I found myself enjoying the theoretical aspect of the subject matter. As luck would have it, when the professor divided the class into teams, she assigned me to a team with Andrew, Madeline, and Greg, another dear friend from my learning team.

Seated in my swivel chair at home one afternoon, I was absorbed in the assigned Corporate Finance case, when I noticed my phone light up with a message notification. The message was from Nikhil. After much agonizing, in 2017 – five years after our break-up – I had decided it was time to dial back our communication even further. This decision came after he made sure I was the first friend he shared the news of his engagement with, a gesture that felt like a disquieting echo of our past intimacy. Though the passage of time, physical and emotional distance, and shifting circumstances had extinguished any embers of romantic feeling, I still found it difficult to let go of the memory of being the sole focus of his attention. But I could protect myself. With the all-consuming demands of business school to scale, I reasoned that it was finally time to reduce Nikhil's presence in my life.

He'd responded calmly and rationally when I'd initiated a frank conversation about my decision that we should have less involvement in each other's lives.

"Yeah, that makes a lot of sense," he said, his voice betraying neither relief nor regret. "Do whatever feels right for you, and you know that nothing between us will change. So take your time." A small, selfish part of me had hoped for more – perhaps just a moment of hesitation, something to indicate that Nikhil would feel the void my absence would create. His composed demeanor and deliberate

efforts to ease our situation only added to my confusion, making it harder to navigate the shifting landscape of our relationship gracefully.

In those first raw days, it took every ounce of effort to resist the temptation of reaching for my phone every time something new happened in my life that I wanted to share with Nikhil. However, as the year rolled on, whether due to the demands of business school or all the friendly banter with the Sweethearts, my desire to involve Nikhil in my inner world gradually diminished. While we still kept each other updated on the highlights and lowlights of our lives, the voltage of the daily lights dimmed.

Although Nikhil had invited me to his wedding, which had taken place earlier in the week, with careful consideration, I thought it best not to attend.

The flashing unread message on my phone piqued my curiosity. It was from Nikhil. I tapped the notification to see a thank-you note from him for my congratulatory email to the newlyweds. *Ah, the sweet satisfaction of doing the right thing.* I returned to re-read the congratulatory email.

Dear Nikhil and Layla,

Congratulations on being newlyweds!!! The wedding looked and seemed like it was a great success, both for family as well as friends' enjoyment and undoubtedly yours first and foremost too :)

Believe me, I am very happy indeed that you found each other. Layla, I've been very impressed that you not only accepted but chose to love Nikhil despite all the baggage he came with. Your acceptance made things a lot easier for me and surely for Nikhil too.

I wish you both much happiness and contentment in the years to come.

Much love,
Tarini

I looked up from the screen out the window, at the ashen plumage of a robin flitting across the sky.

But quickly, my attention returned to the email thread I had opened. Layla had replied not long after.

Dear Tarini,

Thank you so much for your sweet note! It means so much to us to have your love and blessings. It was a great weekend, mostly because Nikhil attracts such loving and kind people into his life!

Just as you are impressed that I've accepted Nikhil's "baggage" (though I would choose to call it history and life experience!), I am grateful that you have been open and accepting of me, and nothing but kind and welcoming to me. I know it must still be tough, but I'm so grateful that Nikhil has you in his life as a dear friend and loved one. You are so wonderful, and you helped shape and support Nikhil into becoming the man he is today (and I know you still help and advise him a lot!).

You are so awesome and impressive, and I hope that we will get to see you and hang out sometime soon!

Love,

Layla

Feeling a sense of tranquility in my heart, I closed my eyes. A newfound peace resonated within me. I was genuinely happy that Nikhil had found a kind and thoughtful partner.

But soon enough, I shook myself out of my reverie and looked upon the week's long Corporate Finance case that I still needed to read – *and* understand – before I met up with Andrew, Madeline, and Greg that evening – we had to divide responsibilities for the case report our team had to submit.

In the first year we met, Andrew discovered both my cultural and personal sides, thanks to countless long, meandering conversations about life and jazz – whether in school corridors, at coffee shops, or during brunches at the Oriental Pantry or P&M Market. We lost ourselves for hours planning his various house shows. But the thought of him learning of my cognitive limitations – which Madeline and Greg were already privy to as my learning team colleagues – made my stomach churn. Would understanding become pity, ease become awkwardness, friendship become a burden?

In our conversations throughout the year, Andrew got wind of my deep love for New York City and listened intently to my life story. Meanwhile, I was awestruck to learn that his younger brother was a reputed trumpet player in a New York-based brass quartet called the Westerlies. A month before his graduation, Andrew offered to accompany me to Brooklyn's Flatbush neighborhood to see the Westerlies perform at the Owl Music Parlor. I could hardly believe my luck.

Giddy with excitement, I had to remind myself to play it cool and not appear overeager lest he get the wrong impression. Even though NYC was only a two-hour train ride away, a day-long trip was no easy feat for me. There are always a million hurdles in my path that inevitably spill over to affect my companions. While my family bears the weight of my limitations with stoic acceptance, a reflection of unconditional love, friends are free to choose if they want to walk the path beside me. It is my responsibility to make sure they understand what standing by me really entails. But the trip to New York felt like Andrew's goodbye gift to me before the graduation of the class of 2019, and I knew I had to try to make it work.

But first, I had to make an awkward request. Would Andrew sacrifice his plans to crash at his brother's place in NYC and instead accompany me back to New Haven after the show? Holding my breath after summoning the courage to ask, I hung in that precarious space between vulnerability and response.

A familiar heaviness settled in my chest as I watched his expression shift. He tilted his head and made a series of gentle inquiries to better understand the complexities at the heart of my simple request. I knew what he must be thinking – our other classmates, regardless of gender, traveled solo by train and cabs without a second thought. I understood his hesitation. Hailing a taxi in New York, which I would need to do to get to and from the train station, is as routine as breathing for most, and unlike Chris, Andrew hadn't yet faced an accessible taxi disaster with me.

Fumbling over my words, I explained to Andrew that I felt safer traveling with someone whose speech could be understood when mine couldn't, who could see above the crowds, and jump up to get help when required. I also mentioned having experienced my wheelchair's wheels getting stuck in the gap between the platform and the subway in DC, and needing strength to pull it out. My family and I had concluded that the NYC subway was dangerous and out of the question, relegating me to the less budget-friendly option of cabs to get around the city. With soft "mm-hmms", I could hear Andrew's brain working to understand my needs. He uncrossed his arms and leaned forward.

"Tarini, I go to New York all the time. It's really no big deal for me to not stay there one Saturday night. Of course, I will travel back to New Haven with you."

Positioning my wheelchair in the assigned spot, I waited for the conductor to secure it in place, ensuring it wouldn't slide. As the train doors clanged shut, it finally sank in that this really was happening.

I was going back to New York City as a regular person. Andrew turned to look at me, he seemed to know just how important this trip was to me.

Andrew had learned that the Arts in Management student club had planned a trip to New York that same day to see an exhibition of the neo-expressionist artist Jean-Michel Basquiat at the Brant Foundation in the East Village. I was thrilled when he proposed we check out the exhibition before heading to the show, and especially excited when I realized the gallery space was just a fifteen-minute walk from the building where I'd lived in NYC.

I could sense this trip to the city with Andrew would be a memorable one. I had planned a day full of activities that would appeal to both of us. We wanted to fully experience the present moment and create lasting memories while at it. It was also an opportunity for us to truly experience a slice of each other's past.

With Andrew's help, I would recreate my New York City vibe – one that I had deliberately left behind, much like my relationship with Nikhil. Both had left indelible imprints on my character. Watching my friends' lives progress – with mine also progressing, albeit on a different, more solitary track – wasn't easy. Yet, Andrew's choice to spend an entire day with me in the city showed me his willingness to invest in our friendship, making the time we spent together more meaningful.

As we talked, a word coined by friendship expert Shasta Nelson surfaced in my mind: "frientimacy". It describes the concept of building deep connections between friends. It's not about the number of interactions but the depth of trust, vulnerability, consistency, and positivity. As we had laughed and made plans during our time together at SOM, I felt a strong bond with Andrew and a renewed sense of trust.

The train arrived at Grand Central Terminal, and as we stepped out onto the platform, Andrew turned to check if I was still behind him. From there, we headed upstairs to the Main Concourse, with its impressive architecture and iconic constellation ceiling. Memories flooded back, including those of a younger version of myself running up the same staircase. I took in the vibrant hustle and bustle of the city with a sense of loneliness, acknowledging the void within me that had persisted for seven years.

By now, I had grown somewhat accustomed to the shape of life bestowed on me. There is a mismatch, though, between how I see myself and how I believe I appear in others' eyes. Despite my physical limitations, I see myself as quite the catch – a woman with much to offer. But the world seems to view me as shattered glass. A partner could choose to help me piece back the shards, though it would be a laborious task. I wouldn't wish the weight of my brokenness on another, but I also wish I hadn't internalized some of the ableism that remains so pervasive in society.

I heard Andrew calling out to me from a distance, "Tarini, where should we meet the accessible cab?" Goodness, it'd slipped my mind that a potential accessible cab debacle awaited.

As it happened, there was none. Instead, the city spun a perfect restorative spell around me. Not only did I slip back into my former New York City skin, but I also painted fresh hues on the canvas of the present moment. After a poignant yet regenerative day in the city, we returned to Grand Central Terminal at around 11 p.m. that evening. I'd spoken to Mama about my late arrival before making the trip. She responded with gentle understanding, which I appreciated. Opportunities to roam without familial oversight were rare.

Andrew led the way into the station, holding open the large doors. Before entering, I looked around, taking in for the last time that day the sights and sounds of the city that had given me the most precious two years of my life so far. I said a silent goodbye to the place I'd once called home and whizzed in through the open door.

Therapists, yoga gurus, mindfulness apps, spiritual friends, and my own mother have all advised me to breathe in the taste of the present and cast aside the past, for it will never return. My heart and head collide when I reflect on this sage advice. While focusing on the present moment appeals to me on an intellectual and spiritual level, my heart struggles to embrace the static, pain-filled present moment, given the countless obstacles that hinder my ability to enjoy it any more than I already do.

Andrew leaned back in his seat on the train.

"That was a fun day," he said, his eyes softening. "No hitches along the way, either!"

"Yeah! Believe me, I've literally never had this much luck with cabs." I said, afraid he would now see my caution as unnecessary. How could I explain that I needed a friend accompanying me as a form of insurance? "Thanks for the "backstage pass". I loved meeting the band after the show!"

Andrew laughed. "There was no 'backstage pass'!"

I groaned out loud when the train pulled into New Haven. "Back to reality," I muttered under my breath. As we chatted, I was struck by a sense of foreboding. Graduation Day for the class of 2019 was just around the corner. I was careful not to let Andrew in on my unannounced melancholy at the thought of losing his daily company. His cool demeanor and hip taste had been a balm for me at business school, and I didn't want to spoil the evening with any gloomy thoughts.

We were now at the elevator and Andrew was checking his watch.

"Damn it," I muttered. "We've been waiting for the elevator for over five minutes, and no one else is even at the station at this late hour," I said, vocalizing my fear.

"I'm pretty sure this elevator is broken," Andrew said, his face pinched.

My internal monologue subsided as I realized that this was the obstacle Andrew thought we'd managed to avoid.

"Let's first check if there is another elevator on this platform," I suggested, pausing to glance at our empty surroundings, "and if not, could you please run up to ask someone to fix it?" I suggested. Looking at Andrew, I let out a deep breath I didn't know I was holding.

As Andrew set out to launch his investigations, I dialed my parents to inform them of the situation and assure them I was safe.

Aching to resume its frenetic activity, my brain manufactured the next thing to worry about. Until now, I had been fixating on the last year of solitude awaiting me after my friends graduated. Yet, the familiar dread of social isolation had mysteriously lifted; I found myself strangely confident in my ability to select new Sweethearts. SOM had already performed the initial alchemy – transforming the vast unknown into a promising pool of kindred spirits.

No, my all-consuming worry now revolved around the uncertainty of my future after leaving the safety and familiarity of the inclusive space at Yale. The thought of returning to India – technically my homeland, but not truly home for sixteen years – gnawed at the back of my mind. I had no real community there anymore. Most of my school friends had moved on and out of Delhi. My troubles getting around in New Haven would multiply tenfold in Delhi, where buildings often lacked elevators, roads were potholed, pavements didn't have curb cuts, and accessible transportation remained a distant dream. The difficulty of forming new connections in a society still awakening to disability accessibility, sensitization, and awareness wasn't lost on me. Who would connect with me – someone so disconnected from local know-how, latest fads, and youthful slang? Someone who felt both isolated from daily life and painfully aware of her privilege.

Setting aside my self-sculpted worries, I looked toward the staircase, hoping to glimpse Andrew returning with assurances. Instead, I saw an empty platform stretching beyond, a barren landscape that echoed my despair.

Suddenly, Andrew emerged out of nowhere, and as I'd hoped, assured me that he'd had spoken to the relevant station employees, who said they'd fix the elevator and send it down for us. I breathed a sigh of relief.

But after another agonizing fifteen minutes, I decided I'd better liven up the situation for my friend.

"So much for a smooth ride back to reality, huh?" I said, mustering a chuckle.

Andrew's face bore deep lines of exhaustion.

"Looks like we'll still be stuck here for a bit," he said in a defeated tone.

"I always knew that someday I'd end up trapped with a handsome jazz musician in the dead of night at a train station," I said with a cheeky smile.

Andrew laughed. "Well, you certainly have a way of making things interesting."

We spent a few minutes laughing and chatting, forgetting we were stranded at a train station in the wee hours of the night.

But soon, Andrew's expression turned serious.

"You are an amazing person, you know," he said out of the blue. "Most people in your situation wouldn't have as light and good-natured a spirit as you. Hell, take the present moment. I am all tense and worked up, while you remain lighthearted and able to crack jokes."

Touched by Andrew's words, I met his eyes briefly to allow him to see my appreciation. Then, it was time to reveal the truth about my lightheartedness.

"It's easy to be calm when others are looking for solutions to my problems, and the only thing I can do to help the situation is manage my mood," I said. "And I work hard just for that – you know I'm anything but calm!"

Before we knew it, we'd been waiting on the platform for another half an hour. Andrew suddenly piped up.

"I just had a crazy idea, which could work," he paused, studying my expression before adding, "if you're willing to try."

I raised my eyebrows.

"We can get down from the platform via the ramp there," Andrew said, pointing to the end of the platform. "Then we can cross the tracks on that flat area on the same side and climb up on the platform opposite us. There's a ramp there, too. And then, we can use the elevator on that platform!" he said triumphantly.

"That's insane but brilliant! I'd never usually take a chance of 'walking' across train tracks, but I'm not exactly thrilled about camping on the platform all night," I said, before another idea surfaced. "Wait one second, let me call the Disability Van. Once we're out, it'll drive us to my building for free," I felt a small surge of pride at contributing a solution to our predicament. "That van sometimes takes forever to arrive though. You can get an Uber from my place – probably cheaper, too," I added, trying to be practical."

By the time we reached my building at 2 a.m., Andrew and I had dissolved into exhausted laughter.

"Some adventure!" he said, grinning as he hopped off the van to walk me to my building entrance.

"Thanks for an unforgettable goodbye gift," I said when we reached the front door.

"Don't shoo me away just yet," he teased. "We have forty-five more days of non-stop fun ahead." He knitted his brows together and smacked his forehead playfully. "My bad, I forgot the six days of finals."

18

Anchors in the Storm

Work began around 9.30 or 10 a.m., and my commute to the Harappa Education office was an easy-breezy fifteen-minute journey. The workspace itself was everything I'd hoped for in my last summer internship of business school – an open office filled with the energy of a young, dynamic team. Still, there was no denying the fundamental difference between academic and professional settings. Academia grooms you for the workplace – the supposed final destination. In contrast, workplaces tend to view people more as resources, each serving a particular utilitarian function, with far less of the nurturing support I had grown accustomed to at my university.

Wanting this professional chapter to be as purposeful as the rest of my journey, I was determined not to be perceived as a charity case, someone constantly in need of favors. I knew that rising at daybreak was the only viable option – the only way to carve out enough time to account for the additional hours I needed just to shower, dress, and complete the full ninety-minute stretch of my morning physical rehab. Without this disciplined routine, I wouldn't have enough pain-free moments to get through the day.

Despite my aversion to the Type-A variety – those restless souls driven by perpetual ambition and an almost painful need for order

– I found myself adopting such a mindset. Type-A people also tend to be highly competitive, the one Type-A trait I don't identify with. Yet, to make up for lost time, I became a clockwork mechanism – ensuring my schedule was well-oiled, every minute accounted for, every second planned with surgical precision.

That summer, back in India after the departure of the class of 2019 and facing my final year at Yale, I paused to examine the road ahead. Until then, I'd remained resolute in my desire to work to help smallholder farmers improve their livelihoods. I had long aspired to bring my global perspective back home, to stand alongside millions fighting against deep-rooted systemic oppression. During the first two summers of my four-year MBA, I had tapped into this calling and was drawn to summer internships at the Bill & Melinda Gates Foundation and Oxfam, both in India. At both organizations, I immersed myself in various aspects of agricultural development.

Yet, despite the wealth of knowledge I gained about Indian agriculture, the distance between my desk and the farmers' real-world struggles left me feeling disconnected. I longed to accompany the program managers to the muddy, uneven fields, to talk to the farmers, and witness their challenges firsthand. I couldn't envision a future for myself as an expert in agricultural development while being so far removed from the intricacies of farmers' lives.

I began contemplating paths with fewer obstacles, eventually turning toward education. The shift materialized in an internship at Harappa Education in my home city of New Delhi that summer of 2019 – a calculated step into new territory. Extreme self-discipline overtook me; I longed to make up for lost ground in my career ambitions. Yet, even as I pushed forward, I couldn't shake the feeling of being a step behind, of not quite measuring up to my peers. The nagging insecurity haunted me, and I wished to show both myself and others what I was made of.

Though younger than me, most of my new colleagues had years of experience I couldn't match – six years had slipped by in the wake of the accident. Of course, I had worked and studied during much of that time, but not at my full potential. Now at Harappa, I observed the young workforce shaping the startup's identity with practiced ease, their contributions flowing naturally into the firm's lifeblood. Initially, my interim role felt like that of an understudy, watching from the wings as the seasoned took the lead. But, gradually, I found myself easing into the flow.

Settling into my routine as a summer intern, a solitary figure in the office caught my attention – always there, already immersed in work, when I arrived at my desk in the open space. His goatee beard and sparkling eyes suggested he was in his mid-twenties. Nishant, I later learned, carried an air of quiet purpose that made him stand out from our other colleagues who gradually ambled in. Most of my young colleagues at Harappa were, I discovered, sharp, friendly people who didn't bat an eye at my various disabilities. They wove me into the fabric of their days – lunch breaks, after-work plans, casual conversations – until I felt myself becoming part of their collective story. Yet something about Nishant's focused presence drew my curiosity deeper, sparking a wish to understand the person behind the morning stillness.

One day, Nishant beat me to the office again, his energy out of place for a Monday morning. As Vinod, ever-helpful, pushed my wheelchair inside, Nishant dropped his work, rather uncharacteristically, to saunter over, and engage Vinod in friendly Hindi banter. Vinod had been a guiding light for my family during our darker days, and watching Nishant treat him like a brother in our carefully hierarchical society lifted my spirits. I decided not to tease Nishant about overlooking my presence in favor of Vinod. As I chatted with Nishant, I learned the reason for his timely arrival to the office – he followed a strict schedule, including a rigorous running routine before the start of the workday, building towards a distant finish line he dreamed of crossing. Though we were different, I recognized something familiar in him. Could we be friends?

To glimpse the less stoic side of Nishant, I decided to ask him during lunch break if he could teach me some contemporary Hindi slang. I was out of touch, having been away for so long. To my surprise, he responded to that, too, with a methodical plan, suggesting I create a Google Sheet on which he could enter different phrases for me. It wasn't difficult for him: Hindi was his first language – the one he used with his parents and many friends. What stood out was how Nishant approached even the smallest task with a sense of organization and structure. As the office came alive with activity, I noticed colleagues turning to him to settle office disagreements and provide clarity.

"He must be quite a clever fellow," I thought.

Nishant revealed he was on Harappa's founding team, explaining his colleagues' reliance on him. I learned he was from Uttarakhand and planned to pursue a graduate degree in the US. Excited about the possibility of a meaningful connection opening up, I offered him my help.

In the final month of my summer internship, I pivoted to brand strategy – an entirely new territory I was excited to explore. Nishant had been noticeably absent from the office these last weeks; a health emergency had called him to his father's side. When I learned of the five-hour ambulance journey from Dehradun to Delhi, my heart sank for Nishant. Being an only child, I imagined him sitting alone with his father on that endless ride, carrying the weight of the world on his shoulders. I desperately wanted to help him in any way I could, to return some measure of the kindness that had surrounded my own family during our crisis.

I reached for my phone, unsure of what practical assistance I could provide, but extended my support anyway. As we spoke, Nishant painted a vivid picture of the dire state of emergency services at hospitals in Delhi.

"It's not just long queues, but scarcity of beds and *extreme* demand." Healthcare systems across the globe are broken, with both the developing and the developed worlds having unique inadequacies. Yet, rather than sitting slumped in a corner, Nishant displayed a remarkable poise in finding solutions to the insurmountable problems posed by the medical crisis.

During his father's hospitalization, Nishant had to prepare for his upcoming Fulbright Scholarship interview. With modest resources, he had navigated the challenges before him to pursue his dream of getting a graduate degree in the US. Being invited for such a prestigious interview was no ordinary feat – it felt like he'd chanced upon some sort of Nishant magic wand.

Channeling my knowledge gained from seven and a half years of lived experience in American higher education, I offered my help by conducting a mock interview for him. Despite all his troubles, Nishant exuded a calm self-confidence. A tide of certainty swept over me upon hearing his thoughtful, articulate answers. There was no doubt in my mind that he would shine as a top candidate for a prestigious university. On sharing this sentiment with him, I was greeted with an endearing snort of laughter.

Even as life swirled with uncertainty, when everything seemed in flux, and despite all my fears of returning to India, I found again what I should have known all along: adult friendships can take root and flourish, becoming anchors steadying us through any storm. Looking back, I was simply witnessing the relentless march of life. The voids left by absences gradually give way to the arrival of new entities – reminiscent of nature's aversion to vacuum

– birthing particles to fill the void. Friends may depart but others can arrive to fill the emptiness – not as substitutes but as distinct, new relationships, much like a proton to an electron.

One sweltering summer night in 2019, I lay in darkness during a power outage, with only the weakening whir of the overhead fan to break the silence. Heat pressed against my skin, and I longed for the refreshing respite of air conditioning. A flapping T-shirt became an impromptu fan, offering little relief as I waited for comfort like a parched plant awaiting life-giving rain. I was at the mercy of my weak inverter while my neighbors luxuriated in their generator-assisted, air-conditioned havens. The fan did little to prevent my nightclothes from sticking to my body. The steady drone of their generator filling my ears, I closed my eyes and imagined the cool air emanating from the air conditioner washing over my sticky skin. Relief from discomfort was all I craved. But then my thoughts drifted to our cook, and the countless others like him, who had to endure the unforgiving heat without even the meager solace of the fan during an electricity outage. Although this thought ignited gratitude for the gentle whirring of the fan overhead, my sweat still lingered, as did my envy of the neighbors' comfortable existence.

My mind wandered away from the searing heat to dreams of my graduation ceremony at Yale. I pictured myself surrounded by family and friends, though many were scattered far and wide across the globe. Then, an idea sparked: why not gather thirty friends from my past and present for one magnificent celebration in May 2020? A graduation that would double as a reunion, allowing me to celebrate this milestone. After all, if I couldn't journey to them, perhaps they could come to Yale and share in this milestone moment. How innocent those plans seem now. How unaware I was of what May 2020 would bring.

Within days, the power outage faded into an anecdote. I was back in the sun-drenched halls of SOM, exhilarated and trepidatious in equal measure. I immersed myself in the quotidian rhythms of student life – morning coffee runs, afternoon study sessions, evening gatherings – knowing this pattern would soon belong to memory. Each moment felt more precious for its impermanence. There were new adjustments, too: a new class to know. Students who had entered SOM in the fall of 2018 would graduate with me in 2020. Some friendships were forged but not as many as before.

Nishant and I continued chatting and our friendship deepened after my internship ended and I returned to Yale. Our exchanges revealed the intricacies of Nishant's personality, and despite our different backgrounds, we found several striking similarities in the values we held dear and in our outlook on life. That we were different in many ways made our friendship all the more interesting, and each difference offered a fresh perspective on the world.

One morning, amid our usual messages, Nishant casually shared a screenshot. My heart leaped when I opened it – an acceptance letter to Harvard's Graduate School of Education. Excitement overtook me, pure and immediate, even as I found myself unsurprised. Of course, he would reach for Harvard; it fit perfectly with the quiet determination I'd witnessed those early mornings at Harappa.

I had big hopes for Nishant's future at Harvard – imagining him slowly unwinding from his intense work habits as he discovered the richness of campus life and the joy of new, diverse friendships. But COVID-19 rewrote these hopes, as it did for countless students worldwide. When Harvard announced its shift to virtual learning, I gently urged him to wait – to defer until he could walk those historic paths himself, breathe in the living energy of classroom debates, and feel the pulse of campus life beneath his feet. Through both our unexpected transitions – mine back to India after SOM, his plans suspended in time – Nishant remained a steadfast friend, offering quiet wisdom as I found my footing in a world turned sideways.

As I looked toward my future beyond Yale, an interwoven web of motivations guided the direction of my life. At the forefront was a need for safety due to my persisting difficulties with stability, which made it necessary for me to return to Delhi with my parents. Yet alongside this practical need lived a deeper calling: to build something meaningful in India. By some gentle twist of fate, my new friend shared this vision, his understanding of India's education landscape both deep and current. I had already begun turning toward this field, drawn to its possibilities, and it wasn't long before Nishant's encouragement pushed me further, leading me to consider a career in education.

While Nishant returned to Dehradun to weather the lockdown with his parents, my family planned to return to Delhi soon after I graduated, flight restrictions permitting. A bizarre relief settled over me at the thought of not overlapping with Nishant in the same city. Now that he was more than just a colleague, I couldn't bear the thought of him witnessing how confined my Delhi life could be. I felt the tug of an ironic smile as I dared to face the absurdity of my situation – craving distance from a blossoming friendship coupled with the fear of isolation. Still, with an ocean between us, I clung to the hope that our friendship would endure.

In my final year at Yale, my focus shifted from enjoying school life to the mechanics of applying for jobs in my home country, where I had not yet worked as a full-time professional. It felt serendipitous to have Nishant by my side, guiding me at every turn.

Since there isn't much student demand for full-time jobs in India after graduate school in the US, I couldn't rely on SOM's magnanimous recruiting efforts to help me secure a job. Instead, I managed to secure a couple of job interviews through networks back home. Hell-bent on painting a wholly accurate portrait of my capabilities, I prepared myself to reveal the full extent of the impact of my injury in job interviews, hoping that exposing my limitations wouldn't eclipse the abilities that remained or my fortitude in the face of colossal adversity. My fears were unfounded. I was offered a job providing me with a platform to make a potentially tangible impact on education policy for schools in India. My business school gamble had paid off.

In-person classes suspended.
No friendly faces.
No bickering.
No bonding.
No human interaction.
Only 24/7 parents.

The pandemic felt like a surreal nightmare. I was jolted out of my self-absorbed thoughts only when I caught sight of news footage from India of hordes of migrant workers trudging long distances back to their hometowns, forced by the government's sudden lockdown imposed on March 24, 2020. The sight of the exhausted and expressionless faces of the men, women, and children shook me. Suddenly, my dismay at not being able to gather my loved ones to celebrate my graduation seemed wholly trivial.

Yet, it *was* eventually celebrated – virtually – in the spirit of the times. Christine, my friend from the class of 2018, who was Chair of Student Life at SOM before she graduated, had a track record of organizing events to foster camaraderie among students and the school. To my surprise, as my dreams of getting friends from across the globe together in New Haven unraveled, she promptly offered to help organize a Zoom graduation party for me in April, even though the official graduation was still a month away.

Throughout April, Christine and my friend, Alex, both coincidentally Wellesley women, worked tirelessly to plan and coordinate the virtual celebration. On the day of the event, I logged onto Zoom to find myself surrounded by the faces of loved ones from all over the world. My family, friends, and teachers had all gathered to celebrate my accomplishment. Even my therapists and doctors had taken time out of their busy schedules to attend and celebrate with me.

The sight of the little rectangles on my screen – all eighty-seven of them with smiling faces in them – moved me beyond what I had thought possible. Among them was Nikhil, his rectangle no larger or smaller than any other, a visual truth I hadn't expected to find meaningful. It was a fitting symbol of the reality that now existed – his place in my life was now on par with that of my other close friends.

Andrew's screen lit up as he started the celebration by riffing on his saxophone.

Then, a chime sounded as a new participant joined the call. I had been told there would be a surprise chief guest, but I had no idea who it was. I was speechless when I saw it was Indra Nooyi, the former CEO of PepsiCo. She is an alumna of the Yale School of Management herself. Upon reading my story, which my brother had penned for Christine to pass on to Ms. Nooyi, she decided to participate in my graduation celebration. She spoke movingly, recounting my journey for all the attendees. Tiny goosebumps erupted on my arms when she addressed me:

"We are humbled by you, your courage, your fortitude, by what you have already achieved. We are excited about what you will do next, because today is the first day of the rest of your life."

Taking a deep breath, I tried to hold on to this moment. My eyes wandered back to the attendees – falling on Isabel first, who was now thriving at UN-Habitat in Nairobi and had found a Kenyan partner. I spotted Davis next, who'd joined the ceremony from Chicago. After graduating from community college, Davis had enrolled at the University of St. Francis, where he was working toward a BA in Registered Nursing. He was on his way to entering his final year in the fall of 2020. Meri was there too, now based in Beirut and still working with UNICEF. Pallavi was there of course, with her one-year-old daughter in her lap, and with Ishan by her side.

The next speaker was Susan Davis. She said she would recount my story by focusing on the period between two momentous occasions in my life – June 1, 2010, when I left Morgan Stanley, to June 2, 2016, when I moved to New Haven to settle in before enrolling at Yale SOM.

She briefly talked about the day she met me in Uganda along with Lois Juliber, the Chair of Mastercard Foundation, and how impressed they had been hearing me speak passionately about how important it was to raise farmers' incomes for the health and education of their families, and my readiness to leave comfort to help further this work.

I noticed all the attendees leaning in, listening closely.

"The person I met in 2010," Susan continued, "before her boda-boda accident in Uganda that night I got on the plane back to New York, and the person I met after, in a hospital in Delhi, in January 2011, were the same. Her essence, her core was, and has always been, the same. No tragic accident could take it away. But she had to learn that for herself. . ."

I felt my eyes misting as she continued.

"Her attributes only became more pronounced and evident.

Her positive perspective,

Her wry humor, and ability to tease.

Her critical, analytical thinking,

Her rapid research capabilities,

Her keen curiosity,

Her compassion,

Her love of agriculture and food. (I mean come on! She later got an apartment in DC literally OVER Whole Foods!)"

I felt grateful for the moment of levity. Susan's words had hit me hard, and the joke gave me a chance to compose myself,

"In January 2011," Susan went on," I was in New Delhi with His Holiness, the Dalai Lama. I asked him to pray for Tarini, and then [I] went to see her. I met her incredible parents, Rakesh and Rasika, there for the first time. I remember telling her, "Hurry up and get better. I need you to get back to work." And so eventually she did. The climb back to health and work was Everest-worthy!"

Susan concluded by introducing the next speaker, Pallavi, who reflected on the depth of our long friendship. She then passed her screen time over to Andrew, who took over the virtual stage again – this time to speak. My parents went last. Mama spoke with deep feeling, maintaining her composure as she usually does. Papa thanked everybody, remembering, as he would, to take the names of practically each of my long list of therapists and doctors, including my anesthetist in Uganda. He ended by pleading with me not to graduate again, citing that my two graduation years – 2008, the year of the global financial crisis, and 2020 weren't good years for the world.

Hoots of laughter followed.

My heart swelled when I thought of the constellation of people, both present and absent, who had illuminated my path to recovery. Each person who had entered my life – every caregiver, friend, doctor, therapist, teacher, understanding colleague, kind stranger – kept my hope and faith in humanity alive.

Fortunately, my spiraling thoughts were silenced when Andrew and Josh's a-cappella group, the Economies of Scale, took over. My cheeks ached from how hard I was smiling. They felt even more strained when I heard the lyrics of a song composed specially for me. I was overwhelmed by the outpouring of love and recognition for what I had accomplished. I promised myself to think of this moment whenever I felt alone in the future.

Shortly after, with friends still lingering and exchanging messages on the screen, I wondered if everyone had their own "villagers" – my private name for this community that held me so carefully – or if it was just me. Recalling my pre-accident years, I dug deep, hoping to uncover whether I would have ever seen my groups of dear friends this way before. While I have always had a close-knit group of friends, it took standing at the edge of existence to truly see their profound role in my life.

Atul Gawande writes in his book, *Being Mortal*, of Stanford professor of psychology, Layla Carstensen's theory on the change in human needs and desires and how it affects our sense of how finite our time is.[16] She called it the Socioemotional Selectivity Theory (SST). The theory suggests that our perspective on time shifts as we age, and we become more aware of our finite time in this world. It all made sense now. The reason I see my friends as my "villagers" now is because of my newfound perspective, subconscious as it may be, on life after my accident. My perspective on life has changed, even if, as Susan correctly said, the essence of who I am has not. My "villagers" hadn't appeared after the accident; they had always been there, ready to support me. It just took a life-altering experience for me to recognize the village that had surrounded me all along.

With my graduation behind me and the pandemic now raging, flights to India were stalled, leaving us marooned in New Haven until October, 2020 – five months after I should have received my degree in my cap and gown. Amid the sparse distractions of those pandemic months, I teetered on the brink of anxiety as I contemplated the uncertainties of the next phase of my life. The question wreaking havoc in my mind: was it time for my good fortune to turn once again?

Sixteen long years had passed since I had truly lived in India. My time in Delhi after the hospital felt more like watching life through frosted glass – always under watchful eyes. I was there, but absent. Now I faced the daunting task of reconnecting with my Delhi community after nearly two decades of treading non-overlapping paths.

Papa often teases that if I can't find something real to worry about, I'll manufacture new, if not imagined, sources of anxiety. Although he says this in a playful manner, I hate to admit that he speaks the truth – a truth I'm reluctant to acknowledge.

I finally shook myself from my spiral of worry and turned to face what lay ahead. From the plush maroon armchair in my room in New Haven, I immersed myself in the recently enacted sixty-six-page Indian National Education Policy (NEP), 2020, trying to gain a foothold in my new world of school education in India.

As I read, I wondered what unique perspective could I – shaped by both East and West – bring to India's school education policy. Yale's accommodations, though generous, were, after all, mandated by federal law. Without these accommodations, I wouldn't have been able to function on the same footing as my peers. I found myself wrestling with a paradox: why are workplace accommodations not talked of in the same breath as those in educational institutions? If the purpose of higher education is to mold us into capable professionals, shouldn't the workplaces that await us also strive to create an environment that unlocks our full potential?

My curiosity led me down a digital rabbit hole, where I learned that workplace accommodations were enshrined in law on both sides of the globe. The Indian Rights of Persons with Disabilities Act of 2016 mirrored the spirit of the US Equal Opportunity Employment Commission – a federal agency established in 1964 to guard against workplace discrimination. Both frameworks shared a powerful core concept: "reasonable accommodations".

This phrase, I learned, carried far more weight than its bureaucratic tone suggested. It wasn't just legal jargon, but a commitment to fundamental fairness – a promise to make whatever adjustments were needed to level the playing field, provided they didn't place undue strain on the employer. The ultimate aim of these accommodations is to open pathways for individuals with disabilities to enjoy the same rights, and the ability to exercise them, just like anyone else.[17]

I willed myself to embody the superhuman power of Nietzsche's "Übermensch"[18] and adopt this magical mindset – not just to weather what lay ahead, but to flourish in spite of it. The philosophy felt both ancient and urgently modern in those strange days.

Being trapped in my room was not doing me any good. But COVID-19 had shut the world down, and my options for clearing my mind were limited. Determined, I rose from the chair to walk up and down the corridor outside my apartment. Despite my extroverted nature, I dreaded running into strangers in the hallway and engaging in awkward small talk. But here I was, aching for even a glimpse of a stranger's face.

By this point, walking with my quad cane felt so natural to me that unlike before, I no longer had to choreograph each movement. This freedom let my thoughts roam as I plodded down the empty hallway. Not a person in sight. No strangers, not even a neighbor's shadow. I couldn't help but wonder what was becoming of humanity.

With measured steps, I made it to the hallway's distant window. I closed my eyes and hoped to find some sort of balance, but the world seemed to spin around me. I wobbled, dreams threatening to scatter as my heart ached for a thousand wishes. But I steadied myself, my grip tightening on my faithful cane as I tried to clear my mind. My inner voice reprimanded me for mentally shutting doors on myself when they had just barely creaked open. Instead of a thousand wishes, I settled on a single wish, one solitary hope that may guide me forward. I wished for the courage to embrace my truth, to evolve with the world around me, and to find happiness amid its raging chaos. In that moment of clarity, I understood something profound about both life's storms and placid waters – they are best navigated with others beside you.

Walking back to the apartment, it seemed as if a veil had been lifted from my eyes. *I have unintentionally already succeeded in evolving along with my life-changing circumstances. If only I could transform those unintentional actions into deliberate ones to build a future as radiant as the one my present successes had revealed to me.*

The colors of the setting sun seemed to waltz and weave, echoing Nietzsche's wisdom: "I want to learn more and more to see as beautiful what is necessary in things; then I shall be one of those who makes things beautiful."[19] Only by learning to see the necessary as beautiful could I sculpt this life into its own fierce masterpiece. Tracing the golden threads of my Yale memories, I was struck with embarrassment – it was high time for my pity party to clock out. In my quiet reflection, a kaleidoscope of memories of the past four years unfurled before me – the laughter shared with countless friends, woven with the fierce loyalty of my core village, those who had walked every rocky mile with me, wheelchair and unyielding pain in tow.

A decade after the crash that rewired my brain, my life had found its own peculiar rhythm. Yale's hallowed halls had welcomed me, wheels and all, yet while my peers danced through their days with effortless grace, my world moved to a slower tempo, punctuated with pain's recurring staccato. Still, my family refused to let four wheels dictate the borders of my world. They became masters of improvisation – turning airports into familiar territory, transforming hotel bathrooms into accessible havens, their smiles never wavering even as their shoulders bore the weight of these daily adaptations – all so I could sample the sweet taste of freedom once again.

And oh, how their devotion bore fruit: I had reached a level of recovery that allowed adventures I'd thought impossible – exploring Mexico's vibrant streets not once, but twice, and visiting Colombia, Turkey, and Switzerland, all in my four years at Yale. These weren't just trips, they were expressions of defiance against the boundaries my injury had tried to impose on me.

A memorable encounter during my visit to the ancient Mayan city of Uxmal came flooding back. My family and I stood, perplexed, at the foot of the majestic pyramid, contemplating how to descend the steps, gentle as they were, with my wheelchair, to best view the sound and light show in the Nunnery Quadrangle. Just then, our gaze caught the attention of a rugged European tourist who, without hesitation, unburdened himself of his backpack and stepped forward. Clad in a black vest and khaki pants, the compassionate stranger approached us and offered to lift my wheelchair down the steps – with me still in it. Now, freed of his gear, he summoned a few other men loitering nearby for assistance, and off we went.

The strangers' benevolence added an ethereal quality to the already magical spectacle of the Uxmal sound and light show.

All the same, I am acutely aware that overreliance on my caring circle may at times be limiting, casting shadows on my independent spirit. The human spirit is like a bird, born with a desire to fly solo but sometimes requires others' help to learn to fly all over again. I have learned to fly with clipped wings, and this burden is mine alone to carry. Work remains to make peace with this different flight pattern.

I entered my apartment from my walk in the hallway to find Mama in the open kitchen, her smile bright despite the tears brought on by the onions she was chopping for dinner. Her grace in life's unexpected turns never fails to move me – like the sudden transition to living in the US when her heart was still in India with her loved ones and her cultural roots. At Yale, without the company of friends and relatives, her spouse absorbed in his teaching world, she rarely complained, save for the occasional outburst. Instead, she crafted her own garden of belonging by immersing herself in auditing classes. Mama wandered through Art History's painted corridors and Greek Mythology's ancient tales. She wove friendships with neighborhood women, their footsteps echoing in New Haven's quiet museums. Then came a surprise that delighted both my father and me – she enthusiastically volunteered to sing regularly in the church choir at the Yale Divinity School. Her hands even found new rhythms in the School of Music's Javanese percussion ensemble – Gamelan – performing regularly at formal musical events throughout Yale's sprawling campus.

I wished for a similar adaptability to life's shifting seasons.

"Pom! Come join your Papa."

I turned my head to hear Papa's voice calling out to me. He was seated at the table adjacent to the kitchen, leafing through a jumble of academic papers strewn across the surface.

He pulled out the chair closest to me. Though I hate to admit, in this age of glowing screens, it's a rare occasion when I give my family my full attention. I am always plugged into something seemingly more pressing or desirable. Yet, sometimes, like at this moment, I did savor the present in my parents' company. The rhythmic tap of Mama's knife against the cutting board ceased as she crossed the kitchen to join us.

Collecting a stack of papers and clipping them together, Papa looked up, smiling.

"The three of us are having a good time through the pandemic, being locked in together, aren't we?"

Acknowledgments

I am deeply grateful to my writing community for ensuring I didn't throw my hands up on the countless days of solitary writing. I consider myself incredibly fortunate to have crossed paths with some remarkable people who graciously extended me their help when I was operating in the dark. In order of their appearance, I'd like to express my gratitude to the following people in my writing community:

- Tara Khandelwal, the founder of Bound, India's largest storytelling platform
- Mohit Parikh, the MVP of my author journey; Bound writing coach
- Michelle D'Costa, former Head of Learning and Editing, Bound
- Kanishka Gupta, my matchless literary agent and founder of Writer's Side, whose guidance, belief, and skill were nothing short of extraordinary
- All my brilliant editors, starting with Anushree Kaushal, my first professional editor and a freelance powerhouse
- Janani Ganesan, my second professional editor, Writer's Side
- Anjali Puri of Juggernaut Books, my final professional editor, who just gets it.

I could never have written this book without the friends who spurred me along at different stages of this journey. As they say, the journey is as, if not more, important than the destination – thank you all for graciously enduring my incessant nagging and for supporting my writing in your own unique ways. In order of appearance in my writing process, I'd like to thank:

- Christine Chen
- Nishant Singh
- Kizito Davis
- Meri Poghosyan
- Nikhil Sood, star beta reader (maintaining the changed name for consistency)
- Roxane Debaty, star beta reader
- Trisha Meili
- And last but nowhere near the least, Aarshiya Chaudhry.

I extend my heartfelt gratitude to the following people for generously carving out time from their busy schedules whether to help me navigate the intricacies of the publishing process, read and offer thoughtful feedback on my manuscript, or open doorways that allowed my story to reach you. Suffice it to say, your invaluable support spared me countless hours of frustration in attempting to decipher the nuances of the querying, publishing, title discovery, copyediting, and cover design journeys.

- Chiki Sarkar, Parth Mehrotra and the entire Juggernaut Books team: thanks for your incredible and unparalleled personalized attention.
- Paro Anand
- Meru Gokhale
- Liaquat Ahamed
- Meena Ahamed

- Suhel Seth
- George Skaria

I am deeply indebted to my various professional mentors and workplace leaders, who played crucial roles in cultivating a healthy writing life for me. Their contributions went far beyond conventional mentorship – from those who pored over my early drafts with microscopic attention, to those who opened their office doors to provide me an opportunity to get out of the house in the year I was a full-time writer, and from those who injected flexibility into my work schedule for uninterrupted time to polish my manuscript, to those who turned what might have been a lonesome journey to a joyous shared one. In no particular order, I would like to express my sincere gratitude to the following individuals for going above and beyond:

- Susan Davis
- Pramath Raj Sinha
- Shreyasi Singh
- Deepa Kapoor
- Nidhi Reddy
- Lokesh Anand
- And last, but far from least, my friends at Jetri and Harappa

George Orwell is known to have said: "Writing a book is a horrible, exhausting struggle, like a long bout of some painful illness." I found a cure in reading for inspiration, motivation, reflection, and learning. In crafting this book, the following authors and their works contributed to one or more aspects of this journey, each in their own unique way. I owe each of them a sincere debt of gratitude:

- Suleika Jaouad, *Between Two Kingdoms: A Memoir of a Life Interrupted*; Suleika's memoir was the immediate catalyst for my choice to record my own story in a similar style. Thank you, Suleika!

- Trisha Meili, *The Central Park Jogger*
- Liz Murray, *Breaking Night: A Memoir of Forgiveness, Survival, and My Journey from Homeless to Harvard*
- Elyn R. Saks, *The Center Cannot Hold: My Journey Through Madness*
- James R. Doty, *Into the Magic Shop: A Neurosurgeon's Quest to Discover the Mysteries of the Brain and the Secrets of the Heart*
- Akwaeke Emezi, *You Made a Fool of Death with Your Beauty*
- Hanya Yanagihara, *A Little Life*
- Donna Tartt, *The Secret History*
- Ocean Vuong, *On Earth We're Briefly Gorgeous*
- Mary Karr, *The Art of Memoir*
- Vivian Gornick, *The Situation and the Story: The Art of Personal Narrative*
- Jonathan Rosen, *The Best Minds: A Story of Friendship, Madness, and the Tragedy of Good Intentions*

Much gratitude to my aunt, Malati Shah, and my cousin, Vivan Shah for brainstorming potential titles with me, playing with potential cover designs, and for putting up with my barrage of back-and-forth text messages.

Finally, above all else, I wouldn't be an author today without the unconditional love and support of my parents, Rasika and Rakesh Mohan, my brother, Rasesh Mohan, and my new sister-in-law, Sabah Usmani. Each has helped in countless ways, literally speaking, throughout my author journey and beyond.

Notes

1. A matatu is a shared taxi in Kiswahili
2. The Kiswahili word "muzungu" is used to refer to a white person, and depending on the context, can refer to anybody "wandering around", i.e., all foreigners, which is why I was referred to as a muzungu too. I recall Davis telling me that I was referred to as a muzungu also because of how I dressed, which he described as resembling the style of a white person.
3. Sujal Parikh's Blogspot blog, September–October 2010, http://sujalparikh.blogspot.com/2010/.
4. Hemiparesis is a condition that affects the muscles on one side of the body, caused by damage to the brain. Hemiparesis may also affect the muscles used for speech, which is so in my case.
5. TBR: To Be Read (books).
6. Andre Gallois, "Identity Over Time", The Stanford Encyclopedia of Philosophy, ed. Edward N. Zalta, Spring 2011. http://plato.stanford.edu/archives/spr2011/entries/identity-time.
7. Tarini Mohan, "Because Accidents Don't Only Happen to Others", Indian Express, June 22, 2012. https://indianexpress.com/article/opinion/columns/because-accidents-dont-happen-only-to-others/
8. Spasticity is a condition in which there is an abnormal increase in muscle tone or stiffness of muscle, which might interfere with movement, speech, or be associated with discomfort or pain. Spasticity is usually caused by damage to nerve pathways within the brain or spinal cord that control muscle movement (NIH).
9. Norman Doidge, The Brain's Way of Healing: Remarkable Discoveries and Recoveries from the Frontiers of Neuroplasticity (a James H. Silberman book), Penguin, Kindle edition. p. 10.

10. K.L. Briggman, M. Helmstaedter, W. Denk, "Wiring Specificity in the Direction-Selectivity Circuit of the Retina", Nature 471, 2011, https://pubmed.ncbi.nlm.nih.gov/21390125/.pp. 183–188.
11. National Institutes of Health, Major Accomplishments by Date, "Identifying a Promising HIV Vaccine Target", 2012, https://irp.nih.gov/accomplishments/identifying-a-promising-hiv-vaccine-target.
12. Carl Gustav Jung, Synchronicity: An Acausal Connecting Principle, Princeton University Press, 1960.
13. The concept of the collective unconscious was introduced by Carl Jung. The term is used to describe a theoretical construct that represents the shared, inherited reservoir of knowledge and experiences that all human beings possess. According to Jung, the collective unconscious is a deep layer of the psyche that is beyond the individual's personal unconscious.
14. Lil Wayne, Drake, "Right Above It", I Am Not A Human Being, 2010.
15. T.S. Eliot, "The Fire Sermon", The Wasteland, ed. Michael North, W.W. Norton, 2001.
16. Atul Gawande, Being Mortal: Medicine and What Matters in the End, Henry Holt and Co, Kindle edition. p. 95.
17. The (Indian) Rights of Persons with Disabilities Act, 2016, pg. 7, https://legislative.gov.in/sites/default/files/A2016-49_1.pdf
18. The Übermensch, German for "Overman", is a concept in the philosophy of Friedrich Nietzsche. In his 1883 book, Thus Spoke Zarathustra, the character, Zarathustra, posits the Übermensch as a goal for humanity to set for itself. The Übermensch is a being who has overcome the limitations of traditional morality and religion. They are free to create their own values and live their lives on their own terms. The Übermensch is not a perfect being, but they are constantly striving to become better. They are not afraid to challenge the status quo and to create new possibilities for themselves and for humanity.
19. Friedrich Wilhelm Nietzsche, Thus Spoke Zarathustra: A Book for All and None, Cambridge University Press, 2006.

